THE LAST PARALLEL

Also by Martin Russ:

Breakout: The Chosin Reservoir Campaign, Korea, 1950

Happy Hunting Ground: An Ex-Marine's Odysee in Vietnam

Line of Departure: Tarawa

Half Moon Haven

War Memorial

Showdown Semester: Advice From a Writing Professor

THE LAST PARALLEL

A MARINE'S WAR JOURNAL

MARTIN RUSS

FROMM INTERNATIONAL
NEW YORK

First Fromm International Edition, 1999

Copyright © 1957 by Martin Russ

All rights reserved under International and Pan-American Copyright Conventions. Published in the United States by Fromm International Publishing Corporation, New York. First published by Rinehart & Company, Inc., 1957.

LIBRARY OF CONGRESS CATALOGING-IN-PUBLICATION DATA

Russ, Martin, 1931—
    The last parallel : a marine's war journal. — 1st Fromm International ed.
      p. cm.
    ISBN 0-88064-237-8
    1. Russ, Martin, 1931– . 2. Korean War, 1950–1953—Personal narratives, American. 3. United States, Marine Corps—Biography.
    I. Title
    DS921.6.R8   1999
    951.904'2—dc21   99-10089
                                                CIP

10 9 8 7 6 5 4 3 2 1
Manufactured in the United States of America

For
LAVINIA RUSS
and
CARROLL DUNN

CONTENTS

THE LAST
PARALLEL

GROUP ONE

‖‖‖

Camp Pendleton

August 20th, 1952

This is actually Camp Delmar, one of the subsidiaries of Camp Pendleton. Delmar is to overseas-bound marines what Bellevue is to psychotics, and as soon as we get squared away here we will be transferred to one of the bigger hatcheries—either Camp Las Pulgas or Camp San Onofre. Las Pulgas means "the bedbugs." All of these camps are contained within the boundaries of Pendleton.

Our entire working day is centered around the M-1 rifle. We rehearse for hours at a time the four positions of fire: prone, sitting, kneeling and offhand, *i.e.*, standing. Right now we're doing dummy runs, without ammunition, in preparation for our annual reclassification with the rifle. All marines, from helicopter pilots to jeep drivers, are required to fire for record at least once a year. This system is peculiar to the Marine Corps alone. A certain colonel of the air wing, when asked by a newsman what his particular job was, replied, "Rifleman, at present flying a Sabre jet." Which is a bit mealy-mouthed but to the point. He must have had that answer rehearsed.

All marines undergo an advanced kind of infantry training before being sent over, and the rifle is as much a part of that training as are the more complex maneuvers. There is no doubt that a man will forget how to use the weapon to full advantage unless he does use it periodically, and for this reason we are re-introduced to it every year. During the retreat from the Chosin reservoir, early in the war, it was largely due to the ability of cooks, truck drivers, clerks and other rear-echelon people to respond to emergency infantry deployment—while using their rifles to their full advantage—that the march to the sea was such a success.

Following this week of dummy practice, referred to as "snapping-in," we will move to Chappo Flats, the huge post rifle range, for qualification, and then infantry department at one of the other training camps.

The Pacific breakers are audible, and the wash of the waves on the beach can be heard from any point within this small camp. Nearby, big Diesel trucks are roaring down route 101. San Diego is thirty-five miles south. Los Angeles is ninety miles north. A Santa Fe track runs parallel to the highway. There is a tall beacon light on the edge of the camp, much like the one on High Tor, and its revolving ray fills the barracks with light every five seconds or so at night. One of the barracks radios is picking up cool dance music from Hollywood. Sitting here, it is hard to believe that such a place as Parris Island exists.

Last night I said to the clown who sleeps in the next bunk, "Last night I was in New York," and it impressed him somewhat as it should have. Three thousand miles in twelve hours. Oi! And now I have what Dad calls "the itchy foot." O, the dance music, the traffic on 101, the light of the beacon, the sound of the waves. The Constellation took off from LaGuardia at 11 P.M. and made a wide turn over the Bronx. Times Square was easy to spot. Over on the East Side, Shirley Ayers was possibly in bed, and her two kids were surely asleep. I liked to think that Lem Ayers was in his office. It will be fine to read the reviews of *Kismet* any day now.

When the hostess was watching, I threw a soulful look back at the fading lights of the city, a city that means about as much to me as the size of my turds. The hostess was large and resembled LaVerne Andrews of the Andrews Sisters who, in fact, all resemble airline hostesses. Later on, after leaving Chicago, I

4

looked down and watched those distant strings of lights which were the headlights of cars and trucks possibly moving along on routes 40 or 66. I've hitchhiked across the country four times and have traveled over those two highways, and it was strange seeing them from that angle.

The next morning I took a cab from the airport—what a highly civilized place that airport is—to big Brad's house. He is my large uncle (and Sallie is my large aunt). A most puppet-like exhibition took place. The three little dogs, Thatch, Osburt and Sturgess—all crazy as hell—rushed out as soon as the door opened and enveloped my shoes, which I had polished in the men's room at the airport. Anyone who has been a marine will understand about the shoes. This upset me so much that I ignored whoever it was that shouted greetings from inside. The household glassware rattled as the dogs and I hopped about the vestibule for half a minute. Each time I pushed one of the hysterical mutts away he would tumble backwards, beside himself with joy, and then rebound with great energy against my glorious shoes, which I finally removed.

Sallie and the colonel look fine but my grandfather, Gampie, does not. I was inexcusably patronizing to him because of his age and terrible state of health. But it was a shock. His name is Henry Darlington Faxon.

Later in the day I mentioned to him that I was anxious to get to Korea. He roared, "Why don't you speak the truth?" So I told him what I thought to be the truth and it must have sounded as ridiculous to him as it sounded to me. He is a very handsome man, despite a severe stroke. But he is so thin now. I fed him his supper of soft-boiled eggs. He made a slow gesture with his stiff-wristed arm and said, "Yes, this instrument in which I'm supposed to house my soul must be stored with fuel from time to time. But I'm never hungry."

August 26th, 1952

Two nights ago, feeling more uncomfortable than usual about being a virgin, I went into Oceanside and tracked down a succession of rather frightened women, and became progressively bitter at each failure to pick one up. "Can I buy you a drink?" I said to one crow as we both pretended to look into the window of a store. "Naw," she said. "So who are you waiting for?" I asked. "Somebody." The "else" was understood and I slunk away like a ferret.

I made a grotesque face at another girl walking past the west side of the bus station. She stopped and we turned around and looked at each other, walking backwards in opposite directions. I took off my cap and sort of sashayed up to her. After some zombie talk we made a date for the following night. I think I was probably lucky to get booked.

So we met last night and made a nervous tour of the bars. She drank screwdrivers. We walked out to the end of the long pier and pretended to look at the displays of marine life in illuminated tanks. We lay down on the beach and talked goon language and groped a bit. Her name, she said, was Liz Gordon. From San Antonio, on vacation from a cosmetics factory. Dark skin, dark hair, brown eyes, good build, foul mouth. Idiot. When we started to wander back toward town, she said nasally, "What're you panting for?" I said, "Take a guess." God-damned cretin. Her hotel faced the Santa Fe tracks and there, among the sooty weeds next to a railroad siding, we resolved something or other. I was bored half stiff. For some untraceable reason I tried to kiss her before she went into the hotel, but she would have none of it. She left for Texas this morning.

Art Hour:

Sleep, soft child, within your grave beneath the stars.
Perhaps the cat from under the streetlight will tread across your
    blankets of earth.
—an example of the kind of trash I used to turn out to impress the chicks at the Kappa Kappa Gamma house, although this one was thought up while watching an outdoor movie at Camp Lejeune, thinking of Mike Miller. It's the only one I can remember.

6

The bandage is still in place above my right eyebrow, covering a nonexistent cut. One of the men in the barracks asked me yesterday if I had gotten into a fight with a swabbie. I said yes. He asked who won and I showed him my bruised knuckles, which I had scraped back and forth on a sidewalk in New York. He thinks I'm great.

August 28th, 1952
    A letter today from Jane Owens. We were in the same class at St. Lawrence—she will graduate next year. She was Big Sister for two years. Jane was the only one up there who had the right perspective as far as I was concerned: the contrived wildness. She dug it all and saw to it that I didn't get dangerously carried away by the glories of youth. In other words, she didn't take me too seriously. That is, she took me very seriously but only when it counted, or something. This was infuriating at the time, but I would hate to think about the things that would have happened had she not informed me from time to time that I was "SO corny."
    I used to deliver a series of ponderous lectures to her at odd hours. Euphoria 101a it was called. Something to do with explaining to her my peculiar position among the mortal gods. Near the end of the lecture series, she appeared to be taking the thing quite seriously, even to the point of writing down notes and asking questions. One night I dragged her into an empty classroom in South Hall and wound up the course. It went something like this.
    "There are and there have been several people on earth who, through their works, have made the presence of God more obvious to the multitudes. A point of contact is so essential that these several people have become justifiably revered. The multitudes, by instinct, know that the works of these people are representations of His glory even if they are unable to understand the meaning of the works themselves. Question: Who are these people?"

7

I took up the chalk and drew five separate squares on the blackboard.

Jane said, "Well, Christ is one."

"Right." I printed the name Christ within the topmost square.

"And Socrates, I guess."

"Wrong," said I, for no particular reason.

She concentrated. "Oh well, Bach, of course."

"Bach, of course." I printed the name of Bach within the next square.

"William Shakespeare," said Jane. I printed the name. She mentioned several more people including a couple of saints, but I said no to each. Then I patiently printed the name Bix Beiderbecke within one of the squares. This left one box unfilled.

"There is one being on earth," I continued, "who is being groomed for the position of second messiah (twenty-four hundred dollars a year, no vacations). The pattern has already been suggested to him, but it will take a few months for him to comprehend the enormity of his mission." I poised the chalk near the empty square.

"You," said Jane.

"Of course," answered the second messiah, printing his name within the box. Euphoria 101a had drawn to a close. We walked down the dark hallway and Jane said that she would visit me in the death house. Jane is a very good girl. We sat next to each other in two classes and muttered continual asides which to us were sidesplitting, and to us alone. At every meeting of a particular class—Historical Survey of Music—the mere sound produced by our holding back a torrent of barn-yard cackles usually reduced the class to a shambles.

She digs Bach, Couperin, Vivaldi and those guys, and is building up a tasty repertoire of allemandes, gigues, courantes, etc., often working late at night in one of the practice rooms in South Hall. Those rooms are tiny. One night she discovered that I was sitting on the floor behind her, the door not having been opened. I had scaled the outside wall, wearing tennis shoes, and had wormed through the window without making a sound. So corny. But it scared the hell out of her. Of course I told her that I was able to move through solids.

During an exam week, the second winter, we used to talk to each other on the phone at 4 A.M., having crammed all night. The phone at the Kappa Delta House is located near the house-mother's rooms, but Jane was always prepared to pick it up as soon as the bell started to ring. Mrs. Jarret's Garrets—where I boarded—and the Kappa Delta house were at opposite ends of Canton. The town hall, with its sonorous *boing-boing* clock, is in the middle. As soon as this bell struck four, I would begin to dial. We talked until the birds began chirping outside. She would have the phone inside a coat closet and I would be lying on the floor.

We invariably argued. Her anger was intense but controlled. She was so important to me that hardly a day passed in which I avoided working myself into a rage over her. I trusted and depended upon her to such an extent that several times I tried to get her into a fist fight.

On the opening night of *Mad Woman of Chaillot* I was extremely nervous and felt obliged to get loaded on Ron Rico rum. Jane got word of this and fetched me and dragged me roughly to the playhouse. The morning after the first perform-ance the annual acting awards were presented and I got one, thereby suggesting an obligation to become stoned for each per-formance. The third or fourth night I overdid it a bit and had to be carried to the Phi Sig house to be revived, hav-ing passed out after putting on costume and make-up. Jane led the way followed by the four pallbearers carrying the King of the Sewer-men along the sidewalk. Traffic came to a halt. I wore an elaborate suit of rags, a red beard, knee boots, several wool hats—and I was vomiting. Jane didn't have anything to say to me for several days.

During the last thirty-day leave I hitchhiked through the spooky Catskills and went to Delphi, a lonely and beautiful lit-tle town a hundred miles west of Kingston. Jane was not there; she was a councilor at a camp in Cooperstown. I intro-duced myself to her parents and sister, who were very hospitable,

9

and spent the evening there, working everything mechanical in the house, playing a little bop piece on the piano which I knew Jane had played at home, and looking at some of her little-girl pictures. Mr. Owens runs the drugstore in town. I didn't spend the night there.

September 1st, 1952

Reveille sounded this morning at 5 A.M. as usual. The NCO of the day entered the barracks, turned on the lights and blew the police whistle as loud as he could. These guys always seem to feel a compulsion to stride up and down the barracks, vigorously shaking each man's bunk. The "Duty," as he is called, takes the business of waking the troops quite seriously, because the sergeant of the guard is likely to appear a minute or two later to see that everyone is out of the sack. This morning the Duty was a staff sergeant: three stripes and one rocker underneath. He was wearing the .45 pistol and two loaded magazines in his belt.

Trouble. One buck sergeant—three stripes, no rocker—remained motionless in his rack with the covers pulled up over his head. He had checked in from a ten-day leave late the night before. And no one's balance is particularly stable anyway the first morning on a new base. It is one of the most depressing mornings a man ever lives through.

He would not get up. He said quietly, "Leave me alone."

"Who the fuck are you?" said the Duty. "A fuckin' general or something like that there?"

No answer.

"Get the fuck out of that god-damned rack, mate."

No answer. So the Duty said something close to these words:

"Listen, mate. I'll run you up with the morning colors— I'll run you up from here to San Diego. You better GET out of that there rack."

The buck sergeant finally spoke. "I'll get up," he said. "Just leave me alone."

"Leave you alone, my ass."

Most of the men in the barracks were crowded around the

10

scene, watching. Then the Duty rattled off another eloquent line in which he used the word "boy."

The buck sergeant leaped out from under the covers and stood in front of the Duty. A small, well-built man, dressed only in green underdrawers.

"Don't call me 'boy,'" he said. "Don't ever call me 'boy.'"

Whereupon the Duty, in a particularly well-turned phrase, replied, "Fuck you, boy," and fixed his attention on the plate of metal at the end of the bunk, upon which the name of the occupant was stamped. As he was copying the name into his notebook, the other man fell on him, attempting among other things to destroy the notebook. By stepping hard on the other's bare feet and shoving him away violently, the Duty was able to extricate himself from the arms which choked him. Two or three men pinned the buck sergeant's arms behind his back and held him. The Duty was breathless and white with excitement. He withdrew his pistol from its holster, raised it to a forty-five degree angle toward the ceiling, and inserted a loaded clip, saying, "By the authority vested in me, I place you under arrest."

A tall corporal from the South had been quietly making up his bunk nearby, apparently oblivious of the scene; but at this point he lost his temper. Each time the Duty began to speak, the corporal would shake his own bunk very violently, but still pretending that he was making up his bunk for inspection. It was pretty grand; the Duty couldn't finish a sentence:

"The next time you feel like gettin' salty with me"—RHUD-DD—dud-dud—rattle RATTLE-CLANK!—"and believe you me, buster, if I have anything to say about it, you'll be locked up for insub"—RHUD-ud-dud—rattle CLANK, CLANK-K-K! . . . "WHO IS MAKING THAT GOD-DAMNED RACKET OVER THERE?"

"Oh, I was jes makin up mah bunk, Sarge," said the corporal, wide-eyed. He was also arrested, and both prisoners were escorted to the guard shack. I didn't mean to turn this into a half-assed joke. Every one of us in the barracks this morning hoped that the hounded man would smash the authority with anything that was handy. The authority acted suspiciously like a former drill instructor at Parris Island. I suppose that is the only reason why

11

I bothered to write it down; I'm apt to become apoplectic at the thought of Parris Island, its drill instructors and that kind of authority. Since I have only been away from the place for a year, I still cannot talk about it without running around in circles.

Morbid dept. (to continue):
Near one of the corners of a building at San Quentin, there towers a tall green spire, visible for some distance. It is the escape funnel for lethal fumes of the gas chamber. The chamber was purchased from an outfit of some kind (interior decorators) in Denver for a bit over five thousand dollars. A relatively small, square object, it is practically independent of the other walls of the prison. Inside are two metal chairs, not unlike electric chairs. A bucket of acid is placed underneath the chair to be used. At the warden's signal the executioner operates a lever and a capsule of cyanide drops into the bucket of acid. The execution is witnessed by a group of about thirty, through a large window. No one enters the chamber for half an hour during which blowers force the gas out of the room and up the green spire. O.K.?

September 20, 1952
There are certain places in cities which I try to avoid while on liberty. In New York—The Grand Central, Penn Station, the Port Authority bus terminal, the air terminal on Forty-second Street, and anywhere near Riverside Drive. To stay away from anything suggesting departure.

On Aug. 17th at five o'clock in the afternoon—three hours before the bus was scheduled to leave for LaGuardia—I felt the farewell impulse and leaped over the side of Shirley's convertible and abruptly said goodbye to her and her two tremendous kids, Sara and Johno. The traffic light at the intersection of Fifty-ninth Street and Eleventh Avenue was red at that moment and there was a line of cars behind us, some of which like Shirley were going into the country. Shirley called out, "Why don't you walk downtown along the waterfront? It's only a block over, and it's fairly nice and quiet at this time of day." At that particular hour of that particular day there was nowhere I would rather not be than near the Hudson River, near the Weehawken ferry, connected to the Weehawken station, connected to the West Shore Railroad, connected to Stony Point, connected to your hipbone. "Good idea," I said, "so long," and headed straight for Broadway to get into a movie house before dusk.

September 24th, 1952

As a marine, one almost feels obliged to conceal any emotion except anger. To show sympathy for instance would suggest effeminacy. If a marine used the words "lovely," "kind," "please," "thank you," or should he indulge in such a thing as a natural giggle—as opposed to the regulation Homeric roar—he might find either that his conscience bothers him momentarily or that his barracks mates are riding him. The point here is not that I am criticizing this behavior—I'll try that later when I've thought it out—but that it is necessary in order to be "accepted" among the other men. Is it necessary to be accepted among the other men? For me, a corporal, it is.

It is interesting to note the reaction of a man who has accidentally let slip one of the words mentioned above, or who has become unconsciously rhapsodic and realizes suddenly that, if he doesn't shift gears in some way, he is in danger of losing his masculinity in the eyes of his listeners. There are numerous methods for covering up such a mistake. The most effective is to increase the cadence of four-letter words. The word "fuck" will be used three times as often as it usually is, and such a sentence as the following—two guys talking about who can drive a truck better—would not be considered unusual: "Fuck you, fucker. I was behind the wheel of a fuckin' Diesel truck before you ever learned to fuckin' well drive." And the word is often interposed in this manner: "Reveille goes tomorrow at four o' fuckin' clock," and the answer might be "Jesus fuckin' Christ!"

In reference to even such a commonplace thing as a movie, it is a bit difficult for a gung-ho marine to speak of, say, *The Best*

13

Years of Our Lives. We will hear instead about "that there fuckin' *Best Years of Our Lives* or something."

One other common cover-up is a sudden and distinct swagger in the walk. And I'm willing to bet that somewhere on every marine post in the world there is at least one man whistling the tune to "Shave & a haircut: two bits."

A few days ago a group of us were standing around the battalion office, waiting for information concerning our pay records. A pot-bellied master sergeant swaggered in, wearing liberty uniform w/ campaign ribbons. As he spoke to a clerk, we learned that his mother had died that morning and that he was to receive emergency leave papers. He stood about on one foot and then the other, making little expressions of petty irritation with his mouth. The same sort of pathetic routine.

The average marine, if such a condition exists, is definitely not the lad represented on the recruiting poster. More likely he is a small, pimple-faced young man who, because it has been so skillfully pounded into him at boot camp, believes that he can lick the world. He hates sailors, is not averse to beating up homosexuals, and loathes civilians. Nevertheless he is the man most adaptable to combat, the most efficient soldier in the world. If this be the quality of material necessary to fill out the exalted ranks, then more power to them—the drugstore cowboys in search of adventure they can never find working for the telephone company, the civilian failures, misfits and all the others like myself, trying to prove something or other.

Why not play it to the hilt, I say? So I swagger, curse and mumble with the rest. This has nothing to do with respect, a word rarely applicable around here. The trick is to be a bit awesome.

September 26th, 1952

When I came into Gampie's room last weekend he didn't know who I was at first; his nearly sightless blue eyes were wide open. I identified myself and he said, "Well! Good afternoon, GRANDSON—and killer." He is a Quaker and so gentle a man that

14

it is difficult to imagine him as an old-time prairie man, whose father was a saddle maker. The story is that Jesse James, one of our boyhood heroes, raided a fairgrounds near Lawrence, Kansas, while Gampie and his father were selling saddles to cowboys and range men. Anyway, he is appalled at my desire to go to Korea. It would be negligent for me not to think out the reasons for wanting to go, but I haven't done it yet. It is imperative that I do and that I write it down before leaving.

George Berry is a saintly old man who has worked for the Faxons for many years. When Gampie suffered the stroke, George left Kansas City for good in order to come to Santa Monica to take care of him. He has been in Santa Monica long enough now to have made some friends and knows his way around town pretty well.

Saturday is his day off. I was sitting in the kitchen with Sallie when he came in at 2 A.M. last Sunday morning. He was absolutely stoned, eyes beet red. The best way to describe him physically is to mention that he looks quite a bit like Louis Armstrong. He launched into a routine much too great not to have been used in a vaudeville act somewhere.

Appearing in the kitchen doorway, he removed his old dress fedora with a D'Artagnan flourish and went into a low bow. An extremely low and happy bow—so low in fact that instead of recovering from it he slid gracefully on down to the floor and collapsed deftly into a heap. Sallie turned icily back to the dishes, having decided that no comment was called for. George cheerfully gathered himself together, rose to his feet and moved upstairs, followed by one of the mad dogs.

October 2nd, 1952

Suicide is not a rare occurrence in the Corps. When I was with the 10th Marines, an artillery regiment at Camp Lejeune, our battalion sergeant-major shot himself through the head with a pistol one morning.

When the 10th was engaged in amphibious maneuvers and anchored off Norfolk, a marine hanged himself from the fantail

15

of an APA-type troopship. A member of our battery, standing the dog watch, saw him suspended under the stern of the neighboring vessel. He said that the figure swayed slightly from the roll of the ship and the early morning breeze.

Three or four months ago two men from this base stole a civilian car and had a ball with it for a few days before jumping from the window of a San Diego hotel, one to his death.

Being what is known as a short-timer and also being a fairly active optimist, I'm at peace with service life; but I won't deny that I sometimes feel at least the outer fringes of despair brought on by loneliness, a feeling which the long-timers must have to fight regularly. Only once did this oppression amount to anything serious. We were based at Little Creek, Virginia, during those morbid landing maneuvers. One night, on shore but confined to the area, it seemed that I couldn't identify myself to myself and I got panicky. The heat and humidity were almost unbearable. The only thing I could think of to do was to call Shirley Ayers in Stony Point and make small talk for a few minutes. Alec was in Rochester and I didn't know the number. The small talk helped. I'll have to tell Shirley about that sometime. Then I went over to the slopchute and drank some beer to get sleepy.

The life was then and is now so unreal. I'm willing to go along with the unreality of it as long as I am able to wake up every so often. This is here. And I'm part of here; but I'm only certain of this when I'm grinding out these stilted notes.

Here at Camp San Onofre, the Training & Replacement Command—we left Delmar a couple of weeks ago—people constantly remind us that we are Korea-bound. AWOLs occur once in a while and disciplinary measures are severe. The training schedule is intense. This is what I've been leading up to:

Yesterday afternoon we hiked out to a silhouette target range and fired at variously grouped one-dimensional figures that would pop up on a distant hillside. We were practicing fire-control and all of us had a chance to give the orders concerning the volleys. At four o'clock we were assembled. The surplus ammunition was collected and the lieutenant inspected the cham-

16

ber of each man's rifle, a usual procedure. We marched back to the campus and immediately set about cleaning our weapons. There was to be a rifle inspection at quarter past five and, following this, liberty cards would be passed out.

A private from Indiana, Wesley Nordhagen, lived in the adjoining tent; a large, pudgy man who had cried and nearly fainted once during an all-night maneuver. His tentmates say that Nordhagen did not begin cleaning his weapon but instead sat on the edge of his cot with his chin resting on the muzzle of his rifle, the butt of which rested on the ground. He remained in that position for some time and then asked what time it was. He was told that it was five thirty. He squeezed the trigger of his rifle and an armor-piercing slug went through his head.

There was no reaction from any of the tents for about five seconds. I was putting my rifle together at that moment, and as soon as the report sounded we all stood still. We could hear mountain music from one of the radios in another tent. Soon a crowd of men was shuffling around the company street, trying to find out what had happened. Several people were shouting for us to go back to our tents. The sun had gone down and I remember noticing how cold it was. The first sergeant barred the entrance to Nordhagen's tent. There was a great commotion inside and the hanging electric light bulb was jostled many times so that it cast swinging shadows on the men waiting outside. An ambulance from sick bay drove into the dirt street, and we made a wide path for it. Nordhagen's buddies carried him out in a blanket and loaded him into the back end of the ambulance.

The captain spoke to us this morning after muster, referring to "last night's unsavory incident," and he mentioned that we will probably take part in a military funeral. I know nothing about Nordhagen except that the men called him Mary Jane.

October 15th, 1952

Sallie's three dogs are all faggots. Most of their day is spent cruising around that low level of theirs, and despite all the maneuvers it usually works out that Sturgess is drag queen for

17

Osburt. Thatch is rough trade and is violently jealous of Osburt. Gampie howls with malevolence whenever the boys enter his room. They love him, of course, and carry on most of their camping in his room.

Last week we fought the "five-day war," during which we made a series of attacks, and then defended positions in the mountains. We climbed about like mountain goats and slept for a short while each night under the stars. *Exhausto sum.* The weight of a fully equipped combat marine is fantastic. I'll try not to exaggerate—I don't really know the figures. Here is a rough estimate of the weight of the separate pieces and the total:

> field marching pack—50 to 60 lbs.
> loaded cartridge belt w/canteen—15 to 20 lbs. (BAR belt)
> helmet, clothing and shoes—10 lbs.
> BAR (Browning automatic rifle)—20 lbs.
> armored vest—7 lbs.

A total of approximately 110 lbs., supported—in addition to my own weight of 175 lbs.—by two feet.

Last Wednesday, three of us, all corporals, drove down route 101 to Tijuana, Mexico, located several miles below San Diego, not far across the border. There is no shore patrol or military police in Tijuana, and the border guards make a feeble inspection of each car that passes through the gates. The local police, however, have a reputation for strictness, especially concerning American servicemen. If a marine or sailor is thrown in jail there, he will remain locked up for the duration of his sentence. The usual procedure is to turn a man over to the MPs or SPs, but not in Tijuana. If sentenced there, he will serve his term there, and is considered AWOL until set free. In other words, his home base is not under obligation to escort him back across the border.

The town itself is about the size of Nyack. Its main street, Revolucion, is gayly lighted—a gaudy dreamlike avenue if one doesn't look too closely. From bright little stands at almost every corner tacos, and enchiladas—crusty, greasy, delicious little pies of many ingredients—are sold. We came across two vendors, standing beside striped black and white donkeys, selling a tremendous variety of wares, mostly souvenirs. The donkey is used to haul the bulky, clanking stand.

We ran into several little boys who were selling chewing gum, and one who was trying to peddle his sister. Taxicab drivers lolled about the curb, some of them muttering propositions as we passed by. "Twenty French virgins; come and look 'em over. No charge to take you there." "Chinese girl for you, marine." We were almost tripping over pimps as we moved along the street. *"No tengo dinero,"* we would say. We have no money.

We had bought a fifth of Seagram's in Oceanside and were flying by the time we reached Mexico. The names of some of the bars: Sloppy Joe's, Aloha, El California, Oscar's, San Souci, La Reforma, La Cucaracha (the cockroach), Los Angeles. The Cockroach was our first stop. Four women slithered over as soon as we were seated. In the dimly lighted joint they all looked like dolls. Overgard was too shy to talk. Shanahan and myself tried a mixture of pidgin Spanish and sign language, but we didn't ask them to sit down. We decided to leave; we wanted to look over the bevy of beauties. Shanahan removed his arm from around one of the girl's knees and we stood up. *"Lo siento; no tengo dinero,"* I said dashingly to the one I had been leering at. She rumpled my hair, or rather brushed it with her fingers, there not being enough to rumple. "Cheapiscotty," she said. Cheapskate.

In the men's room a boy tried to sell me a prophylactic kit, and an ancient attendant sat behind a little table on which was displayed a variety of goodies including candy, gum and tobacco. As we left we noticed that a policeman was standing unobtrusively in one of the corners of the bar. In almost every bar the cast was identical; the girls, the young boy, the old man, the policeman. The light was always dim, but the women were either grotesque or beautiful.

At El California we found a more sophisticated atmosphere, not that this was what we preferred. After dancing a few appalling mambos I decided to sit and listen because the group sounded good, a mixture of Machito and Henry Busse. Overgard waved me over to his end of the bar where he was seated with a very lovely girl named Dolores. She was about thirty, smartly dressed and had bright eyes. Her hair was short and compact. Overgard wanted me to explain to her that he used to drive a medium tank at Lejeune which was named "Mia Dolores." She spoke very little English and Overgard was having difficulty. Before long I gave up trying to horn in; she was obviously much more interested in Overgard, who has a pleasant face. I was content to sit on the floor in the corner and sometimes interpret. The place was lit in a most peculiar manner. I was too besotted to notice the technical arrangement, but it seemed as though a blue light emanated from the cracks in the tile floor. Overgard became visibly embarrassed when the woman propositioned him for ten dollars. I found Shanahan, doing a bad imitation of Gilbert Roland, and we left without Overgard.

Our last stop was El Baron on the southern outskirts of town, somewhere in the direction of the stadium of the bullfights. We were immediately enveloped by five jaded monsters through which we waded to the bar. This was a sprawling crude joint, and I tried to drink inconspicuously between two Mexicans. Shanahan had been captured and was doing Gilbert Roland again at a large white table. Feeling a wave of drunken something or other, I grasped the arm of a young girl standing behind me, having decided upon something or other. Her name, she said, was Alicia and she was nineteen. It was the bare feet that got me, although she was the proud possessor—she silently asserted—of generous mammae. She asked for a drink and then produced a small stiff piece of white paper which resembled a grocery-market receipt. On it was typewritten:

$$\begin{array}{r} .25 \\ \underline{.25} \\ .50 \end{array}$$

"Twenty fi' cent—me. Twenty fi' cent—bar," she said. A sort of introductory ticket, but I would not pay for this. We had another drink. Hers was, I am certain, diluted Coke. Mine was, I

20

am not certain, gin and tonic, which I had misguidedly decided to be the most civilized drink. Her price was five dollars and the *chambre d'amour* would cost two more. Only after considerable animated bantering was I able to lower the price to three dollars, although the bull-pen fee remained fixed. With the facial expression of a frog she said, "*Vamanos.*" We went out the rear entrance, leading through a stinking kitchen where two elderly women were making—I'm sorry to say—tortillas. A sour old gentleman was seated there behind an ornate cash register. He collected the two dollars and rang it up on the machine. I stole a tomato from a bin in the meantime. The old gentleman gave the girl a key and we walked out into a large unlit patio. I tried to give the tomato to the girl—SO nervous—but she didn't dig it at all. Room number sixteen.

Alicia had one gambit to offer. "When you coming back, baby?" My reply I think summed up the entire proceedings. "Horse shit," I said. *Non erectus est.* I left the room none the worse for wear—so to speak. The adobe archway leading to the street bore the words "*Adios, Amigos.*" I sat on the curb with a headache but no remorse. Shanahan came out and we drove off. We found Overgard waiting near a bridge. He didn't say a word.

Just across the border, next to the shore-patrol shack, there is a small wooden building labeled SANITARY STATION, referred to as the pro station. Inside, the main feature is a long metal trough, knee high, with several faucets operated by foot pedals and a number of soap dispensers, salve dispensers and towel dispensers. The standard operating procedure was plainly printed above each spigot and an SP hovered about, available for questions. We were required to add our marks to a log book, a record of the number of men who have used the pro station, and the name of their base. Camp Pendleton we noticed was definitely in the lead.

And so we leave Old Mexico, with its picturesque fishing villages and its Old World charm, and as we say fond farewell let us remember the quaint adobe buildings and the laughing faces of the women of Tijuana as we sadly watch them disappear into the setting sun.

October 27th, 1952

We drew the full complement of cold-weather gear this morning. What marvelous sturdy equipment. I had dreaded being cold in Korea as much as I dread combat, but it seems that we will be well padded, at least against the weather. We are being transferred to the cold-weather training camp located in the Sierra mountains. Here is a list of the equipment we received this morning:

    canvas clothing bag, waterproof
    mountain brush (small whisk broom, for mud and snow)
    polarized sunglasses
    trouser suspenders
    shell gloves (rough chamois)
    wool gloves, two pairs
    mittens w/trigger finger
    mitten inserts
    winter underwear (long johns), two pairs
    parka w/hood
    cotton cap
    wool scarf
    alpaca pile-lined vest w/zipper
    high-necked wool sweater
    cold-weather trousers, two pairs
    mountain sleeping bag
    thermal boots

The cost of this gear is $126.13 per man.

There is a certain thrill in making up one's pack. First, one never knows whether everything will fit. It almost always does but only after a contest of strength. Second, a fair amount of skill is required in order to adjust the various straps. Considering the feel of the straps, their sturdiness and material, the process is not unlike that of harnessing a horse. A great deal of tugging and clamping and readjusting. There is never room to spare. It seems as though there is exactly enough room. This is especially true in the case of the seabag or duffel bag as it is called in the army. Every time I make up a pack I'm reminded of an incident at Parris Island during boot training.

We were being transferred to the rifle range the following morning and had been instructed to pack our seabags, and to include our scrub pails—that is, the scrub pails had to go in the seabag. One member of our squad decided that this was impossible, as indeed it almost was. He offered to bet ten dollars that no one could pack his seabag with the pail so that the lock would close. I accepted the bet and nearly ruptured myself in closing the bag after an hour or so of careful packing. Later that night he and I made another bet. He was certain that the first words of the Bible were: "In the beginning the word was God . . ." When he discovered that he was wrong, he announced in anger that he would settle neither bet. We argued for several minutes until I threw a full knapsack in his face and asked him to come outside for a waltz. He was white with anger but did not come outside, saying that he would kill me before we left the island. I didn't press him for the debts thereafter, and he didn't kill me, so I guess it was a tie.

Marching in formation to chow this noon, the platoon sergeant, in order that the column avoid collision with a series of erect sewer pipes, gave the following command: "Guide down on in through over there."

November 12th, 1952

The new cold-weather training camp is located in and around the area of Pickel Meadows—elevation sixty-eight hundred feet—named after Frank Pickel, an early settler. Two bivouac areas have been established high in the mountains overlooking the meadow. The highest peak is nearly ten thousand feet above sea level. The Sonora Pass, or the present junction of U. S. route 395 with state highway 108, is visible from many points along the steep ridges. Reno, Nevada, is ninety-five miles to the east.

This area is breath-taking, literally and figuratively, for the air is rarefied. The mountain streams yield the sweetest water I've ever tasted and the coldest, for there are large fields of snow about.

Within several days we have climbed a semicircle of mountains with Pickel Meadows below us. We have been attacked at least twice a day by a group of "aggressors," who are marines permanently stationed here. Most of them are Korean veterans, and some of them speak a few words of Chinese, which they yell during their charges. The other night one of them yelled, "Tluman iss a bassard!" Their tactics are conducted along Red Army lines, their charges preceded by whistles, yells, gongs and bugles. We all use blank cartridges, of course, and are very brave. The worst thing that could happen would be to get captured by the aggressors; they are rough on prisoners. Two nights ago, while on guard duty, I caught an infiltrator crawling toward our camp. I chased him for a full minute, thinking what I would do to him when I caught him, but he got away.

Early this morning we simulated an all-out offensive against the aggressor. Individual preparations were carried out after sunset last night. Then we huddled around untactical fires and bitched about the cold. A lieutenant shuffled sideways down the steep slope and sat with us around the fire, looking into the flames and listening to our conversation for a minute or two. Then he rose and began descending toward the neighboring blaze. I mumbled, "Thank you, Henry the Fifth." The lieutenant halted and turned halfway around. The outline of his body was visible against the sky, his hooded head bent forward as though he were trying to remember something. Then he straightened up jerkily, in what was probably a silent guffaw.

We have had more judo and bayonet work. Judo, though fascinating, seems unnecessary, unless the occasion should arise in which a Chinese and myself meet in the dark, both unarmed. This is unlikely.

There are coyotes around here. They travel in packs and produce the wildest and eeriest variety of noises I've ever heard an animal make. They wail, sob, scream, bark, growl, laugh.

I was thinking how great it would be to return to these mountains someday. God, it's beautiful here! Was thinking about bringing some sturdy babe up here and crunching about the snow looking for deer.

November 14th, 1952

Autumn has me just about ready for the cleaners. The seasons ignore Pendleton and I'd almost forgotten it was fall, but we couldn't very well miss it at Pickel Meadows. Autumn stones me much more than spring. And in summer, just hand me a seabag full of peyote and I'll gladly hibernate in a cool cave. We lit a pile of dead leaves up there one evening, which was a great mistake. Nobody said a word, but we all swaggered about for a few minutes and I knew where I was—back in the neighborhood, in Buffalo, burning leaves.

The stage shows here at T & R have been good. Les Brown, Champ Butler, June Christy. Butler, an ex-marine has a personable style with a beat, but his choice of songs is lousy. June Christy stole the show. Her intonation is terrible, but who cares. She and Jeri Sothern are real fine. Christy is going to Korea. USO.

I have given some thought to the matter of sleeping with a woman in a sleeping bag and have decided that one would barely fit which means that she would not be welcome for any length of time. A slight twinge of claustrophobia would lead to utter panic under such conditions. An interesting way to die, yes, but if a woman were able to wriggle in with me, the poor dear would soon find that she was trapped in a glorified strait jacket with a shrieking, kicking, clawing, hysterical maniac.

When a sleeping bag—or portable womb as I call it—is occupied, it resembles a tremendous green cocoon, and when the occupant moves around, the thing becomes exceedingly grotesque. Sometimes we have Fun & Games at night and become the Sleeping Bag Monsters and hop along, a foot at a time until Sergeant Sir comes in and chastises us. But I fool him. He can say anything he wants because I settle down in the portable womb and I know where I am.

November 15th, 1952

Here is a rough account of the carryings-on of the First Marine Division from their first entry into the Korean war to the present time. The source material is an article in an annual USMC publication, from which I'll quietly lift whole paragraphs, clichés and all.

The North Korean forces crossed the 38th Parallel in June of 1950. At the request of the United Nations, American troops came to the aid of the Republic of South Korea. Army troops landed at Pusan, at the southern tip of the peninsula, and held the enemy in check for a time then lost considerable ground. [I don't mean to slight the Army. This article is concerned primarily with the general action of the 1st Division.] At one point the Americans held only a small perimeter around and including Pusan. The setback was unexpected.

In August the 1st Provisional Marine Brigade—a reinforced regiment—landed at Pusan and within five days advanced twenty-six miles against the enemy. During the months of August and September the Brigade fought together with the 24th Infantry Division along the Naktong River line and inflicted heavy losses. The brigade was then withdrawn to Pusan where it was joined by other units of the 1st Marine Division in preparation for an amphibious assault of Inchon, a seaport located halfway up Korea's west coast. Inchon is to the capital city of Seoul what the Piraeus is to Athens, the distance and direction are practically identical.

On the morning of September 15th a battalion of marines landed on Wolmi-do island, which guards the approaches to Inchon. (I'd like to say something about Salamis but it's not true.) In less than two hours the island was secured. On the afternoon of the same day the rest of the 1st Division landed at Inchon and by the following morning had captured the town. Strategic Kimpo airfield was taken on September 17th. Four days later the combined UN forces entered the capital city.

After driving the enemy to the north and securing protective high ground, the marines were relieved in the Seoul-Inchon area by Army troops, who with other UN units continued to advance across the peninsula toward the sea, thereby cutting off the North Korean forces south of the 38th Parallel; from this point on, guerilla action behind the lines became intensive.

On October 25th the Tenth Corps—of which the 1st Marine Division was a part—landed unopposed at Wonsan, a harbor located halfway up the east coast of the peninsula. Their mission was to strike northward as far as the Manchurian border, clearing away enemy pockets of resistance. General MacArthur .expressed confidence in the prospect of returning home by Christmas just give the news please.

In their intensive drive northward the marines of the 5th and 7th regiments reached Yudam-ni on the western edge of the Chosin reservoir by November 27th. The reservoir is approximately as large as Lake Tahoe. The marines were preparing to continue the drive northward when a new and much more formidable enemy struck unexpectedly, with concentrated power.

Three divisions of the Chinese Communist Forces had crossed the ice of the Yalu river, the border between Manchuria and Korea, to join the North Korean troops. Guerilla units that had been harassing the Tenth Corps during their drive north now consolidated behind the surrounded UN troops.

Under the direction of General Oliver P. Smith, USMC, the 5th and 7th regiments prepared to spearhead the breakout.

On December 6th one of the most famous incidents in Marine Corps history commenced. The Chinese continued to pour in troops, blocking the escape route from Yudam-ni to Hagaru-ri. Having made their initial attack with three divisions (the fools), the Chinese utilized six other divisions in the surrounding movement. It has been estimated that our troops were outnumbered eight to one. General Smith's units consisted of approximately 9800 men including an attached group of 130 British Royal Marines.

For seventy-five miles, over tortuous roads and high mountain passes, the marines fought their way through hordes of encircling Communists, in weather so cold that weapons

27

jammed and many men were put out of action through frostbite. In spite of snowstorms which prevented air support, 30-degrees-below-zero temperatures, mountainous terrain, and an enemy vastly superior in numbers, the unit advanced through enemy roadblocks past Hagaruri and Koto-ri until they reached Hamhung on the sea. They set up a trophy there and sacrificed to Hermes. At Hamhung an evacuation, not unlike Dunkirk in urgency, commenced. Guns of the 7th Fleet made barrage on the hills overlooking the city, while rear units held off the oncoming Communists. More than 200,000 troops and civilians were loaded aboard ships of ʌvery description. The last unit to embark were members of the Navy underwater demolition team and marine bomb-disposal groups who had remained in the city setting booby traps and mining the waterfront.

General Lemuel C. Shepherd, commandant of the Marine Corps, had this to say concerning the Chosin reservoir breakout:

"The opposing Chinese forces were so punished by the marines as to constitute no further threat to our cause. I believe that by no stretch of the imagination can this be described as a retreat, since a retreat presupposes a defeat—and the only defeat involved in the battle was the one suffered by the Chinese."

The cat that said, "Retreat, hell! We're advancing in another direction," was quite serious. Perhaps the most noteworthy accomplishment in regard to the breakout is the fact that the marines brought their supplies, their wounded, and most of their dead back with them. It is generally known that the Army unit left a great deal behind. I have listened to many bitter personal stories concerning the behavior of the Army troops during those two weeks. The easiest way to get into a fight with a soldier is to mention this to him.

Following the evacuation of the Tenth Corps from Hungnam harbor the 1st Marine Division went into reserve with the Eighth Army in southern Korea. Early in 1951 the marines destroyed for fighting purposes a North Korean division that had infiltrated into the Pohang-Andong area.

Next, the division passed under the control of the Ninth Corps and spearheaded the northward drive of a movement known as Operation Killer, on the east-central front. Following this, Operation Ripper occupied the division, with the marines pushing northward again into positions along the 38th Parallel. Other marine sectors of combat were Inge, Changhang and the high ground north of the Punchbowl.

I have left out a hell of a lot. I presume that soon after the Punchbowl operation the 1st Division occupied the western sector where they are operating at the present time.

Marines in general seem to be disappointed that Stevenson did not win the election. It is believed that Eisenhower will extend the military tour of duty and also lower the pay grades. He also expressed an intention of bringing the Korean war to a close, which suggests a full-scale offensive, an ominous prospect if there ever was one. It is probably for these vague reasons that the news of Eisenhower's victory was received so glumly.

November 17th, 1952

I met a friendly English blonde one night at the Millers' and we got along fine. She considered it depressing that I was going to Korea, so I got fractured and stumped out "Foggy Day" on the piano. She was gracious enough to attempt to sing along in seven keys. Between cadenzas I mentioned to her that she ought to be a singer and that it might be delightful for us to go outside and talk or something. A large fool in a black turtle-neck sweater appeared and escorted her back to the lines. I believe she had held my twitching hand. I saw an ad in the New Yorker today that announces her appearance at the Maisonette. Celia Lipton, a very fine singer indeed. She should have told me that I ought to be a marine.

A letter from Shirley today. I picked it up when we returned from field problems—problems in the field—and became so excited by it that I lay on the bunk with my cap over my eyes and remained that way until taps. The sleeping bag is warm and conducive to dreaming. I dreamt the following dream:

29

Shirley was showing me through an extremely ornate house across the Hudson, a practical set by Lem. She wore a hat like the one on Nerfertiti. Her bedroom (watch it) was located on a lower level and had no door, as a dining room in a small house usually has no "door" to the living room. I sat on the floor and we talked. She dusted the pictures on the wall and invited me to come to a dinner party. I asked whether or not her mother would be there and was told that she would be. I declined. (I don't see the connection between her mother's presence and my refusal. Perhaps I subconsciously retain the slight embarrassment I felt when her mother turned to me at a formal candlelit dinner and asked me if I had ever been to Madrid.) Scene change: in an expensive bar. I was wearing an Ivy League uniform; button-down shirt, regimental-stripe tie, Brooks Brothers jacket and charcoal grey trousers. Shirley came in with a bundle of packages, wearing a Rube Goldberg hat. She balanced the packages on a bar stool and handed me a blue slip of paper, on which were written the reasons why I should come to the dinner party. One of them was that her mother would not be there. I apologized and explained that I could not make it. She began arguing politely when reveille sounded. Mother once said that the two most boring topics of conversation were one's dreams and one's operations. That is correct.

Shirley reminds me of Judy Garland. There is a photograph of her in a storeroom on the third floor of the Ayer's house that is a gasser. It looks like it was taken in the fall in New York. Shirley is about thirteen years old, is wearing an old sweater, is standing on roller skates talking to two or three grownups. It is a great picture.

I have said goodbye to Aunt Sallie and the colonel. At the door, I had intended to say, "Well, thus ends phase four in the life of Jean Valjean," but I was so nervous about leaving, that, "Well, thus ends life," was what came out. And I got all balled up trying to explain what I meant. There is so much to be said about Santa Monica that whatever I say won't begin to cover it.

The atmosphere of the town is suited to retired people, like a huge clean and neat sickroom. But then I was only inside one house, the focal point of which was the sickroom of my grandfather. But there were other things which made that town seem empty. Saturday night, wandering in and out of the bars along Wilshire, Santa Monica Boulevard and Broadway, looking half-interestedly for a girl. I found one once, a drunken college girl about ready to pass out. I followed her down the street, near the end of Broadway, and carried on a shouting logorrhea until she sought refuge in a hotel lobby. When I realized that I was frightening her, it frightened me and I left. She didn't even let me call her a cab.

The stores in Santa Monica close early in the evening, and the shopping district, from the Sears building to Wilshire, is almost desolate. Even so I managed to wander through this area every Saturday evening, looking in at the unlit store windows and the little displays that moved. Sunday was usually spent killing time until I had to hitchhike back to camp. For a long while to come Sunday afternoons are going to be accompanied by a feeling that it's time to go pretty soon.

Hitchhiking back was always something of a dream sequence. Those crazy, brightly lit, haut-monde towns south of L. A. with that Benzedrine of a highway, U. S. 101, connecting them. Hermosa Beach, Redondo Beach, Long Beach (where it seemed as though a perimeter of homosexuals waited, in the area of the Long Beach circle, to encircle the hitchhiking serviceman each Sunday night), Balboa, Laguna Beach. Always lots of marines and sailors waiting beside 101. And how about the oil fields around Long Beach! They looked marvelous at night.

Two or three weekends ago a well-dressed young man in a convertible picked me up. As we started up he said, "Do you want to go to a gay party?" I said, "Sure. I'm . . . not gay myself, but I'd like to come along." He brought the car to a rapid but graceful halt. He reached over and opened the door for me and I got out. "Good night," he said.

I don't think I want to see Santa Monica again or even

Southern California. I'm fairly certain that I won't see Gampie again.

We board the *General Wm. Weigel* at the San Diego docks tomorrow.

GROUP TWO

▌▊▊▊

En Route

November 21st, 1952;
aboard the USNS General Wm. Weigel, *at sea*

Naturally there is an albatross following the ship. It has been gliding gracefully along, several hundred yards off our bow, since we left San Diego three days ago. He often flies in fairly close, especially when a garbage dump is made. Each day there is prolonged firing of machine guns and BARs from the fantail, a drill in which all of the marines on board will have taken part before we dock at Inchon. "Ancient Mariner" be damned; I can hardly wait.

This vessel is inhabited by 3,300 marines, most of whom are cruddy, partly seasick, slightly homesick, and certainly bored. The troops, for recreation, write letters, read Mickey Spillane or the Bible, gamble, play "Red River Valley" or the Marine Corps hymn on harmonicas, look at the sea, or look at each other.

The sea is for the birds. The state of seasickness is definitely a suicidal one. Therefore I want to die.

The troop compartments—oh God the troop compartments. Understatement of the year: They are crowded. The racks —stretched canvas, designed specifically to avoid any support of the sacroiliac—stand four to six high and are so close, one on top of another, that one's nose, pelvis, knees and toes are partially flattened when the man above moves around. The man in

33

the uppermost tier is in some cases the most fortunate, unless he happens to be located under one of the continually glaring lights of the hold. He can at least stow his personal gear in the rafters.

The aisle between each tier is wide enough to permit only one-way traffic, which means that each man must stow his equipment on his own rack. Our gear consists of the following articles: a greasy life belt, a full combat pack (haversack, knapsack and blanket roll), a rifle, a cartridge belt (with canteen, first-aid pack, bayonet). This, we feel, is exactly like being interred in a sarcophagus, complete with provisions for the afterworld. No, it is more like an exercise in yoga. Each morning we "awake," having been "asleep," and stare into the oily face of the poor bastard in the adjoining tier—if he is visible through the surrounding rubble. As yet I have not felt obliged to speak to my neighbor, and frankly, if he decides to speak first I am going to tell him to go to hell.

The hold—the troop compartments—carry a static odor of sweaty feet and vomit. The Hour of Charm. Twice a day we are herded up on deck so that the catacombs can be swabbed and inspected. We lie around in semi-catatonia until this moment arrives, and a nasal voice whines over the intercom: "All marines in troop compartments *will* report on deck." Almost invariably some wag begins mooing like a cow. This is picked up by several others until, by the time the ladders and passageways are crowded, the compartments echo with what sounds like a herd of driven cattle.

Having taken part in maneuvers and knowing what life is like aboard a troop transport, I sanctimoniously purchased a fifth of I. W. Harper bourbon during the last weekend in Santa Monica, to use when the waves of self-pity arrived. Some thieving, lecherous, opportunist son of a bitch stole it almost as soon as we left the harbor. I should have bought morphine instead, and hidden it in my shoe.

Our company shares mess duty with another company; two days on, two days off. The other company stands guard duty. Three companies take care of the cleaning details. The others are relatively free except for weapon and equipment inspections.

In the galley, three other corporals and myself are responsible for the swill which the troops use to wash down their food, allegedly coffee. None of us will drink our own product.

We pulled out of San Diego harbor at 6 P.M., November 17th. The Third Division band, in dress blues, played a few marches and a blaring "St. Louis Blues." There were twenty-seven civilians on the dock. As we began to get under way the band played the Marine Corps hymn (musically unsound, yet inspiring). There was not a dry eye among us, except for one tall corporal who, like the ghoul in a Chas. Addams cartoon, was leering gleefully, having officially commenced his quest for the True Masochistic Cross.

Two young women were standing alone under a wharf light near the end of the pier, waving. I won't forget their faces, or their figures, for a long time.

December 2nd, 1952

Last night some of us watched *A Tale of Two Cities* on what is wishfully referred to as the Promenade deck. Watching the movie was like attending pre-dawn meditations at a Cistercian monastery. The only way one could see was to kneel, consequently everyone knelt. It would have been literally impossible to have left in the middle of it. The movie was good. The sunset was great; vivid red—and the air was balmy. Once the sun touched the horizon it disappeared rapidly and the color of the water was like no color I've ever seen. We have passed several tiny uninhabited islands, craggy masses of rock. Three or four times we have seen the distant lights of a ship at night going the other way. At sea they say the horizon is eleven miles away. Tiny schools of phosphorescent sea life are brought to the surface by the wash of the ship, which can be seen at night if you lean over the side.

This morning at 4:30, after filling the coffee kettles, I went up on deck and was unpleasantly surprised by a cold wind and a startling sight. There they were, the mountains of Japan, with the moon hanging above them. It was a real barrelhouse sight and I imagined hearing a tremendous Oriental GONG. The Forbidden Far East. The cold wind and the sight of the mountains mean that we will be in Korea soon.

By sunrise we had anchored off Kobe. A kind of Mr. Moto came on board from a motorboat, dressed impeccably and just as inscrutable as hell, and piloted the ship into dock, next to the Mitsubishi warehouse—where the Mitsubishi bombers and Zeros were once manufactured. The 1st Marine Air Wing replacements disembarked here, and a few Army officers were taken on board. None of the other troops were allowed on shore. Kobe is apparently an industrial city and is built upon a string of hills backed by a mountain range. It's not a beautiful city but certainly looks fascinating.

We are somewhere between Kobe and Inchon now. The captain of the ship gave a nasal speech over the intercom this afternoon. No one paid any attention until the end, when he got carried away: "You men . . . are about to enter . . . the Far East theatre of operations. . . . As United States Marines . . . you will conduct yourselves . . . accordingly (long pause). . . . Most of you men . . . will return . . . in due time (voice low, choked with sincerity). . . . Some of you . . . will not . . . Good hunting. . . ." There was a two-beat pause below deck, then someone tittered. Someone else roared. In a matter of seconds, hundreds, maybe thousands of grimy, homesick men were screaming with hysterical laughter. The vast hold of the ship echoed in a most unmilitary manner.

December 6th, 1952

We are anchored in the harbor of Inchon now, and the troops are disembarking by units, boarding LCMs to be ferried to shore. I am waiting below; our outfit will be one of the last to go.

On our way up the coast we came through two fairly heavy snowstorms, but the stars are out now and it is extremely cold outside.

Each man has been assigned to a unit of the 1st Marine

Division, made official by the presentation of IBM cards to each man yesterday, indicating the destination of each. Mine reads "1st Ord Bn"—Ordnance Battalion. A hell of a disappointment. Although my MOS or military occupation specialty *is* 2111, that is, small-arms mechanic, I was counting on being assigned to an infantry outfit. As it turns out, logically, each man seems to have been assigned according to his MOS. Things aren't usually done in a logical manner in the Corps. However, I'll request transfer as soon as possible. I may be an idiot, but I have two immediate goals: to become a member of a line company and to be promoted to buck sergeant.

In preparation for disembarking I'm wearing the following articles: scivvie shirt and drawers, long johns, flannel shirt, utility trousers, cold-weather trousers, pile-lined vest, parka w/hood, gloves and inserts, flannel cap, socks, boondockers (USMC field shoes), and muffler; am carrying the following articles: M1 rifle, cartridge belt w/accessories, field transport pack, seabag (remaining cold-weather gear included in seabag). Personal effects: a wallet (our US currency has been substituted by a military script referred to as Mickey Mouse money), toothbrush, powder, razor and blades, two mechanical pencils, lead, a small flashlight and batteries, this notebook, a roll of Scotch Tape, a cheap 35-mm. camera, three rolls of film, and a pocket book titled *The Greek Way*, by Edith Hamilton.

On the last Santa Monica weekend I spent most of an afternoon browsing through a stack of magazines, looking for a picture or two that I could carry with me. A purely sentimental move. I wanted a picture that was capable of holding my attention when I needed a distraction. I picked out two small cuts, both pictures of Judy Holliday. One is from *Time* magazine, captioned "Old who?— Old Vic." The other is from *Quick* magazine, captioned "Holliday-duped." So she will function as Miss Girl Whom I Would Most Like To Be Sent Overseas WITH.

I'll keep writing until we are called. The compartments seem unnatural and chilly, nearly deserted. Now I miss the other cattle.

I went up on deck to take a look. The shore is not visible.

Many ships, including a nearby hospital ship, surround us. A floating drydock of rough logs has been towed alongside by a civilian-type barge. It is moored on the starboard side. The troops are leaving the ship through a hatch near the water level. They wait on the drydock for the LCMs. The loading area is illuminated by several searchlights. While waiting, there have been two blackouts.

I acquired three friends during the two-week voyage: Cpl. Maynard Keil from Bicknell, Indiana, a radio relay man. He graduated from Purdue, has done a hitch in the Navy. Pfc. Peter Warner from Larchmont, also a radio relay man; spent two years at Syracuse U. forestry school. Cpl. Dan Rossi, from Norwalk, Conn., motor transport; studied at Harvard for a year. Warner is a gentleman of the old school, never complains, stays relaxed, is willing to make it with the euphoria-world and does admirably at it. We both asked to carry BARs on maneuvers at Pendleton and had several private contests to see who could climb a particular hill the fastest. Old Smoky is sixty-eight hundred feet high but we tackled it as a race. We left the rest of the company far behind us, but by the time we got to the top we were crawling in agony. Part of the training program was to climb one of those hills every day. Everyone was in great shape, but we've lost it lying around the ship.

It's getting cold down here. Keil and Warner have left with the 1st Signal Battalion replacements. Rossi is asleep on one of the racks. We two, and another man, are the only people left in this compartment. As Keil and Warner saddled up to leave a few minutes ago I said, "Have a nice vacation. See you next fall."

December 7th, 1952, Ascom City, Korea

The 1st Ord, replacements disembarked last of all, at 1 A.M. We reached the wharf at 1:30 and filed in column along a jerry-built quay illuminated by bare lights on tall poles. We passed underneath a wooden archway. WELCOME TO THE PORT OF INCHON

KOREA was painted on it. The opposite side read BON VOYAGE, but we shouldn't have looked back.

There were more than 3,000 men standing in formation along the waterfront waiting for the *General Wm. Weigel* to be emptied so that they could go home. Several of the throng began a sort of sadistic chant which was picked up from group to group. "You'll be sorr-ee!" rang in our miserable ears. Theoretically we are their replacements.

We were loaded immediately into 6' by 6' trucks. The men going home had lit a few fires despite the possibility of a blackout and they watched us loading. "You'll be sorr-ee!"

The convoy to this camp—Ascom City or Ashcan City—was absolutely the END. Ten or fifteen miles of the god-damnedest panorama I've ever seen. The trucks were open and most of the men buried their faces in their arms against the flaying wind, but I managed to peek out with one twitching eyeball. Is there such a thing as frostbite of the eyeball? How does one describe Inchon? It resembles nothing like any American city. The buildings and streets appear to be in miniature. Even the unidentifiable shapes and the shadows were strange to the eye, that poor blinking eye.

Banners have been stretched across some of the intersections. WELCOME IKE. He's come and gone.

I shudder to think what Inchon must look like in daylight. I'd like to say flatly that I'm hog-wild about what little I've seen of the Orient, but I'd better cool it awhile. I may not be so hog-wild later.

Ascom City is a marine replacement and supply depot. We were issued thermal boots as soon as we arrived. Boondockers provide little protection against the cold and our collective feet were numb by the time we arrived, not to mention one eyeball. We were divided into thirteen-man groups and billeted in unheated tents to sleep from 3 A.M. until 5 A.M. The Ord. Bn. replacements, 145 men, are billeted in one corner of the sprawling camp. A double-apron barbed-wire fence separates us from the outskirts of the rubble of a town called Bu Puang, pronounced

Boo Pee-ong. A wide-open concrete sewer, resembling Brush Creek in Kansas City, runs along the outskirts. It is just on the other side of the fence. A range of bleak snow-covered mountains rise in the distance. Although it is daylight, a thin fog is present and the sky is grey.

I'm seated on an ash can near the fence. Two young Korean women are selling whiskey and leather wallets to a group of marines who are crowded on this side of the fence. The wallets cost three dollars and the whiskey—Seagram's V. O.—costs ten dollars. There are several buyers. The women produce the booze from tremendous pockets of their baggy cotton pants and lean way over the barbed wire to make the exchange.

Same day. 7 P.M. 1st Ordnance Battalion

We began moving out at nine o'clock this morning. Each of us was issued three clips of ammunition. Apparently a guerilla band raided one of the replacement trains last year. We hiked a mile to the Bu Puang railroad station and boarded an ancient Japanese-made train. Before the train pulled out, I walked around outside and investigated a group of civilians who were watching us. Sounds as though I were suspicious; that's not what I mean at all. I couldn't describe the town and I don't think I can do much more for the people. Wretched, clean, filthy, ugly, beautiful, finely made. There.

The Bu Puang station is about the size of the one at Suffern, N. Y. No waiting room.

The old train rattled and clanked and achieved a thundering 20 m.p.h. The cars were filthy but so were we. The seats were hardwood benches with perpendicular backs. No toilet to be found.

Rather than sit with the piles of gear inside, I stood within the open vestibule between two cars and took in all the fabulous sights, as far as Yong Dong Po, across the Han River from Seoul. The train shuddered to a hissing stop in each village to take on or let off civilian passengers. During the short stops children would crowd under the windows of the train screeching, "Hi,

Joe!" or, "Hello! Hello!" Many of them were trying to sell chewing gum and, to those of us in the open vestibule, shoeshines. Some of the older people were trying to sell gaily wrapped Korean whisky, but there were no takers. In a number of hygiene lectures in the past the point has been made that Korean-made booze is practically poison. A white-bearded old man, dressed in long robes and smiling affably, shuffled in among the noisy children holding up a bottle of the local firewater. A marine leaned out one of the windows and indicated that he wished to examine the label on the bottle, and also the seal, to see whether it had been broken for watering-down. The ear-splitting train whistle shrieked, and we started to shudder on down the track. The kids yelled even louder and the old man began stumbling along beside the train. He ripped off the outer packaging of the bottle to show the marine that the seal was intact. He thrust it up toward the open window, but the marine didn't want any. The old man trotted along for a few yards until the train picked up speed. A strand of his coarse hair had dropped down over his forehead. He was as pathetic as the children.

At the next village the train stopped in such a way that the vestibule in which I was standing was lined up with the inter-secting main street. A group of Hollywood characters waited there for the train to move past so that they could cross over the tracks. They were facing the train and, in my position, I was framed for observation—so I launched into a high-school routine for them; leering, bowing, winking, waving, saluting, bowing again. The children giggled loudly, but the old folks remained stone-faced. A ragged old man, wearing an elegant silk scarf and biting upon a long cigarette holder, observed the pantomime with humorless fascination, tilting his head as though he were a dog listening to an imitation of a cat.

The countryside between each village is pretty unreal, a frozen patchwork of fields and rice paddies. We saw many farmers, carrying tremendous loads on their backs, walking along the raised paths which separate the rice paddies. The size of these loads are staggering, usually a collection of brush for fuel, held on the back by a cord encircling the entire bundle. Wisps of smoke rose into the air from the top of each thatched hut that we passed.

The condition of Seoul is a very moving sight; like a vast trash heap. A few modern buildings, but a huge rubble of a town. We did not stop there and went on through three long dark tunnels, during which clouds of soot and smoke filled the inside of our car.

At 3 P.M. we reached the village of Kumchon-ni, unloaded, and walked a mile or so to the 1st Ord. Bn. area, located atop a hill overlooking the town. Here is a rough map showing our approximate position.

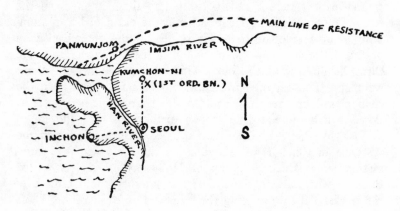

GROUP THREE

‖‖‖

1st Ordnance Battalion

December 10th, 1952

No, I can't possibly remain here. Here are some of the reasons:

1) We live in well-heated six-man tents.
2) Three hot meals a day are served in a warm mess hall less than fifty yards from this tent.
3) The sybarites have built a recreation hall in which movies are shown every evening.
4) Hot showers are available three times a week.
5) There is an organ in the chaplain's tent. An organ!
6) Each tent is wired for electric lights, radios, etc.
7) A PX truck comes around every week and we all scurry down to it and buy goodies & confections and other unmilitary commodities such as shaving lotion.
8) We are allowed a beer ration; one case per man each week. Staff N.C.O. personnel (staff sergeants and above) and officers receive a liquor ration.
9) Our laundry is done for us by the Helot slaves—Koreans.
10) The working day begins at 8 A.M. and ends at 4:30, with an hour for lunch.
11) Breakfast is served at 7 A.M., although one may remain in bed until approximately 7:55. One usually does.

12) It is possible for an enlisted man to buy black-market booze from members of the Korean Service Corps.

O, gone, gone are the days of the Lacedaemonian ideal, gone the crude camaraderie of the Macedonian phalanx. I shouldn't have read Edith Hamilton. O, Death! Where is thy sting at? O, bloody, terrible carnage!

So here I sit, four comfortable miles behind the lines, hanging on my bough of luxury—I quote of course—ripe and undisturbed. I am sitting, Indian fashion, on the cot, smoking a King Edward cigar (I loathe cigars but the WHOLE THING is all an act anyway, I think), half loaded on imported Budweiser beer, a case of which lies under the cot. A Korean named Moon has sold me a fifth of Canadian Club for eight fifty. Wall Street capitalist warmonger, I.

The rumbling of heavy artillery is sometimes audible back here, and at night we have heard .50-calibre machine guns firing long bursts into enemy lines. To us new arrivals, the sound is fascinating. Today a helicopter flew over the camp with a long bundle upon the undercarriage, a wounded man.

The company commander, Captain Brown, a cigar-chewing marine of the Old Corps, interviewed the new men this morning, individually. I made known my urgent and rather corny desire to be transferred into the 0300 field—the infantry. "You are insane," he said, adding that many of us would be sent to line companies before long, but functioning as small-arms mechanics. He mentioned that it would not be difficult to obtain a transfer, once attached to a rifle company. Encouraging. I suppose what I want is to be able to sit in some lonely foxhole, scratching my filthy beard, clutching a BAR, huddled in a corner against the bitter cold, waiting stalwartly for the Chinese to attack. That is correct. Naturally I want to be up there on Christmas eve; then Doctor Masochismo would really be happy.

This tent is on the edge of camp. A wire fence separates us from a collection of thatched huts. A fine little boy who calls himself John lives in one of them. We have made friends and he waits for me on the other side of the fence each day as soon as he gets back from school. The school he attends is in Kumchon-ni. He has taught me some basic Korean: "Hello. How are you? I am well. Thank you. Goodbye. Yes. No. Come here. GET OUT! Food. Water. Beer. What is your name? My name is——. How much? Halt." The kid has beautiful manners and is obviously quite intelligent for his age, which is twelve. According to our way of noting age he is eleven. The Koreans, however, count time in the womb which seems entirely logical.

There are several mounds of earth, covered with weeds, located within the camp. One of them is situated behind our tent. There is another near the fence, and I usually sit on it while talking to John through the fence. They are about four feet high. I used to pee on the one behind our tent until John informed me, with a complicated pantomime, that they are graves.

Panmunjom, the site of the truce talks, is marked at night by a powerful searchlight, a fixed vertical beam, visible to the northwest.

December 25th, 1952

Now I know why I'm so easily satisfied with anything the Corps has to offer. The Corps, and service life in general, is a combination father and mother to us. A kind of immense womb. General Shepherd might justifiably frown on such a comment, but he's been a general a long time. In this setup we simply do not have to fend for ourselves. Everything is taken care of by men of superior rank, and a spiritual ivory tower is not at all hard to find here. This reminds me of a telegram that my brother sent the day I graduated from South Kent: CONGRATULATIONS FONG. IS THIS THE END OF YOUR IVORY TOWER?" Fong was my nickname.

I've got a lot on my mind tonight, but it's all vague as usual. I doubt that I'll be able to put it down without sounding flatulent.

A monk (here we go) in perhaps the most urgent grasp for austerity, lives according to his particular standards of poverty,

45

chastity, obedience and, in most cases, silence. While I sometimes profess to acknowledge no standards, these four are always
attractive and sometimes I make a feeble stab at putting them
to use. But it's always just a feint. Whether or not we are poor
here is disputable, although not in the case of the front-line
troops. That we live by the other three is certainly far less disputable. Silence is a personal affectation, the only defense
against the oral warfare of the tent, the chow line and the ordnance shop.

Derision of some kind is never lacking around here. It is
often unadorned contempt. Last night I went on a rapid crusade
against it and committed no less than battery & assault on an
idiot who felt like riding me because I never said anything.
When I asked someone what time chow call blew in the morning, the schmuck childishly mimicked my voice, repeating the
same question. I have spoken hardly a word since arriving and
he must have thought he had found a whipping boy. At that
moment he seemed to epitomize the barbarous attitude expressed so often by enlisted men for various semiforgivable reasons. His truculence was an intrusion on my guarded Christmas
Eve privacy, and that routine had to be cut short. So—dressed
only in long johns, I uncocooned myself from the sleeping bag
and flew across the tent, upsetting water and oil cans on the
way. I aimed a blow at his face which landed on his chest. The
blow. He was too surprised to defend himself. I sat on him and
put my hands around his neck and said something like "I want
you to ignore me from now on. I don't even want to know that
you know that I'm in the same tent with you." Scared hell out
of the poor man.

It's quite possible that I'm the kind of snob that considers
himself "eternally moved" but who is certain that his companions are never moved by more than some evidence of their own
companions' errors, in petty circumstances under which they feel
that they themselves would not err. Thank you, Plutarch. But
this is a common denominator in us all, prodded into action by
the treatment we received at Parris Island. We were broken down

46

into our basic parts there, and it was too much of an effort to observe the Golden Rule. On the southbound train I talked to several other recruits, or boots as they are called, two at least of whom may be referred to as "representing their former environment" fairly well. One, Victor Seif, was a graduate of Maryland U., an astute, upper-class intellectual. Within two hours after crossing the bridge to the island he was as much an animal as Harry Poole, a scarred, tight-lipped Negro from Roanoke; and as much an animal as myself. The fact that I mumble, curse and swagger like the others here precludes whatever introspection one might attach to the actions. The one secure control is silence.

Pfc. O'Neill, from Joliet, is the other member of this tent who maintains near silence. But he is belligerently ignorant, and his rare interjections are out of this world. A few minutes ago we were mumbling something about animals as pets. O'Neill was lying on his bunk, actually swaggering while prostrate. One of the men spoke of his own dog, saying that he strays from home once in a while. O'Neill rose up on one elbow and delivered the following observation:

"Any fucking dog that don't know enough to stay home deserves to have his goddam *ass* blowed off." O'Neill, having been sufficiently stimulated to reveal his acquaintance with the matter—with triumphant obtuseness—then resumed the prone position.

When Truman was mentioned last night, one of the mumblers said, "That bastard? Why he's a fucking crook."

"All right," somebody else said. "Name somebody in politics that ain't a crook."

"Yeah, they're all crooks."

"Christ, there's war with the Democrats and depression with the Republicans."

"Yep. Sure as hell . . . Them son of a BITCHES!"

Cpl. Joe Fernandez drank a beer with us the other night. After he had gone, there were phrases said like "Good man," "Squared away," and "Good guy." There followed a discussion

47

regarding the difference between Mexicans, Spaniards and Puerto Ricans. Someone said, "Ahh, them *fuck*ers is all the same anyhow." The others seemed to agree.

If the service has changed me in any way, the difference is only slight. There has always been a leaning toward cynicism. Perhaps that is an inadequate word to use here because it suggests the jaundiced outlook of one who has suffered; a condition which I have successfully avoided. Or perhaps I am merely self-conscious about using the word. It is the vogue these days: young, cynical men. But I can't use the word "realistic" either; I'm impractical as hell and an escapist to boot.

So the outlook now is one of private, mild but constant mistrust. I expect nothing from anyone and am therefore never disappointed. Oh, horse shit! I watch myself stumble through a daily cycle of unrelated characters: the tough N.C.O., the intellectual, the matinee idol in a war picture, Father Confessor, the dullard, the snob, the monk, the seeker of truth—all these and many more in a single day. (Busy day.) The nucleus of constants is nearly obscure. Egotism and loyalty are the only two. Isn't this chaos of personalities something I have noticed in most of my friends? Yes, indeedy. I'm learning to be intolerant of others but very tolerant of myself. I will never be awed by anyone again, and I retain a crude marine truism concerning the similarity of human feces, which will be a powerful prompter, if a terrible one.

Captain Brown delivered his Christmas speech this afternoon, calling us out of our drunkenness to hear it, weaving in ranks at attention. He said, "At ease. . . . We all of us have been hearing 'Season's Greetings' and 'Merry Christmas' and all that. With us being where we are, we all know about how much those words and phrases add up to. About nothing. . . . I do wish one thing: that you men will have a contented Christmas. That's as much as I can hope for, that you men be contented . . . and that, by God, none of us will be here next Christmas. . . . Tainn-ss-ʜᴜᴛ! Dismissed."

We all weaved back to our hot toddies by the stoves.

December 27th, 1952

My transfer has been approved! HAH! Between January 1st and 6th I'll be shipped to the 1st Marines, one of the three howling infantry regiments of the division. The 5th Marines and the 7th Marines are the other two. At present the 1st and the 7th are on line. The 5th is in reserve. Unless there is an emergency it is always set up this way; two regiments up, one regiment in reserve. The only other regiment in the division is the 11th Marines, an artillery regiment composed of four battalions. Thus, the 1st Marine Division is made up of four separate regiments: the 1st, 5th, 7th and 11th. The supporting units are almost all of battalion strength. Ordnance bn., ammo bn., medical bn., motor transport bn., signal bn., tank bn., service bn., engineer bn., shore party bn., headquarters bn., anti-aircraft company, anti-tank company, reconnaisance company. I'm not informed as to the strength of the 1st Marine Air Wing, but it is strong as hell.

There exists an unpublicized regiment known as the Korean Marine Corps, called KMCs. They are attached to our division, but their higher echelon is filled with American marines. They have a fabulous reputation. They are trained in our methods of fighting and use our equipment. Incidentally they are very hard on their weapons and don't appear to be interested in cleaning them. Our repair racks in the ordnance shop are constantly filled with weapons from the KMCs.

About that emotional binge on the last couple of pages. It was mostly because a transfer at that time seemed untenable. Since entering the service on November 1st, 1951, I have tried by every possible method to join an infantry outfit. After fourteen months of duty I'm still not there, but close. On our second day at Parris Island we were given forms to fill out, on which we were permitted to indicate preference as to military occupation specialty. I asked for infantry duty and, during an interview that same day made it quite plain that I had absolutely no mechanical aptitude WHATEVER and that I had entered the Corps to be a gung-ho roaring marine. I was sent to ordnance school at

Quantico, Virginia. At Quantico we were again permitted to make a choice, or rather to state our preference of duty station. As pointedly as possible, I asked for infantry duty and was OF COURSE sent to an artillery outfit at Camp Lejeune where I was used as an ammo man in a 155mm. howitzer crew. I immediately put in for a transfer and the name was added to a long list of other malcontents. Later on I was promoted to corporal and given charge of the ordnance shop of the battery. This move failed to placate me and I promptly turned the shop into an utter shambles, but not out of spite—out of not knowing anything about anything having to do with running anything. One hot, greasy afternoon I stomped into the first sergeant's office and requested mast in a loud and trembling voice. Requesting mast is an involved chain-of-command process by which an enlisted man may personally present a significant complaint to his commanding officer. I rehearsed a speech before appearing in the presence of His Eminence, the colonel. But it all went to hell and I went into an endless plea, starting way back in the days of Homer. Before I got into Xenophon, His Eminence told me to GET OUT! but he granted the transfer to Training and Replacement Command at Pendleton. The training we received there was strictly infantry type and we were led to expect that we would be sent to an infantry unit overseas. Quite logically, however, we were placed according to our occupation specialties. I requested mast for the second time, was held in check by Captain Brown who pointed out that the battalion policy was to hold a man at least three months before considering transfer to a better ward. In the case of the other five armorers, who have already been transferred to line companies, he explained that 1st Ord. bn. had been a casual company, as it is called, in their case, and that they had been scheduled for the line even before they landed at Inchon, having been detained here for purposes of orientation. Naturally I was feeling a bit sorry for myself, hung up in this cozy winter resort. But I haven't quite made it yet. I'm going to the 1st Marines as an armorer and will have to request transfer from there.

December 28th, 1952

According to a detailed Army map which is spread out on my lap there are five narrow-gauge railroads in Korea, all of which are above the 38th Parallel. The southernmost one connects Sariwon with Changyon, a distance of forty miles. Changyon is near the west coast, and the tracks run parallel and not many miles above the 38th. The next one branches off the main line up from Pusan, at Koindong, a village close to the Chosin reservoir. Its tracks run ten miles west and end at the base of a mountain. Interestingly enough, there is no village mapped there. Perhaps it is the private railroad of a leering warlord. Two of the three remaining narrow-gauge tracks are even more intriguing, as seen on the map. They are both situated north of the reservoir, near the Yalu river. According to this map they run from nowhere to nowhere. No village at either end, only mountains. Alec Wilder digs the narrow-gauge world and has traveled far to ride on one. He said that there are very few of them left. We've got to make that trip from nowhere to nowhere someday. The northernmost narrow-gauge track connects Pungsan with Tanchon, a distance of fifty miles. Tanchon is four miles from the China Sea, the east coast. The track from Pungsan joins a 4' 8-½" track at Tanchon and this track goes on to Vladivostok, on Peter the Great Bay, in the Soviet Union.

The town of Uijongbu (Wee-jong-boo) lies east of here, on the other side of the mountains, the nearest big town. Kumchon-ni, where little John goes to school, is about the size of Portageville, N. Y.

The whistles and steam engines of supply trains echo within the valley every night. This particular track is a real production. It spans the peninsula from Pusan—at the southern tip—to Seoul, through North Korea to the Manchurian border where it crosses the Yalu and keeps going as far as Harbin, four hundred miles from the Korean border. At Harbin, it joins the tracks of the Trans-Siberian system, by which a passenger may travel to Moscow and western Europe. The tracks from Pusan to Harbin were laid out under the supervision of the Japanese.

51

Yesterday we knocked off work for a while to watch a funeral procession; a column, moving across the raised path which separates the nearby rice paddy. Ten people in gay, beautiful costumes, wielded a thing that was a cross between the papal blessing-chair, or whatever it's called, and a palanquin. The corpse was sitting in it, covered by a large cloth of vivid red. Some of the pall bearers carried little bells in one hand; two men carried gongs. The sound was incongruous in the freezing daylight. Tinkle—tinkle—tinkleGONG tinkletinkle—GONGtinkle. At the same time they sang an atonal or quarter-tone scale chant. According to Moon, a KMC, the Koreans bury their dead in a sitting position so that they can "see the land they once inhabited." It's a nice idea but why not put a window in the burial mound?

We have watched the Korean kids playing two games. One is a sort of ice tag. They each sit on a board and propel themselves across the ice with sharp sticks, trying to tag each other. The other game consists of bouncing a rubber ball on the ground, using their feet to do so. They compete by seeing who can bounce the ball for the longest time. It is necessary to stand on one foot and none of us can do very well at keeping the ball in motion.

Letter from my brother, Tim:

[I am] for the first time in my army career doing things which are reasonably parallel with my civilian interests. The only drawback is the presence of a boss who is an absolute Number One ten-carat nothing. His imagination is definitely bound to the most unimaginative and overly detailed regular army way of thinking and he makes it just one shade better by being shot at. The bromide about things could be worse is more than true in Korea, and the memory of other jobs is still a bit vivid for me to tell him to tamp his army regulations up his G. I. ass. . . . I hope very much that you will squeeze in time to write me a reasonably lucid letter. Though only a lieutenant, my present position gives me the opportunity to pull things heretofore unknown to me, and I might be able to hop over to Seoul, and on up to the 1st Marine Division to see you. If you were to brief me a bit on what outpost you are manning a BAR on, I might attempt to do it.

At any odds, old fellow, welcome to the exotic Orient. I can visualize you leading a saber charge with Fong-like zealousness now . . ."

He calls me either Fong or Yellow Fang. I used to have fangs but they interfered with the trumpet so Dr. Meisburger pulled them out. Apparently Tim is not on the line any more. He was in charge of a counter-fire platoon, whose job it was to detect the position of enemy mortars and artillery by means of sound equipment.

GROUP FOUR

||||||||||||||||||||||||||||||||||||||||||||||||||||||||||||||||||||||||||||||||||||||||||||

76-Alley

January 5th through 10th, 1953

Now I'm the automatic rifleman of the second-fire team of the ———— squad of the ———— platoon of Able Company of the First Battalion of the First Regiment of the First Marine Division, and it's about time. Although I've only been with Able Company for five days, I consider it an honor to be here.

The 1st Battalion occupies the divisional right flank. The Princess Pat Light Infantry Brigade of Canada are our neighbors to the right. We see them from time to time; they are distinguishable by their natty blue berets. The United Nations line-up, from the Yellow Sea to the Sea of Japan, is as follows, not necessarily in order: 1st Marine Division, Republic of Korea Division, and the following U. S. infantry divisions: 2nd, 3rd, 25th, 40th, and 45th. The Greek, Turkish, French and other U. N. contingents are attached to the Army divisions. The entire production is referred to as EUSAC—Eighth U. S. Army Corps. My brother Tim is an officer of the 45th.

It will be difficult as hell to catch up on the activities of the past few days and nights. This is the world about which boys like Jonathan Ayers dream and when I was his age I dreamt of it, too—of creeping, hiding, listening, stalking, shooting. I have dreamt so many adventures in terrain like this that the whole situation seems familiar, as though I've been here before. This is the most "adventurous and colorful" life of them all, but its morbid aspects stand out and are not to be—cannot be—overlooked. I'd better admit one thing right now. I'd rather be right here than anywhere else in the world. Whether I'm ready for the loony bin or not is beside the point. That's how I feel. When I change my mind I'll say so.

The front, or front lines, are rarely referred to as such. "MLR" is used instead. It stands for "main line of resistance." In our case the MLR is a deep trench, from five to seven feet in depth, running along the ridgeline of the hill mass occupied by our platoon. Theoretically the MLR is a continuous avenue from coast to coast, cutting the peninsula of Korea in half. If this were so, it would not be unreasonable to assume that I could find Tim if I followed the trench east for a few miles.

Our bunkers are situated on the reverse slope of the ridge, out of sight from the enemy trenches. A Yukon stove in each bunker provides heat. It is much more efficient than the pot-bellied type we had at 1st Ord. Bn., although smaller, measuring approx. 3' by 1' by 1'. It is oil-fed from a five-gallon can which rests on top of the bunker. Candles provide light inside the bunkers. The arrangement of the inside of the shelter—the thick wooden supporting beams, the sandbag walls, the crude wooden table, the photographs of beautiful women nailed to the beams, the rifles, ammunition belts, grenades, the candlelight—reminds one of a set for "What Price Glory." It is impossible to keep anything clean; showers of dirt fall each time an incoming shell lands anywhere nearby. These bunkers were probably built more than a year ago and, as far as improvements go, there is not much more that can be done. Fortunately we do not sleep on the ground—this is Rodent City—but either upon raised structures against the wall or in stretchers hung by communication wire from the ceiling.

The microcosm here is the platoon. We have practically nothing to do with the other two platoons of the company. Here is a rough diagram of the ——— Platoon area.

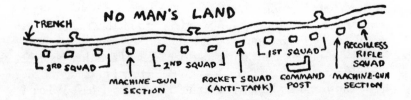

Those three protrusions into No Man's Land are phone emplacements. They are occupied constantly, and serve primarily as points of observation, each commanding a wide view of No Man's Land. Between each phone emplacement there are several "fighting-holes." These are also protrusions but are not covered and/or reinforced as are the phone emplacements. Most of the fighting-holes are provided with grenades—both fragmentation and illumination—and belts of ammunition. These are individual positions, *i.e.*, accommodating one man.

A cutaway view:

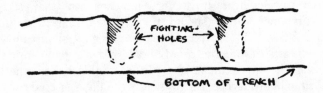

The drawing might be confusing. These are not foxholes; but they are niches or alcoves that have been dug into the forward side of the trench.

I am writing this in the phone emplacement bunker of the ——— squad. It is early afternoon and it is very cold. I might have stayed in the bunker but (a) I'm self-conscious about all this scribbling and (b) the candlelight is too dim. "What, after all, is Art?" someone said at a party, in a resonant voice and with a straight face. "Fuck you," someone else said, in a resonant voice and with a straight face. Looking north, this is what one sees from this position, except for the labels:

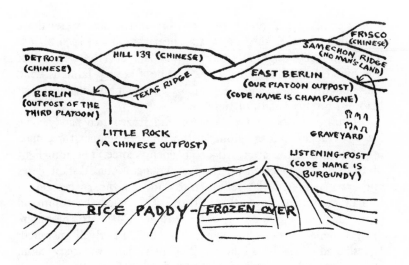

No Man's Land is the space between our MLR and that of the Chinese. Here the distance is approximately eight hundred yards. In some places we are told it is less than a hundred yards.

It is a rule that no green man be allowed in front of the MLR for the first three days. This will give him time to calm his imagination a bit by observing the lay of the land from the main trench rather than going out on a patrol as soon as he arrives. Here is a fine example of why green men are kept on line at first:

My First Night in War

by Martin Russ, 6th grade

Sgt. Barefield, the squad leader, asked me if I would mind standing watch during the night. I would not mind, I replied. At 2 A.M. I was awakened by Cpl. Mackay who offered to stand watch with me until I got used to it. This was a kind gesture on his part, one which I admit considering, not so much from fear of the enemy but from fear that I wouldn't know the method of standing watch—what to say on the phone and so forth. Nevertheless I decided to do it alone. Mackay escorted me up to the phone emplacement and there I sat. His instructions were: don't sleep, don't smoke, keep quiet, stay near the phone, keep a close watch on the terrain in front of the parapet (the window of the bunker, approx. 3′ by 1-1/2′). The freezing January wind whipped through the opening and I found it impossible to sit before it for any length of time.

I heard noises below, down on the frozen rice paddy. The ice was cracking and groaning in the sub-zero temperature, making sounds like the approach of an enemy force. The dim light of the sky was reflected on the ice and occasional distant flares and tracers altered the reflection to add to the suggestion of human movement down there. Terrified, I called the command post. The way one does this is to whisper "C-P" into the phone until someone answers by saying "C-P on." Lt. Buell answered. I described what I had heard. The lieutenant was very calm. "Stay alert and call back if anything develops."

I laid the BAR, loaded and cocked, across the parapet. In one hand I clutched a grenade. I was ready to face the Yellow Dragon.

Noises again! And the wind stirred the ming trees and the dry bushes growing along the forward slope. Several of the moving shadows resembled human figures. I was certain then that a group of Chinese were maneuvering into position for an assault. For one horrendous minute, I aimed the BAR at the nearest upright shadow, awaiting the attack. The ming trees and the dry bushes continued to bob and weave.

In a dry whisper, I called the lieutenant. "Sir, I hear more noises and I think I can see figures now."

"What is your name?" he said. He must have realized that I was a new replacement. I identified myself. He said, "Play it cool, lad." Listening over the phone, I heard him call each of the phone emplacements, alerting them. Seconds later, a shadow down the slope began waving its arms. I pulled the pin of the grenade and lobbed it into the air. It detonated next to the moving shadow. When my eyes again became accustomed to the dark, I saw that the Damned Thing was still waving its arms.

The lieutenant had heard the detonation, or it had been reported to him. "All right, goddamit! Who got shook?" he yelled into the phone, addressing the phone emplacements in general. I whispered back intensely, "But, sir, there are some Chinese out there. I'm sure of it!" He replied, "Get ready, Russ!" and immediately set about alerting the entire platoon sector, including the outpost East Berlin. The two listening posts were instructed to return to the MLR at once. The men on line stumbled out of their bunkers carrying parkas, weapons, ammo, belts, helmets and armored vests. In the meantime the lieutenant had contacted the 60mm. mortar crews, requesting an emergency mission of flare projectiles. Before the mission was fired he called each of the phone emplacements in turn, instructing us to remain well concealed but, as soon as the flares ignited, to observe the terrain on the forward slope of each of our positions. Talking to me, he said, "Are you ready to open fire, Russ? They're probably nearest you."

The mortar crews gave their "On the way" signal to Lt. Buell and he relayed it to us. Three projectiles were discharged from the mortar tubes, making a dull THUNK-THUNK-THUNK sound. In a few seconds the flares ignited, with three sharp POPS, hundreds of feet in the air. The effect which this intense illumination caused was terrifying. All of those shadows, hundreds of them—craters, bushes, rocks, trees—moved irregularly back and forth as the parachute flares themselves oscillated. Unfortunately they had ignited too far forward, and the hill mass of East Berlin cast a huge shadow across the rice paddy. Lt. Buell estimated the correction in elevation that was necessary and relayed it to the mortar people. The second group of flares were perfectly placed, illuminating the forward slopes of the MLR with a brilliant white light. Not a single human, nor a single deer, nor a single rat was to be seen.

The men stumbled irritably back to their bunkers, and I sat in great embarrassment until 4 A.M., when I was relieved by Sgt. Barefield.

Next day

I was allowed to cross the MLR last night to share the relief of one of the two listening posts in our sector. Being in an exposed position, they are occupied only during the dark hours. Both men are required to carry automatic weapons and a load of grenades. One hundred per cent watch is maintained, which means that neither man sleeps. A sound-power is also brought out in order to communicate with the command post, which is, of course, behind our lines. A sound-power resembles a civilian telephone except for a little knob which is turned when one wishes to talk. How it works is a mystery to me. There is no visible power box of any kind; a wire simply runs from one phone to another—sometimes several others, as in the case of the phone emplacements. Obviously the working mechanism is contained within the phone itself. Reception is extremely clear. Contact is established with the CP every fifteen minutes. The lieutenant, or someone else in the command post, calls each of the phone emplacements, then the outpost, and finally the two listening posts. Since the men on listening post are in an exposed position and small in number, they are required to whisper one word into their phone to signify that all is quiet out there: "Burgundy," which is also the code name for the listening post. The position of this post is flexible although constricted to an area of about 100' by 100'. As far as the weather is concerned, the Burgundies are the cruelest watches of all. No blankets are taken out and one must lie upon the frozen ground for four hours at a time.

In order to get out there it is necessary to cross a mine field, laid by U. N. troops months ago. The field is not marked, but Cpl. Mackay, who led the way, knew the path and suggested that I memorize it, in case . . . etc. There are mine fields all over this area, including ones laid by the Chinese. Cpl. Mackay and I both heard the sound of digging last night, while on Burgundy. The sound came from the direction of Samechon ridge, about two hundred yards away. Mackay said that it was probably a mine-planting detail. They did not approach us. If they had, we could have spotted them coming from some distance away. We were set up near a fork in the path.

Every third night our squad mans the outpost, East Berlin, accompanied by a machine-gun section and a radioman. The forward slope of this hill is extremely steep and covered with rows of barbed wire. Sgt. Barefield said that East Berlin has been attacked once since the platoon has taken over this sector, an interval of ten or eleven days. The attacking force approached along Texas Ridge. Our machine gun is set up so that it covers that ridge. Nothing happened in the way of action the first night I went out there, although I had a nightmare. From the top of that hill we have an almost unobscured view of the Chinese MLR, and all was quiet. This is the general layout of East Berlin:

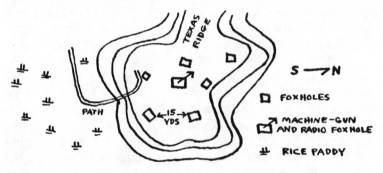

As soon as the sky begins to lighten, the squad—with a machine gun, it is actually a reinforced squad—withdraws to the MLR, except for two men who remain hidden in one of the holes throughout the day. These two "lay-outs," as they are called, are relieved by the next squad that night. I am interested in standing this particular watch. I can't determine what their function is, since they must hide in a hole all day.

Almost every night we are exposed to the Chinese methods of psychological warfare, which are hysterically funny and never fail to increase our morale. The Chinese have set up an ampli-

61

fier unit on the hill known as "Detroit." The "treatment" commences at 6 o'clock and continues intermittently until about 8. Last night, as an opener, the loudspeaker blared forth with an Oriental version of an American jazz number of the Roaring Twenties. I nearly fell off my stool. I failed to recognize a single Western instrument. The tones were produced by reeds and plucked strings. We have heard real Chinese music over short wave from Peiping, and it is tremendous; but this was merely a poor imitation of our own music. The first number is played to attract our attention and possibly to give us time to call out our friends. As soon as the record ended, a man began speaking, in English. I don't think I've ever been so fascinated by anything in my life. He sounded like Victor Sen-yung and all those other Oriental cats that appear in Hollywood movies, screaming things like "Maline! Tonight you die!" or "O-kay, Yank!" (steering his Zero fighter into a kamikaze attack) or "You im*pet*uous *Ameli*cans arr mos' *amm*irabeer (admirable). . . . *Howeverr* . . ." etc.

What this man said was roughly this—very much like this:

"Marine officers and men. . . . A happy New Year to you from the Chinese People's Volunteers and the Korean People's Army. . . . This is a season of peace and joy. But there is no peace or joy for us in Korea this season."

". . . We must leave Korea to the Koreans . . . We of the Chinese People's Volunteers have come here only to defend our borders of Manchuria. *We* are not the aggressor. . . . We too are thinking of our loved ones, and of our homes. . . . Listen . . ."

No one will believe me when I get back—but, by God, they played "There's No Place Like Home" next. This was almost too much. "Incongruous" doesn't begin to cover it. The number was performed by a trio of women, accompanied by a deathaphone, a senilaphone, and a b-flat farthorn. My musical training is enough for me to know that the harmony was precisely wrong. As I remember, the tonic chord was repeated throughout the piece, without a change of key. The loudspeaker is some distance away and is apparently turned slowly on a swivel mount. When the speaker is turned away from us, obviously we cannot hear too well, particularly when the wind is blowing, and it always is.

Next, Victor Sen-yung again, but we could hear only isolated phrases, "her arms again," "bombs and germs, a typical . . .", "after the fall of the Japanese and Nazis."

When I was in college, a friend of mine got on a Victor Sen-yung kick. He was obsessed with the Oriental way of speaking English and did wonderful imitations. I picked it up from him and together we did private routines which consisted, I remember, of talking to each other in an excessively polite manner for several minutes—exchanging pleasantries, bowing, etc., and then suddenly, very suddenly, screaming inarticulate insults at each other in terrible wrath. This was our conception of the Oriental.

Before Christmas, we are told, the Chinese played carols for us, including a few Bing Crosby records. These nightly lectures are fascinating but I notice that none of the older men—as opposed to new replacements—bother to come out and listen. The demoralizing effect is nil. While on outpost or Burgundy watch, the thing becomes a bit spooky, as though something's going to happen, and it tends to make the men more alert.

Next day

Another treatise: Although the Browning automatic rifle is the most formidable individual weapon that we have, it is nevertheless heavy to carry, therefore unwieldy. The mobility of our machine guns is also hindered because of their weight. In both cases this includes the weight of the ammunition. A loaded BAR belt, with its twelve magazines, weighs nearly as much as the weapon itself, which is 20 lbs. In a machine-gun section, a number of men are used as ammo-humpers—a waste of manpower. Army ordnance is experimenting with the use of compressed gas as a propelling force. It is possible that these units of pressure could expend enough energy upon release to force a stream of slugs through a barrel, thus eliminating powder, cap and cartridge case. However, the U. S. Ord. Dept. is notoriously sluggish in its acceptance of new ideas, more liable to requisition gadgets than to accept modifications in functioning.

This fall, for instance, the supply section of 1st Ord. Bn. received a shipment of several thousand cold-weather triggers for M-1 rifles. They were distributed among the line companies and consequently discarded by most of the men. The gadget looks like this:

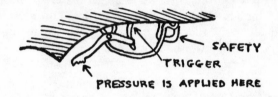

SAFETY

TRIGGER

PRESSURE IS APPLIED HERE

Although cold-stiff and thickly gloved fingers can manipulate the cold-weather trigger more easily than the original trigger, the gadget blocks the free path of the safety mechanism. If the safety is set on FIRE, an accidental discharge is liable to occur because the cold-weather trigger is not protected by a guard. Also, considerable slack need be taken up, as compared with the light hammer release pressure of the original trigger. A waste of money. I have spoken.

Idea: In place of the conventional 20-round BAR magazine, why couldn't a 30-round magazine be developed and substitued? (The Thompson sub and the M-2 carbine, incidentally, accept 30-round magazines, and the Chinese burp gun uses a 35-round magazine.) The normal unit of fire for a BAR is 260 rounds; that is, a belt of twelve loaded magazines plus the one in the weapon itself. This belt that I have in mind would accommodate eight 30-round mags. Including the ninth magazine—in the weapon—the new unit of fire would be 270 rounds. The weight of ten extra cartridges would be negligible and the fire power of the weapon would be increased enough to warrant adoption of the new equipment. Under battle conditions, the time required to change a magazine is about seven seconds—a hell of a long time when an assault squad is depending on the steady fire power of this weapon.

Here is a run-down of the personal weapons used by marines in Korea:

M-1 rifle, or Garand: 30 calibre. Ten of the thirteen men in a marine infantry squad rate this weapon. The Corps was the first outfit to adopt the M-1 and they have used it since the last days of the Guadalcanal campaign, when it replaced the Springfield '03. The M-1 is gas-operated and accepts a clip of eight rounds. Functioning is semiautomatic, requiring no manual operation except for the squeezing of the trigger and the loading of the clips. In other words, a clip is emptied by eight successive squeezes of the trigger; no cocking is necessary. Weight 9.5 lbs. Accurate range is 500 yards.

This weapon is habitually praised, undeservedly so. The M-1 is not dependable. Often, very often—during prolonged firing—the semi-automatic functioning fails and awkward manual operation is necessary. I have seen this happen as a man test fires his rifle, immediately after cleaning it. Nevertheless, the M-1 is probably the finest military semi-automatic weapon in the world. General Patton thought it was the best weapon in the world, period. But nothing is in the same league with the BAR.

Browning automatic rifle 1918 A2: .30 cal. Three of the thirteen men in a marine infantry squad rate this monster. Each fire team is built around this weapon.

The affix 1918 A2 signifies that the weapon was adopted in 1918 and that two additional modifications have been made since. The weapon was designed by John Browning as the result of a need for an individual automatic weapon by the AEF. Only a small number of them reached France before the armistice.

The Army infantry squad rates only one BAR. The entire squad of nine men is built around it. The Army is considering adding another.

BAR is gas-operated, the functioning fully automatic. The rate of fire may be adjusted by means of a small lever on the left side of the piece. When the lever is set on FAST, the weapon will fire at the rate of 550 rounds per minute. When set on slow, 350 rounds per minute. With the latter setting, the shooter—if he is experienced—can squeeze off single shots if necessary. BAR is completely dependable.

A buffer mechanism in the stock absorbs much of the recoil, which becomes less than the kick of a .22 rifle. The rear sight is graduated up to 1500 yards, for long single shots. A burst of fire will hold its pattern for about 600 yards.

The BAR is actually a portable machine gun. Its mount, for prone firing, is an adjustable bipod, extending below the muzzle. The bipod may be folded parallel to the barrel. In most cases it has been discarded, although it is extremely useful in defensive fighting. The accuracy of the weapon is increased by it. BAR costs $385.58.

U. S. carbine M-2. .30 cal. Staff noncommissioned officers (staff sergeant, gunnery sergeant or technical sergeant, and master sergeant) and commissioned officers rate this weapon. A contemporary of the M-1 rifle, the carbine originally functioned semiautomatically, from a magazine of 15 rounds. It was called the carbine M-1 then, and had been designed to supply the need for a light, short-barreled weapon to be used by troops occupied with combat duties other than actually shooting at the enemy, i.e., officers, truck drivers, headquarters personnel, etc. A later modification enabled the carbine to function automatically, and the 30-round magazine was developed. Carbine is gas-operated. Sometime I'll have to write down what this means. The carbine does not fire the same ammunition as the M-1 and BAR. Carbine ammo is about half the size. The slug is of the same width (.30 cal.) but much shorter.

Carbine weighs approx. 6 lbs. Its accurate range is 200 yards. The main advantage is its tremendously rapid rate of fire, something like 650 to 700 rounds per minute. But this is a very undependable weapon. Due to its light weight, the internal parts are small and fragile, and subject to malfunctioning, particularly in cold weather. The piece just won't work in freezing weather. When operating properly, the 'bine is perfect for night action, when rapid fire at short range is needed. Because of its small slug and light powder charge, the carbine has poor "stopping power."

Springfield rifle, M1903. .30 cal. Each marine infantry company rates two of these, the old World War One workhorse. They are equipped with telescopic sights, cheek rests, and in some cases, bipods. Used only for sniping. The Springfield is more accurate and more dependable than the M-1, but it is manually operated, firing single shots from a clip of five rounds. Accurate range is 600 yards. '03 weighs 6 lbs.

Thompson submachine gun. 45 cal. The Thompson has terrific stopping power—firing the fat .45 slug—but very limited range; up to 100 yards. The rate of fire is almost as rapid as that of the carbine. Tommy gun weighs 10.5 lbs. Accepts a magazine of 30 rounds. It is a short, easily maneuverable weapon. Great for night fighting, particularly ambushes. No better weapon for street fighting. Because of its extremely short range, the Thompson is rarely used in daylight unless by an assault squad. This weapon is not gas-operated; instead it functions by means of its own recoil.

Thank you.

Two days later, in early January 1953
The ——— platoon staged a raid several nights ago. I've put off writing about it for one or two vague reasons.

The raiding party was divided into four groups. Each group was briefed separately by Lt. Casimetti, the company executive officer. A volunteer was needed from our group to do a zombie job and I was chosen. The general mission of the unit was to capture a prisoner. The specific mission was to assault an enemy outpost known as Little Rock.

COVERING SQUAD	ASSAULT SQUAD	TWO MACHINE-GUN SECTIONS	STRETCHER BEARERS
Code named "Pepper" 7 men; Lt. Buell in charge.	"Sugar" 13 men; Lt. O'Dwyer in charge.	"Salt" ? men; Sgt. Kovacs in charge.	-eight South Koreans.

The diagram shows the placement of each group as the unit moved out in column. This was strictly a volunteer deal; nobody was included who didn't want to be. At dusk I ate a can of beans and a candy bar and dressed in the following manner: long johns, socks, windproof trousers, fur-lined vest, sweater, flannel shirt, armored vest, armored shorts, field jacket, scarf, thermal boots, helmet and gloves. I had cleaned the BAR and magazines that afternoon. It was very cold and I did not apply any oil to the parts, using instead a tiny amount of graphite, which will not freeze in any temperature. The parka, although much warmer than the field jacket, is cumbersome and for this reason I did not wear it. I carried four grenades.

The entire unit was assembled by ten o'clock, near the ——— squad phone emplacement. The covering squad, of which I was a part, was the first section to leave the MLR. Lt. Buell had said this to us: "We'll bring everyone back. I can promise you that if someone gets lost we will stay out there until we find him. . . . Remember, 'gung ho' means 'work together' . . . Let's go. . . ."

I was surprised to hear the phrase "gung ho" used seriously. Although it is the unofficial battle cry of the Corps, it is almost always used sarcastically. One speaks of a new recruit, or a man fresh from Parris Island as being "gung ho"—ready to take on the world but not really knowing what the score is. It is a Chinese phrase, and up to this time I was unaware of its meaning.

We filed out through an opening in the sandbags and climbed down the steep, icy slope, supporting ourselves by a rope bannister attached to iron barbed-wire stakes. Without the aid of this bannister we would have slid all the way to the bottom. Halfway down the slope we encountered the barbed-wire entanglement which protects the entire platoon sector. As far as I know, there are only two openings in it; one for the Burgundy reliefs and the one which we made use of that night. Both openings are blocked by a removable section of wire which must be taken out and then replaced as a unit moves through it. One at a time, we passed through and continued the descent. At the edge of the rice paddy we re-formed the column and moved across the ice and frozen turf to the foot of East Berlin. The temperature may have been below zero; the mucous in my nose was frozen. Fortunately there was no wind. Actually, the wind helps to cover the sound of movement and is usually welcome, but not in such cold weather. At this time of the year, the moon does not rise until after 5 A. M., and so it was also almost pitch-black.

We made the climb to the top of Texas Ridge and turned left. The terrain up there is covered with little pine trees, and it was necessary to move quite slowly. Even so, we made a hell of a racket—which made some of us extremely nervous. The element of surprise would be lost, but there was nothing we could do. If we weren't crunching through patches of snow, we were crunching through patches of dry leaves. Moving west along the ridge for about two hundred yards, the point of the column came upon an intersecting path, a path which came from the direction of Hill 139, a Chinese position. One marine was left here, to wait in the bushes near the intersection and act as a listening post. The Chinese also move about in No Man's Land at night and, as I mentioned before, their recent attack on East Berlin was launched from Texas Ridge, probably by means of this particular path.

Two hundred yards further, the point man reached the top of a saddle which drops off to the right. A saddle is usually nothing more than a good-sized groove in the earth, on the ridgeline of a hill. In this case it looked as though a now-extinct stream had caused the erosion. Climbing down the slope, within the long saddle, several of the men slipped on the ice and slid for some distance before grasping a branch. This must have been terrifying to the first three or four men. If one of them had gone all the way to the bottom he would have found himself sitting on the edge of an unfriendly rice paddy, on the edge of an unfriendly mine field. All this commotion angered me; I visualized groups of Chinese on Little Rock preparing themselves leisurely while we stumbled and slid toward them. Looking straight ahead, one could see the huge black mass of hill Detroit. Little Rock is an extension of this hill. Then I slipped and slid, and couldn't stop. The four grenades were attached to the rear of my magazine belt, within an empty canteen cover. It wouldn't have surprised me if one of the pins had worked loose; I was sliding on my butt at the time. Somebody grabbed me before I crashed into Lt. Buell. When the unit reached the bottom of the slope—a distance of about 50 yards from the top—the lieutenant told me to go back to where the other man had been left, the temporary listening post. This was the "volunteer" thing I mentioned. I wasn't too crazy about wandering around out there by myself, and I still don't think it was a sensible idea, but I went—of course—and caterpillared back up the slope. I came across a thing—I don't know what to call it: two dead trees, with a piece of rope strung between each. I learned later that this had been used by the Chinese to hang propaganda pamphlets.

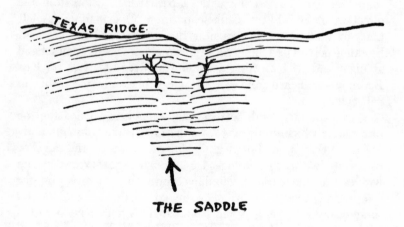

THE SADDLE

My "mission" was to wait there with the other man (*en-fant perdu*) for the second unit, the assault squad, and report to Lt. O'Dwyer that "Pepper has reached check point four." (Sir.) But I never made contact with the temporary listening post because Lt. O'Dwyer's unit had already passed him and he, of course, fell in at the rear of the column. I heard them coming from quite a distance away and I hid among the trees; for two reasons. First, I didn't want to get blasted by their point man—in case he hadn't been informed as to who I was; second, because there was always the possibility that this wasn't Lt. O'Dwyer's unit at *all*. So I lay there, getting more and more nervous, for still another reason; I hate to scare people, and I knew that the point man of the assault squad would be ready for the cleaners after I challenged him. When I saw him, about twenty yards away, I said "Log," the password, in a speaking voice, and lying flat on my stomach. It was the lieutenant himself, a cool cat. He only pointed his carbine at me before saying "Book," the countersign. As the column passed by, I fell in at the rear. When we reached the top of the saddle, I was told to climb down and inform Lt. Buell that "Sugar is at check point three." (Sir.)

We remained where we were for several minutes, both units, awaiting the regimental T.O.T. (Timed on Target), the first of two pre-raid barrages. The impact of this volley was tremendous, including ten 4.2-inch white phosphorous projectiles which blasted the top of hill Detroit. The illumination allowed us to view our objective, Little Rock, a wide terrain finger running south from Detroit. A mine-detector operator from 1st Engineer Battalion had volunteered to clear a path in the minefield. He was accompanied across the paddy by another volunteer, a BAR man from the ——— squad named Carl Pugnacci, a pfc. They disappeared into the darkness and we waited. The presence of the mine-detector man seemed to indicate that none of our patrols had entered that area for some time. Fifteen minutes later they returned, having cleared a path. What a precarious stroll that must have been. They had crossed the paddy to the bottom of the Little Rock slopes.

I was again ordered to climb the saddle, to inform Lt. O'Dwyer that a path had been cleared and marked, and that the covering squad would begin crossing as soon as I returned.

The column was formed and we began to cross the paddy, maintaining an interval of five yards between each man. We crept along a series of ridges, no more than two feet high, called dikes. These little humps of earth are part of every rice paddy I've ever seen. They separate the little fields where the rice once grew, forming terraces to hold each shallow body of water. They are irregular and intersect at many points. It would have been possible to take a wrong turn were it not for the strip of white cloth that the mine-detector man laid down for us to follow.

As we made the crossing I became conscious of a peculiar odor, not an unpleasant nor unfamiliar one. It was not a corpse, not a plant, not fertilizer. I don't know what it was, but it was vaguely familiar. There is a sort of old wives' tale that it is possible to smell Chinese soldiers from a distance because they eat garlic; but it was not that.

The only audible sound was the echo of distant shelling and infrequent machine-gun fire from our MLR. The Panmunjom truce light was visible to the west; its vertical beam illuminated the low-ceiling clouds above. Not a sound from the Chinese position.

At the base of Little Rock we found a wide intersection of two paths. Another drawing:

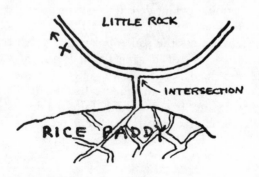

Lt. Buell immediately pointed out our defensive positions. It was necessary for the mine-detector operator to precede each of us. I was placed in the position marked "X" above. Cpl. Medve was placed on the other side of the path. The two of us guarded that avenue of approach. While Medve was being placed, the mine man found his first mine. The detector produces a continuous humming sound, which increases in volume and pitch if a metal object is passed over. The noise is uncomfortably loud, even when no metal is near. There is also a dim green light somewhere on the instrument which is visible for several feet. After five minutes of chipping away at the frozen turf, he uncovered the mine sufficiently to disarm it. I haven't found out yet what type of mine it was. Altogether, he uncovered three of them at separate points along the path. We noticed that the path was loosely covered with straw, probably in order to conceal any evidence that mines had been planted.

Little Rock is not a large terrain feature. The distance from the base of the slope to the enemy trench, as we learned later, is not more than one hundred yards.

Lt. Buell called Lt. O'Dwyer on the prc-6 (the Army calls them "walkie-talkies") and told him that the covering squad was in position. Within a few minutes, Lt. O'Dwyer's unit appeared and silently filed along the path, between Medve and myself. These were the poor bastards that had to make the assault, thirteen of them—one squad. The mine detector preceded them as far as the jump-off point which, to our unpleasant surprise, was no more than twenty yards from where Medve and I lay. Leaving the path, they climbed this short distance up the slope. We could barely make them out, moving around, getting into position for the assault. They were in echelon formation:

It was very cold now because we were not moving. The field jacket meant nothing against that wind. I was so cold that when the second mortar barrage commenced, I thought of the explosions as fires, warmth. The barrage was startling: a flurry of 60mm. shells whistled through the air and screamed downward into the area above the jump-off point. The ground shook with the impact and more shells came plummeting down. The trajectory of a mortar looks something like this.

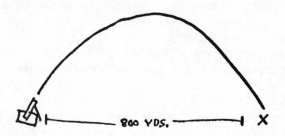

Roughly, a 60mm. mortar shell is as effective as two hand grenades. The barrage ended and we lay completely inactive for two hours. I was confused as to the effectiveness of this tactic (said he dryly). I dreamt of cocoa, Ovaltine, milk toast, coffee, hot buttered rum.

The machine-gun unit, led by Sgt. Kovacs, had been set up on Texas Ridge, two hundred yards behind us. At 3:30 they commenced fire; sudden, rapid overhead fire. I was ready to meet my Maker at this point. When I finally realized whose fire it was, I noticed that every fourth round (bullet) was a tracer and that the red streaks of light illuminated the terrain. The strike zone of the machine guns was the same as that of the second mortar barrage. This overhead fire lasted for one or two minutes. When it ceased, several things happened at once: As we learned later, Sgt. Kovacs moved his men swiftly to another position along the ridge. As they were moving out, a number of Chinese mortar rounds raked the area which they had just left, and the place-

74

ment of this barrage looked perfect—the Chinese have the reputation of being expert mortarmen. Due to Sgt. Kovacs's foresight none of his men were injured. And at the same time, Lt. O'Dwyer and his men began the assault.

First each man heaved a grenade in the direction of the enemy trench, and then they moved in a skirmish line up the slope. The Chinese were ready; they must have heard us coming. Concussion grenades—we carried none—began exploding above us, flurries of them. Thirty would be a good guess. The ground shuddered and the dead leaves on the branches shook with the rushes of air. Next we heard the sound of two or three BARs and a group of carbines. Next—and it was in this order—we heard the BRRRRP! sound of one Chinese pp-S or "burp gun" as it is called. This was followed immediately by a burst from a carbine. That was all; there was no more shooting. The actual fire fight could not have lasted more than twenty seconds.

While all this was happening, I got up on my knees, to give the blood a chance to circulate, to see what was going on, and to be ready to move somewhere else in a hurry. Cpl. Medve yelled, almost hysterically, "Get down, you stupid shit!" A moment later a figure appeared along the path. We challenged him; he gave the countersign and moved past us. Another figure, perhaps the same man, came up to us from the rear, carrying a stretcher and followed by two Koreans. He said to us, "Let's go. We need help." This man was probably a Navy corpsman. In file, we climbed the slope and came upon a group of four men, kneeling and crouching around a fallen marine. I noticed that the remaining members of the assault squad had formed a hasty line of defense, facing the top of the hill. They were prone. According to one of these men, with whom I talked later, this defense line was less than thirty yards from the enemy trench.

The Koreans helped extend the long stretcher. There was complete silence as we lifted the man onto it. He moaned softly as we began to step down the incline. The last concussion grenade exploded above us, but near. The force of the rushing air smacked into my right side and I lost balance. We dropped the stretcher. The wounded man rolled out of it and turned over once before coming to rest against a prone Korean. We reloaded the stretcher. He had stopped moaning and had in fact stopped living. At least he died between the time we put him on the stretcher and reached the bottom of the slope, if it makes any difference. I thought that I could see steam rising from the blood on his face and throat. When we reached the intersection of the paths we were relieved by the other Koreans. Medve and I returned to our former positions on either side of the path. The dead man's name was Mathew Hood.

Three other wounded men were brought down the hill. The first was unbearably pathetic. He was supported by two men, and was jiggling like a puppet, his arms around the shoulders of each. His head hung loosely over his chest and he made a feeble attempt to say something cheerful. We heard him make a little joke as he moved by, but I didn't hear what it was. He was lowered, shoulders first, onto a stretcher, and he crumpled like a rag doll. The second man was unconscious. The third was Lt. O'Dwyer, with a bullet in his leg. When I first saw him, he was seated on the ground. Someone brought a stretcher and he was loaded onto it, but he insisted on sitting even then.

It is difficult to put into words the urgency of the situation. The remaining members of the assault squad moved past us. They walked backwards, peering intently at the skyline. This bothered me very much. It was at this point that I began to get really frightened. I saw no reason why the Chinese would not follow us. Lt. Buell appeared and told us, the covering squad, to remain where we were, and that he would give us the word when to pull out, which would be after the stretcher-bearers had crossed the paddy.

Once more Medve and I crawled forward and lay down on either side of the straw-covered path. My weapon had been cocked for some time and I clutched a grenade. A minute or two of breathless listening, then the lieutenant crept up to us and whispered, "Move out!" The three of us practically ran to the edge of the paddy, found the marking of white tape, and stepped up on one of the dikes. Again the peculiar odor.

We walked backwards, but moved fast. On the other side of the paddy, we found that the Koreans were having great difficulty in lifting the stretchers up the icy saddle. Lt. O'Dwyer was still sitting up on his stretcher, which was resting on the ground near the edge of the paddy. Lt. Buell came over and said to him, "Well, so O'Dwyer finally got hit!" The other lieutenant chortled quietly. He showed no sign of pain until they lifted his stretcher. Somehow, a section of communication wire had become twisted around his leg, the injured one. I was lying nearby and rose to unwind the wire. He handed me his carbine bayonet and held the wire taut as I hacked it apart.

Lt. Buell had the good sense to find another avenue of withdrawal, twenty yards to the left. The stretchers were moved to that area, and the ascent was begun with less difficulty than before. Both officers prodded the Koreans severely, swearing at them in their own language.

Meanwhile Pfc. Hogg and myself lay on the edge of the paddy and covered the withdrawal. It was at this time that I was most frightened. We heard strange noises and thought we saw movement on the other side of the paddy. Hogg lay ten yards to the left of me, and we both were lying across a strand of communication wire, although neither of us knew it. Whenever one of us moved, the wire moved also, causing a moment or two of real panic. It sounded as though someone were crawling among the weeds between us. Hogg and I were the last to pull out, but this was an accident. Hogg is also a new replacement.

While we were making the ascent, Pfc. Jack Cole dropped his helmet and it tumbled down to the paddy. He looked after it for a moment as though he were considering going after it. Hogg said, "Leave it, man; leave it."

A reconnaissance patrol was sent out the night before this raid, and it was their responsibility to find a suitable route for withdrawal. They thought they had found one but nosiree. During the hassle with the stretchers, we waited more than ten minutes at the foot of Texas Ridge. Had the enemy followed us, had they made even a small counterattack, we would have been sufficiently bottled up for them to have caused considerable damage.

When we reached the ridgeline Lt. Buell turned to us and said, "Christ; I've left the sound-power back there." I offered to go back across the paddy and retrieve it. This was a well-calculated risk; I assumed that if no one had been sent out to follow us by then, no one would. Furthermore Little Rock is an outpost and would not be left unguarded. But I was distressed as hell at his hesitancy to say no. He reminded me that I had severed the communication wire myself—around Lt. O'Dwyer's leg—and that it would be cut again when we reached the MLR. The only lost equipment then was the hand-phone.

Reforming a column along Texas Ridge, we retraced our route and reached home at 5:30 A.M.

Most of us crowded into the command post and drank coffee and ate sandwiches. There had been a death, and some of the men looked sick. Others pretended to be casual about it. Others appeared to be callous. All four casualties had been sent to the rear area before we arrived. Obviously the "raid" was a failure. The support barrages probably caused some damage, and one member of the assault squad swore that he hit the burp gunner—who was the only Chinese that actually fired. These facts, balanced by our own score of one dead, three wounded, do not sit evenly. And no enemy prisoner. It was the concussion grenades that halted the assault in its tracks.

I won't deny that I was excited as hell about taking part in the raid. When the bombardment and the shooting started, I was so god-damned fascinated by the idea that people were out there who were trying to kill each other that I wasn't afraid—a stupid ass. Not appalled, fascinated. During the withdrawal, when I saw that people were hurt and that one of them was dead, I became very much afraid.

January

Back at 1st Ord. Bn., I collected the following bits of cheer; news items from *Stars & Stripes*, the overseas paper.

Information from Chinese Nationalist observers:

Siberian railway lines are jamming with heavy military traffic. The Kremlin has promised to mechanize 50 Chinese divisions. Observers along the railway lines have checked 300 heavy Russian tanks, and 100 artillery pieces of 125mm. to 152mm., en route to Manchuli and Changchun, cities near the North Korean border.

The Soviet commander of Russian forces in the Far East is Malinovsky. He recently inspected the Korean front for the third time. His first tour occurred shortly after the invasion of South Korea; his second followed the entrance of the Chinese into the war.

The estimated number of Chinese troops in North Korea is 1.2 million. When the Panmunjom truce talks began, the number was estimated to be 750,000. At least 80,000 Soviet troops are massed in Manchuria.

Soviet submarines are displaying increased activity near the China coast in the Yellow Sea. The total number of operational Soviet submarines based at Vladivostok (one hundred miles

from the Korean border) is 100. Ten of the newest type schnorkels have been spotted in recent weeks at Port Arthur. Observers have reported that more than 100 Russian MIG-15 fighter jets have landed at Mukden and Antung, flown by Russian pilots. A considerable number of new Russian jet bombers have been spotted over Manchuria.

Mother! I want to come home.

To point out how close Vladivostok and Port Arthur are, I'll copy this map.

Panmunjom is a neutral zone. No planes are allowed to fly over it, and no armed troops other than U. S. and Communist guards are allowed to enter the area. From our platoon sector, looking several miles to the west, we can see a number of balloons which serve to mark the neutral zone in daylight. They are flak balloons, the kind used by the British in World War Two.

Social notes from all over:

We have a young man with us named Dunbar Bloomfeld who is as afraid of rats as I am of cobras. He crawled into his sleeping bag the other day and found that a rat had moved in during the night. When we awoke to go on watch, we found that Bloomfeld was sitting in the middle of the dirt floor writing letters, and possibly his will. He was surrounded by burning candles—to keep the phalanx of rodents at a distance. In his lap was a loaded .45.

January 20th, '53

Propeller-driven planes of the First Marine Air Wing fly sorties over enemy positions every day. These missions are called "air strikes." Hill Detroit received an air strike last week.

An observation plane, a Piper Cub (poor little fella; goes about 60 m.p.h.), arrived an hour before the strike and snooped around a bit. When he withdrew, the striking force—three marine Corsairs, each carrying a napalm bomb, droned into sight over the hills. The lead plane peeled off, way, way up, and roared downward. The acceleration was gradual, with the motor straining. The pilot adjusted the axis of flight in line with Detroit. The dark object attached to the belly of the plane broke loose and gained its own momentum as the Corsair leveled off and climbed back into the clouds. The napalm bomb ripped into the reverse slope of Detroit, a perfect shot. Huge billows of orange flame, surrounded by even larger billows of black smoke, appeared above the ridge as the muffled report of the impact reached us. The other two Corsairs jettisoned their loads in the same manner, then reformed and flew away in a triangle formation.

Napalm is jellied gasoline. It spreads and burns; it seeps down into trenches and is a perfect weapon for trench warfare. This is why the Chinese trenches are so deep. We have been told that the depth of some of the trenches on Detroit are between 15 and 20 feet. Steps of earth lead up to the individual fighting-holes. To enable the men to escape the napalm, deep caves have been dug in the side of the trench and some of these caves are used as living quarters by the Chinese. These caves correspond roughly to our "bunny holes," which are only large enough for one man to huddle in during a mortar barrage. Bunny holes are usually dug so that a man can jump from his fighting-hole into the bunny hole without having to move very far. This is how it is usually set up: a cross-section drawing of the trench and us with X-ray vision:

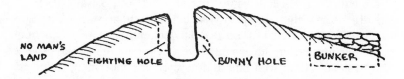

If the feces really hits the fan, there are three points through which a man can run for the hills—rear exits in the trench called "bug-outs."

The Chinese anti-aircraft units have a reputation for great

accuracy. Against observation planes, they send up fused projectiles that explode in small puffs of white smoke. Against diving planes, such as those three Corsairs, they send up armor-piercing projectiles of high velocity. When a Corsair dives, the ground actually vibrates from the muzzle blasts of the concentrated fire power of the Chinese weapons. The noise is tremendous; a series of CRACKS. Their anti-aircraft weapons are probably similar to the *pom-pom* or *ack-ack* of British warships. Both, I think, are automatic and fire multi-barreled blasts at a single target.

This is what I've been leading up to:

The wreckage of two Corsairs lies within our company front: one is in No Man's Land in front of the ——— platoon sector, the other is behind enemy lines. The former wreckage is visible eight hundred yards or more to our right front. Its engine, tail and fuselage are scattered over the rice paddy at the foot of a large enemy-held hill called Frisco. The wings are nowhere to be seen.

The other Corsair crashed far behind Detroit, probably more than a mile behind. It was knocked down yesterday. I didn't see the crash dive but everyone heard it. A terrible noise. We rushed up to the trench in time to see the pilot floating downward under his parachute. He was directly above hill 139 and was drifting west and north. He was frantically maneuvering the shrouds in a futile attempt to change his direction. He was bareheaded and wore a dark flying suit; also dark flying boots. Despite his desperate effort, he descended into that area between Texas Ridge and Little Rock—that rice paddy with the peculiar smell. The horrible thing was that if he had landed approximately two hundred yards nearer, he would have been temporarily safe. That is, we could have seen him and covered any movement he made. It was dusk when he disappeared behind the ridge, growing darker every minute. If it had been night, he might have evaded captors until we got out to him.

However, seconds after he floated out of sight, we heard the strange metallic sound of a Maxim machine gun, a Russian-made weapon. CHUG-CHUG-CHUG-CHUG; four rounds, fired from the Detroit or Little Rock area. It seemed obvious that the weapon would not have been fired unless the Chinese gunner had spotted a target. How helpless the pilot must have felt up there in the air, with groups of Chinese watching his descent.

A little man called Dutchy was sprinting up and down the trench, trying to assemble an emergency rescue patrol. "We'll never make it in time," somebody said. "Besides, that Maxim probably got him." Dutchy yelled at him, "We'll bring back the fucking body then!" By that time S/Sgt. Cruz arrived. I think every man in the platoon was standing in the trench, waiting. Cruz strode through us, picking out men at random. With a minimum of preparation, nine of us departed. No time for organization. Some men went without parkas, some without gloves. One man—I won't mention his name—found that his BAR magazines were empty, except for the magazine in the weapon. In my case, the magazines were filled halfway. (In order to release the pressure on the magazine spring, it is advisable to remove eight or ten rounds when the weapon isn't being carried. Otherwise the spring becomes weak.) We even forgot to bring a stretcher.

We slid down the slope, dog-trotted across the ice, and scrambled up to Texas Ridge. No one was the least bit concerned with being stealthy. We crashed in among the pine trees. I got the feeling that the men were out of their heads, literally; that if we had encountered any Chinese it would have been the end of them. Just before we reached the saddle, Cruz motioned us to a halt and we lay down, panting hard and listening. Not a sound. It was almost dark now. A call for two volunteers was passed back. Not me. I wouldn't have gone down in that paddy again to meet Jesus Christ. We had rustled bushes, tripped over twigs, broken off brittle branches, crunched through snow, and fallen through the ice. Mao Tse-tung could have heard us in Peking. Two men volunteered immediately and S/Sgt. Cruz leading them, they disappeared into the dark. They were extremely quiet, as marines can be when they want to.

'Ten or fifteen minutes passed before they returned. They had reconnoitred the base of the ridge but had seen nothing. Cruz moved us west for several yards, then halted us. We were amazed when Cruz in a loud, clear voice, shouted, "Hey, marine! Where you at?" No answer. He shouted the same thing again, adding, "Can you hear me?" Perhaps it is unfortunate that Cruz has a strong Mexican accent. The Chinese have been known to call out to us in English. For this reason, our Navy corpsmen are always called for by a code name, or by their nicknames. I read an account at Pendleton of a group of stretcher-bearers who were captured at the Chosin reservoir because they went out of their way to find a man who was yelling "Corpsman!" It turned out to be a Chinese. So it occurred to me that perhaps the pilot was hiding somewhere out there, thinking that it was a similar trick. There was no answer, and we returned to the MLR at top speed.

An hour later, a weird light was turned on, illuminating a wide corridor of sky to our left. The strongest part of the light fell on the forward slopes of Detroit and hill 139. Its source was a powerful searchlight, atop a tank, that had been driven to a hilltop far behind our lines. Although the beam was greatly dispersed at that distance, it was obviously aimed at the area in which the pilot had disappeared. The Chinese hills looked very ugly under that white light, stark and ghostly. They gave the impression that there was nobody around, and that illusion is a strange one, knowing that they are honeycombed with caves and trenches that we cannot see. This was a sort of beacon for the benefit of the pilot.

Throughout the night the men on outposts East Berlin and Berlin, as well as all men on listening posts, were especially alert. I stood watch in the phone emplacement, and heard men calling in at irregular intervals to report noises they heard, out in the paddy. These sounds are heard every night, but last night we all imagined and hoped that the pilot was out there, wandering toward the source of the beacon. But everyone had heard the sound of that Maxim. Just before dawn the light was extinguished.

January 26th, 1953

My sister Kate and I remember George Berry as a most gentle and humble man, with a sense of humor both humble and gentle. He was a sergeant in a labor battalion of the AEF in 1918. Not long after the war he began working for Gampie and Grandmother Gatzi in Kansas City. He was married five times. I don't know how many kids he had. He was Gampie's chauffeur, uniform and all. I used to drive to the office sometimes with them, and drive back with George who loved that crazy boulevard overlooking the railroad yards and Kansas City, Kansas, across the Kaw river. Gatzi died in 1947 and Gampie had a stroke a year or two later, and went to California to live with Sallie. George asked to come out and be his nurse. He worked hard at it; Gampie was irascible as hell and very sick. On those weekends from Pendleton, I was always aware that George was aware that he was an old colored man in a crowded little house. He embarrassed me constantly—unintentionally—by his extreme humility.

He used to own a dusty little Willys car in Kansas City and he would drive Kate and me around town on Sundays. We left K.C. in 1940, when I was nine, but I used to write to George once or twice a year. They were terrible, patronizing letters. I was going through the same "Crusade for the Colored People" that my sister is going through now. Also I was obsessed with jazz. I would ask him to write about Jay McShann, Count Basie, Eddie Durham, Jimmy Lunceford, Lips Page, and some of the other great Kansas City musicians, figuring that since he was colored, etc. He wrote two letters in return and, as far as everyone who read them was concerned, they were priceless documents, to be stored in a vault. Three pages of painfully scribbled words, telling me what he remembered about growing up and becoming a man, in ink. I lost the letters.

When I was sixteen I hitchhiked back to K.C. to see the Faxons and George drove me around town that night, in the Willys. I had an old record called "Joe Turner Blues," a song about the ghost of Piney Brown, a great blues singer who appears every once in a while on a certain corner in the colored section of town. We drove to that corner, 18th and Vine, and George let me get out and stand on the sidewalk. Piney Brown's ghost wasn't around, but it was one hell of an experience for a sixteen-year-old boy.

I could go on and on about George Berry, but there's not enough time. This is part of a letter from Aunt Sallie, received today:

> . . . This is *not* good news. George, who really admired you, died of a heart attack on Christmas day. He came home after a real fine Christmas eve with his friends. He looked tired, so I urged him to go upstairs and rest (you know how sweet I can be), so he went saying, "I really went to town; and tried to bring it back with me. C'mon, fine puppies." Then about 3 in the afternoon I got worried about him—Brad went upstairs to awaken him but he was fast asleep indeed. My, how I miss him—and so do the fine puppies. Enough of that.

February 1st, 1953

We were withdrawn from the MLR early last Friday morning in order to prepare for a raid—a daylight raid. On half an hour's notice, we were saddled up; carrying only sleeping bags, toothbrushes in some cases, and weapons and ammo belts. The replacement platoon, or "clutch platoon" as it is called, arrived, the morning watches were occupied, and we departed.

Trucks were waiting for us at the company supply point, located several hundred yards to the rear. We boarded them, one man at a time, and sat silently while the others climbed in. We were packed together under the canvas canopy. In a few minutes, the trucks were roaring across 76-Alley. The headlights were not turned on until we reached the end of the small valley, and we did not smoke until then, the valley being under observation from Chinese lines. As soon as the "smoking lamp was lit," as we say, the men began talking in an animated way. The general apprehension concerning the raid probably contributed to the urgency of the humor. The glow of cigarettes was the only light visible and, under the disguise of darkness, I laughed as coarsely and maniacally as I used to at prep school late at night. The interchange of crudity was so intense that we panicked ourselves in the back of the truck with some surprising ribaldry.

It turned out to be a clear day, and later that morning we gathered in an outdoor classroom, several miles behind the lines. We sat on the ground and listened attentively to a major from division headquarters. There were fifty of us gathered around him. I glanced around once or twice and thought: This is a fine collection of soldiers, probably more capable than any in the world.

Our objective, the major revealed, was hill Frisco. Our mission was to capture a prisoner. The 1st Marine Division opposes the 65th Army of the CCF—Chinese Communist Forces —and another unidentified Army. It is the 1st Marine regiment that faces this unidentified unit. S-2 (Intelligence) might be able to learn its designation if a member of that unit were captured. Three S-2 men attended the meeting and would also accompany the raiding party.

Frisco is not an outpost, it is a segment of the Chinese MLR. Heavy support weapons would be available; a flight of Corsairs on call for close air support—the forte of marine aviation—and all regimental artillery units as well as heavy mortars. The raiding party itself would be accompanied by two flame-thrower tanks and three gun tanks. As we learned at Pendleton, tank-infantry co-ordination is a complex method of attack, requiring that the troops involved be acquainted with numerous details.

The major unfolded a large map of the target area, not a regulation military map, but a simplified one, done in water colors. Two peons held it up against the wind for all to see. The schooling lasted two hours, during which the major and Lt. Buell outlined the entire operation.

Here is a condensation of the schedule:

At 5 a.m. a machine-gun section, with two guns, leaves the MLR and occupies Saugech'on ridge (incorrectly spelled before). They set up their guns and wait. When notified by radio that the gunners are ready—to provide covering fire if needed—the assault platoon leaves the MLR. When they reach Saugech'on ridge they will form three skirmish lines and wait.

The five tanks are now waiting behind the MLR, on one side of 76-Alley. All troops remain silent and immobile until thirty minutes after sunrise. At this time the tanks pass through the MLR, advance to the eastern end of Saugech'on ridge and move around it. From this point on they will be under enemy observation and probably under enemy fire. The three gun tanks will commence fire, at "targets of opportunity." The two flame-thrower tanks will cross the paddy and begin to climb Frisco itself. When they are close enough, they discharge their floods of napalm at pre-assigned target areas and then back away in reverse gear, covered by the gun tanks at the bottom of the slope.

The three gun tanks now begin the ascent. This is the signal for the first wave of infantry—one squad—to leave Saugech'on ridge. The distance from the foot of Saugech'on to the base of Frisco is about forty yards. When the first wave reaches that point, the second wave moves out. These two waves follow the gun tanks up the slope, at a seventy-five foot interval, until the tanks come to a halt halfway up the hill. The third wave then leaves Saugech'on, crosses the paddy, and deploys at the base of Frisco, ready to provide either reinforcements or covering fire for the withdrawal. They will also be used as stretcher-bearers if necessary.

The first and second waves move through the stationary tanks, employing the tactic of "fire and maneuver." (Normally involving two separate units, fire and maneuver is a shuffling movement designed to provide a mobile unit with covering fire from an immobile unit. When the mobile unit reaches a point where some terrain cover is available, they deploy and immediately lay out a base of fire over the enemy objective. This provides cover to the formerly immobile unit, which now moves forward through the base of fire—that is, the now immobile unit —until they find terrain cover for themselves. This seesaw movement continues until the objective is reached, and both units make the final assault together—what's left of them.)

Near the lip of the enemy trench, Lt. Buell yells a command and each of us throws a grenade into the trench. Following the explosions, two men, each carrying a satchel charge—twenty pounds of TNT—crawl forward and drop their parcels in the trench. Following these explosions, which are concussive, the two squads rise, rush forward, and enter the trench.

A detailed method of clearing the trench was outlined. Aerial photographs of the Frisco, showing the trenchlines, were passed around for us to study. Something like this:

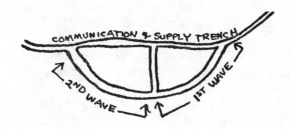

Before noon chow, the major led us out to an open area which resembles the objective. Nearby was a smaller duplicate of Saugech'on ridge, with a paddy in between. We rehearsed the entire operation in slow motion. After chow we went back and continued the dry runs until late in the afternoon. Several weak spots were detected and ironed out during a critique. Although the tank crews were present, the tanks themselves were not used during the rehearsal.

The flanking movement of the second wave—our squad—appeared to be the bottleneck of the assault. It required great co-ordination for thirteen men to shift from an echelon formation into a single skirmish line. It sounds easy, but the terrain made it difficult and we reworked it many times.

At 4:30 a dress rehearsal, minus ammunition and costumes, was staged. During the approach phase two men from our squad

—Cpl. Paul Medve from Baltimore and Pvt. Tony Colia from Galveston—broke into a violent fist fight over a trivial misunderstanding. The lieutenant did not see this. By this time most of the men were pretty depressed.

After the final run-through we regrouped and hiked to another area, where we were given ammunition. There each man test-fired his weapon, firing into a deep ravine. Most of the M-1 rifles had been replaced by automatic weapons for the raid. Three men in each squad were issued Thompson submachine guns. Vincent Lo Castro of the ——— squad carried an Army .45 calibre "grease gun" plus an M-1 rifle. Our squad carried the following weapons: 4 BARs, 3 Thompsons, 3 carbines (M-2) and 3 rifles. My own BAR cranked off two magazines into the ravine as efficiently and as noisily as a motorcycle engine, kicking up a cloud of dust and pebbles three hundred yards away.

Returning to the area and our tents, we set about cleaning our weapons. Later we picked up our unit of fire—the ammunition for the raid—from the supply people. Each man received four grenades and as many rounds (bullets) as he wanted. Sgt. Barefield, a trusting soul, said "Thank you" when given his.

At 7 P.M., the night before the raid, a chaplain came and held special services for the raiders. His assistant passed out mimeographed papers on which was printed the following mawkishness:

> Lead on, O King Eternal,
>> The day of march has come;
> Henceforth in fields of conquest
>> Thy tents shall be our home:
> Through days of preparation
>> Thy grace has made us strong,
> And now, O King Eternal
>> We lift our battle song.

The music to this is an old, beautiful hymn which we used to sing at South Kent at the end of each term. It, along with "Now the Day Is Over," used to gas me (man). #172 in the hymnal. I may be stuffy, but I didn't like the idea of this hymn being sung with those words and in those circumstances—as though we were about to be led to the sacrificial altar.

The service shook up Cpl. Charles. He had taken part in the last daylight raid and he had been wounded severely in the butt and sent to the hospital in Yokasuka, Japan. We all felt that he should be allowed to sit this one out.

The conversations in the tents that evening were morbid as hell; some clumsy puns referring to our forthcoming rest in a grave or a hospital.

I'm afraid I missed the point of this entire production. Nervous yes, but only as nervous as I used to get before a crew race at South Kent. With the exception of mortar barrages and long distance snipers, I have thus far avoided what is referred to (for lack of a better phrase) as the baptism of fire. I was tremendously excited, but wouldn't allow myself to think about the danger involved.

I was sitting on the ground inside the tent, filling magazines by candlelight, when Lt. Buell thrust his head and shoulders through the tent flaps and said, "The raid has been postponed indefinitely. Pack your gear and be saddled up in thirty minutes. We're going back to the line."

General shouting, and bedlam. I won't bother to analyze my own reaction; I remember that I went outside and wept. Carl Pugnacci found me outside, swearing bitterly. He said, "I know what's bothering you. You're *sorry* the raid's been called off." That is correct.

Four hours later, at 3 A.M. I was creeping along the base of Saugech'on ridge, a member of a reconnaissance patrol.

February 3rd, 1953
Something happened during the Little Rock raid that I forgot to mention. While the stretcher-bearers were climbing sloth-like up that icy saddle during the withdrawal, an aerial photography plane chose that moment to take some pictures. A huge five-second flare, corresponding to a flashbulb, was dropped each time a picture was taken. Although the plane was half a mile to our right, the entire countryside was bathed in brilliant illumination, and we could easily have been seen from Little

Rock or Detroit. The light was not unlike sunlight. We expected a mortar barrage to follow but apparently no one saw us.

As a matter of fact the photographs taken by the spotter plane were probably the ones that were passed out to us during the briefing for the raid on Frisco.

Each company sector is named, or nicknamed after the prominent terrain feature within it. In this case the general front is known as 76-Alley. Roughly speaking, it is a long narrow valley which cuts into the much larger valley that is No Man's Land. I have no real knowledge of the terrain to the east, but here is a diagram anyway:

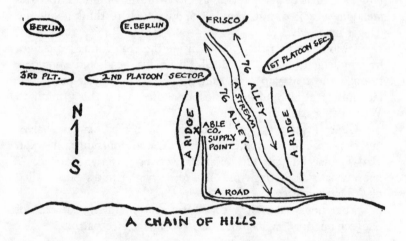

From the drawing, rough as it is, one can see that 76-Alley is open to enemy observation. The narrow valley is about one mile long. At its northern end is hill Frisco. At its southern end is a low chain of hills. The dirt road leading to the Able company supply point is completely exposed. In order to evacuate daytime wounded, or to bring in emergency supplies, trucks and jeeps must speed across the open terrain. Whenever they do, they are fired upon by a Chinese weapon that is set up, well concealed, on Frisco. This weapon is a 76-millimeter recoilless rifle, a comparatively light field piece of low velocity and great accuracy. In the past month, three of our vehicles have been knocked out by this weapon.

Some time last week, a group of marines crossed the valley in daylight, en route to the portable shower unit located behind the low chain of hills at the end of 76-Alley. There is a way of reaching the showers without crossing the Alley, but it is a tortuous, barely accessible route, and most of the men didn't bother with it. The Chinese didn't usually fire upon one or two men crossing the valley, or maybe they didn't see them. On this particular afternoon there was a group of them, fifteen or so. When they were about halfway across, a 76 shell exploded nearby, and they dispersed and went for cover. There followed a 76 barrage. It is a terrible sound. Being a low-velocity weapon, there is a great deal of noise before the round lands. According to the unofficial report, eleven of those men were hit by flying shrapnel; one of them died. Now it is a "court martial offense" for anyone to cross the Alley, unless they are in a vehicle.

The portable showers are a real luxury. One enters the steam-filled tent, undresses, and freezes one's respective gonads. But the water is warm. When one is finished, fresh clothes are passed out.

Another capitalist whoremonger item which is available is the mess hall, located directly behind the Able company mortar positions, approximately five hundred yards behind the lines. A hot meal is served between the hours of 11 A.M. and 1 P.M. Most of the men make it. Carl Pugnacci, who has the makings of a fanatic, runs to chow with me each day. It is a hard run, up and down slopes. One day a breakfast is served; the next day a lunch; the next a supper. It is by far the most enjoyable part of the day. Table manners aren't exactly Edwardian, but we have a ball sitting around exchanging impossible combat tales. Whenever a patrol makes contact with the enemy, the members of that patrol are the centers of attention at chow the next day. Needless to say, contacts with the enemy are rare.

93

February 4th, 1953

Lately I've been writing on top of our bunker, despite great ribbing from the others. No place else to go; candlelight is too dim, and the main trench is too windy. The real reason why I don't sit up in the phone emplacement any more is because I was fired at by a sniper yesterday. It is quite an honor, and a weird experience. I wanted to stand up and shout, "What, after all, *is* Art?"

I mentioned somewhere before that two men remain out on East Berlin during the day. Cpl. Paul Medve and I had that peculiar watch yesterday. It is rough. One must lie in the bottom of a hole for the day. The only obligation is to make contact with the command post by radio every thirty minutes. C-rations are carried out by the two men the night before. They stand the regular outpost watch with the rest of their squad throughout the night and then are left out there from before dawn until after sunset, when they are relieved by the next night's regular outpost watch. It is important that there be no sign of life on East Berlin during the day. Should the Chinese find out that there are two men out there, it would be a very simple matter for them to take prisoners. As far as I know, the forward slopes of East Berlin are not visible from any point on our MLR. These slopes are however visible from hill 139 and Saugech'on ridge. Two Chinese, say, could sneak out to the base of East Berlin before dawn, and remain quietly there until the outpost force is withdrawn, except for the two "lay-outs," as they are called. Then, under cover from any number of automatic weapons positioned on either Saugech'on ridge or hill 139, the two Chinese could climb the slope—which as I said is not visible from our MLR—and peek over the edge of the hole, saying, "Come with us, malines; you are plisoners." I have an acting exercise prepared for the occasion. I will roll over slowly, look up with a bland expression, and say "Get out," and then roll over again. You will? Why couldn't an entire platoon of Chinese occupy East Berlin in this manner during the daytime? They could, very simply. They would have trouble staying on as soon as they were discovered, but they'd have a ball taking it.

The process of elimination is something of a problem for the two lay-outs, who are obliged to remain in a hole for twelve hours. C-ration boxes are used for potie-potie. Never mind what happens with number one.

East Berlin is a very crude outpost. The Chinese have trenches; why don't we? Also, there should be some way in which the lay-outs could keep watch on the forward slopes. Yesterday, each time I called in to the command post, I felt like saying, "No, we haven't been captured yet."

The other night, when our squad had the regular watch on East Berlin, the message came over the radio that the regimental commander, a full colonel, would be escorted to the outpost that night to inspect the fortifications. There wasn't much we could do in the way of preparation, except to collect the empty C-ration boxes and cans and throw them further down the slope. Sgt. Barefield came to each man's hole and said, "If the colonel comes up to your hole first—challenge him. Throw him the password. We got to impress him some way." Pugnacci said, "Can I shoot him if he don't give the countersign?"

Around midnight someone heard the colonel approaching and the word was passed around from hole to hole. The colonel reached the summit near Pfc. Dunbar Bloomfeld's hole, so Bloomie had to challenge him. We all listened carefully. "HALT!" he said. "Who goes there? . . . sir."

The colonel, escorted by a fire team, came around to each hole for a minute or two of Good Guy conversation. Standing above our hole, he asked us where we were from, etc., and what we would do if a mortar barrage commenced right now. Pugnacci and I knew what to do. We scrambled into the bottom of the hole and whimpered around in there until the colonel graciously ordered us to come out. Then he left, to receive his combat pay and Dingleberry Cluster for valour in action.

This was the night I did setting-up exercises on the skyline, with BAR: deep-knee bends, up-in-arms-shoulders, all of them. Pugnacci frowned on this.

I counted the grenades that are stashed around our hole. There are thirty-eight fragmentation grenades, four phosphorous, and three illumination. Let 'em come; I'm ready. (O, Youth, Youth!)

There are a number of M48 trip-flares along the base of East Berlin. One went off the other night. It might have been a deer or a rat, but we quivered until dawn, clutching armloads of grenades.

February 6th, 1953

The original purpose of a reconnaissance patrol is to gather information concerning the enemy; their morale, equipment, position, and the surrounding terrain. In this Korean campaign, after many months of stationary warfare, our S-2 is pretty familiar with the conduct of the enemy, and there is no need for patrols to endanger themselves gathering information already obtained.

Certain things, however, must be checked on by small patrols every night. To accomplish this, each marine platoon on line sends out a nightly recon patrol. The general mission of each of these patrols is completed when the unit's company commander has been assured that the tactical situation in regard to the immediate enemy sector is the same as it was the previous night. These patrols are the means by which our side can detect any movement of the enemy toward us; whether they have established a new outpost, or planted a new mine field, barbed-wire entanglements or dug feeder trenches, etc.

Recon patrols are sent into No Man's Land to gather information and are therefore obliged to avoid contact with the enemy. They are instructed not to return fire unless absolutely necessary, and to withdraw immediately if possible.

Since I got here I've participated in two recons. The first was directed at a prominent terrain feature called the Cork, located fifty feet beyond—west of—the icy saddle that was mentioned in the account of the Little Rock raid. Once a marine outpost, the Cork is now sometimes manned by the Chinese as a listening post. Previous patrols have heard the sound of digging in this area and it was (is) presumed that the Chinese are preparing this knoll for use as an outpost. Our specific mission was to determine the amount of digging accomplished, if any. The Cork is barely visible from several points on the MLR. It is a small knoll which rises above Texas Ridge.

We left the MLR at 11 p.m. and reached the oft-mentioned saddle around 12:30. Moving like worms, we didn't make a sound. There were seven of us—volunteers, I will never fail to add. Sgt. Connant in charge. Two men were detached and sent forward to see what there was to see. The rest of us waited at the top of the saddle. Twenty minutes later the two men returned and reported that there was no sign of life on the Cork. The column moved forward. It was an extremely dark night, but while passing along the ridge I noticed a vague sort of shape off the path, on the right side. It was a small structure of some kind. I was too cold and nervous to step out of line and examine it. I learned later that it was a sign which has been seen by two other patrols. According to Barefield, who read it, the sign says: "BEWARE. DO NOT PASS BEYOND THIS POINT." Great!

On the Cork, we found a trench approximately four feet deep, running north—south. I lowered myself into it while the others looked around. One end of it is cluttered with clumps of frozen earth, suggesting that that end was under construction.

On the opposite side of the knoll—the northern side—we found several caved-in bunkers, apparently the remains of the old marine outpost. Also two foxholes. Sgt. Connant would not allow anyone to enter the bunkers. Worried about booby traps.

We returned to the MLR without incident.

The second recon was the one I mentioned as having gone out on the morning that the Frisco raid was scheduled to take place. Our mission was to see what there was to see along Saugech'on ridge. During the briefing, Lt. Buell said that S-2 (intelligence) suspected that "the Chinese have gotten wind of our proposed raid on Frisco," and that this was the reason for its being called off. "So we just might run into an ambush on Saugech'on ridge," he said. Oh—let's not, I said to myself. Some other time perhaps.

Nine check points were established; that is, nine points along the patrol route at which the radioman calls in to the command post, thus establishing the exact position of the patrol at that moment. The leader of the patrol memorizes the check points, and the company commander has them marked on a map in the command post. If, for instance, the radioman called in and said, "We're between check point four and check point five. We are receiving enemy small arms fire from two hundred yards to our right. Request mortar barrage," the company commander would be able to determine the relative position of the enemy and relay that information to the 60mm. command post. Within two minutes, the enemy's position would become the impact area of a concentrated mortar barrage. For this reason, check points are established and observed.

We left the MLR at 2 A.M. and reached the base of Saugech'on at 3:00. The climb to the top was difficult because of heavy foliage and crusted snow. It was impossible to move silently. Fortunately there was a light wind from the north. There were nine of us. Lt. Buell told us to lay down on the ridgetop; this was as far forward as we would go. The Chinese MLR, a terrain finger of hill 139, was not more than two hundred yards ahead of us. It was too dark to see it, but it was there. We were lying in the area that would have been the jump-off point for the Frisco raid. It is interesting that we all heard noises out there, none nearby though. Digging, coughing, clearing of throats, spitting. This reminded me of a piece by Col. Robert Riggs, concerning the health of the CCF (Chinese Communist Forces). The author states that two out of five of their soldiers have tuberculosis, and that one out of five is mentally unbalanced. The human noises we heard out there were fascinating; more fascinating than the sound of that lone burp-gunner on Little Rock. We lay there until 4:30, under a keenly piercing wind, which carried those occasional sounds over to us. We heard no talking. At 4:30 we withdrew.

I now have a picture of my own, nailed into a sandbag next to my bunk, directly above the candle stand. Looks suspiciously like a shrine. It's a little picture of Greta Garbo in a track suit, posing with some U. of Southern Cal. runners. Jane Owens found it in an old copy of *Vanity Fair*. It's hard to talk about, but I've worked out a complex Stanislavski relationship with her. It's one hell of a woman who will stand watch in Korea and eat C-rations. I haven't introduced her to any of the others and perhaps I'd better not. I'm hoping to convince her to come along on a patrol.

If a man is scheduled to go on a patrol or listening post he is allowed to sleep for a while beforehand. Not that this is a living hell up here, but there is always something going on. When there is a silence it is horrendous, and usually wakes anyone up. For some reason, the occasional shell bursts, the intermittent machine-gun fire, distant mortar barrages, all seem cheerful, but I better drop it right there. Many times we have heard machine gunners communicating to each other, sometimes several miles apart. A gunner who wants to do this will fire the following pattern:

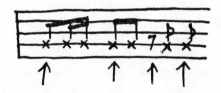

and another gunner will answer it. Sometimes it is passed along down the line, and this carries for great distances at night.

Distant firefighters are sometimes heard; always at night. We sleep in the morning. Afternoons are spent cleaning weapons, equipment, eating, writing letters, going to briefings, etc. The other night I watched a barrage way over in the Canadian sector, one or two miles to our right. The explosions resembled a number of fireflies, such was the distance. The sound they made was a series of muffled, irregular WWHOMPHS.

I neglected to mention that every rice paddy in this area is heavily mined. In most cases, paths have been found and marked.

February 1953

More *Sturm & Drang.* The ——— squad, plus a machine-gun section, stood watch on East Berlin last night. Pugnacci and I in the same foxhole. I always bring out a can of fruit and some kind of candy or a cookie from the C-ration box; and the night is divided not by hours—thank God I don't own a watch—but by the staggered consumption of goodies. The time was somewhere between the consumption of the cookie and the consumption of the fruit, that is, way past midnight. The word was whispered from hole to hole that someone heard noises. They came from below Hogg and Medve's hole. We all strained to hear. The pre-dawn wind was blowing; I heard nothing except the rustling of dry branches and dead leaves. But there were humans out there. The older men heard them. They say that you can tell after a couple of weeks on line.

Sgt. Barefield made contact with the command post and requested illumination. He was much too frightened and concerned to whisper anything in the way of instructions, and Pugnacci and I didn't have the slightest notion as to what was happening, except that someone had heard noises, which usually turn out to be either the wind or deer or rats.

In the meantime, Hogg and Medve were peering over the lip of their hole and both of them saw a figure, or so they reported later. One of them heaved an illumination grenade in the direction of the figure. We all heard the POP as the spoon snapped off. Pugnacci and I hunched down in the hole as it ignited. From Hogg's account of what he saw, he might be expected to have white hair. As soon as the grenade ignited, he looked down the slope and saw the face of a Chinese who was trying to conceal himself among the pine trees. Medve had looked also, but in another direction. He had not seen the face. The Chinese was on the other side of the barbed wire. Hogg began lobbing fragmentation grenades as fast as he could, causing considerable confusion to everyone on the outpost, including Medve. Then two frantic things happened at once. The illumination flare went off high above us, and a Maxim machine gun opened up from Texas ridge, racking the slopes of East Berlin. It became obvious what was happening. The Maxim was covering the approach of an attacking force. People began yelling all sorts of cheerful things: "Get down!" "Goonies!" (Chinese) "Heave all the grenades you got!" "They're coming!" "Jesus Christ!" "What are we supposed to do?" "Heave your fucking grenades!" etc. The Maxim and the grenades made a terrible racket, but the Chinese infantry didn't come any farther. The Maxim fired only about five long bursts, from a distance of one or two hundred yards. I like to think that Hogg's imagination ran away with him, but Barefield said that there *were* people out there. A heavy mortar barrage followed, which Barefield had called for. For three to five minutes the forward slopes of East Berlin were pounded with 60mm. projectiles.

GROUP FIVE

Camp Rose

February 12th, 1953

The First Marines are in regimental reserve now, and will return to the line on March 5th—so we are told. Before I describe this grand area, here is an account of a recon patrol that worked two nights before we went into reserve.

Sgt. Cruz was the patrol leader. The entire ——— squad plus Lo Castro and Ankers, of the ——— squad. Lo Castro had volunteered and literally forced Ankers to do the same. Lo Castro is Ankers's keeper. Ankers needs one. He is a real pathetic little fella from Chicago, and he is like a retarded child. An orphanage graduate. He is good, but Lo Castro—Castrate, everybody calls him—watches over him in a rough fashion, making sure that Ankers cleans his own weapon, that he understands what is said at a briefing, etc. Ankers talks like Mortimer Snerd and his face is not unlike that of a Cyclopean mole.

I stole an M-2 carbine back at 1st Ord. Bn., taking it out of the shop a piece at a time. The larger pieces—the barrel and receiver group and the stock, I hid under a tent flap and retrieved at night. Since I was issued a BAR on line, I had no use for the carbine. Ankers asked for it and got it. But he never volunteered for anything and Castrate finally made him come along on this patrol. More about Ankers and his keeper in a moment.

The mission of this patrol was twofold. As I mentioned during the account of the Little Rock raid, there is a path along the top of Texas Ridge and also a junction of that path with another one—running north. We were to take that path, the one running north down the forward slope of Texas Ridge, as far as we dared. Lt. Casimetti put it in different words at the briefing, but that is what he meant. The captain wanted to know whether or not there was a listening post on or near that path. Also, we were to reach a position where we could observe hill 139 in order to determine whether there were feeder trenches emanating from it. A feeder trench is one that branches off a main trench and cuts down into No Man's Land, providing a semicovered entrance and/or exit for patrols.

We departed at 10 P.M. and reached the junction near 11:30. As we crept along the ridge, Lo Castro kept saying, "Get down, Ankers." Apparently Ankers didn't dig the idea of walking in a crouch. Hard on the back. At one point, the word was passed back to deploy while the point man investigated something. I passed the word back to Lo Castro, who relayed it to Ankers. But Ankers was in a real fog; he kept on moving, kind of wandering around. Lo Castro whispered viciously, "ANKERS! GET DOWN!" Ankers heard him but stood still, frightened. Lo Castro rose slowly and went over to him. He whispered again, softly but with great intensity, "Get—DOWN—ANKERS!" Ankers was tremendously confused and Lo Castro's attitude made him angry. With the voice of a five-year-old, he whined, "Wul . . . Yew ain't down, goddamit Lo Castrate!" His voice echoed back from the other side of the paddy. They both disappeared from view. Lo Castro was probably sitting on him.

The path ran down Texas Ridge at a SE—NW angle. At the bottom, there was the same paddy over which the Little Rock raiders had passed, and where the Corsair pilot had vanished. The path became a dike—a raised portion of earth, a two- or three-foot ridge which separates larger sections of the paddy.

At this point the paddy is only about thirty yards wide, and we crossed it quickly, entering a group of small trees and low bushes that border the paddy. I didn't realize it at the time, but we were at the end of one of the long terrain fingers of hill 139.

This was our furthest point. Cruz passed the word back for two volunteers. Downard and Bloomfeld. Medve was left in charge, and Sgt. Cruz and the two volunteers disappeared into the shrubbery.

They returned in five minutes. Cruz, using hand signals, told us to turn around and move out quickly. We learned later that they had not seen anything but that they had probably been seen. They had moved forward less than fifty feet when they heard the sound of a bolt being manipulated. Cruz told the lieutenant that it was a rifle bolt; sounded like the bolt of a Springfield '03, he said.

February 14th, 1953

Today is my twenty-second birthday, but I would rather be eighteen.

Bad news this week. A letter from mother:

> . . . As you can see by the enclosed, dear Gampie also got too tired. As you know and saw, he had been miserable for so long, it would be phony to mourn his death, but for those of us still around, even though expected, it is always a bit of a shock and a definite sense of a vacuum. He was a fine selfless human, a gentle man, a giver always. He left a great deal of love with so many people. And, of course, not a day goes by but some phrase of his doesn't pop up, like "always leave a trail" and "quality, not quantity." So many. Lots of people have commented on how much alike you are. . . .

How much alike! I wish this were so. I would rather be like Henry Faxon than anyone I know. It seems logical that he died in Santa Monica, that huge sickroom for old people. I didn't take the news very gracefully. The letter was on my rack when I came back from the outdoor movie. Hogg was the only one awake. He was reading by candlelight, halfway inside his sleeping bag. I read the letter, then read it to Hogg. I made a terrible leering face and then began laughing, not hysterically, but laughing hard. Hogg was upset by this: he wanted to laugh at my leering face but couldn't allow himself to, although he almost broke up. He was mildly shocked that I could react this way. I don't think I believed that Gampie had died, and I wasn't interested in thinking about it.

This reserve area, Camp Rose, is located one mile north of the Imjim river, which flows east from the Yellow Sea, and about ten miles behind the MLR. The Imjim would prove a serious obstacle to the Chinese should an offensive bring them this far. In this area, two bridges span the river; Spoonbill bridge and Freedom bridge. A detachment of twenty-four men from Able company are guarding Spoonbill.

Last December the Chinese predicted, by means of their eerie loudspeakers, that they would cross the Imjim before Christmas, and that they would have occupied Seoul by the first of the year. To prevent the river from freezing over, so that an army might cross over the ice rather than be channeled across the two bridges (which would have been demolished by then any-way). . . . Going to start over again. Marine amtracks churn up the ice of the river every day so that ice will not form to allow the Chinese to cross over, should they break through the MLR. At 1st Ord. Bn. people would ask, "Is the Imjim froze over yet?" and we green troopers never knew what they meant.

Spoonbill bridge, over which we passed on the way up from 1st Ord. Bn., is a tremendously sturdy structure of steel girders and thick wire mesh. The bridge is actually quite small. Demolition teams are always prepared to blow the poor dear to bits.

The Imjim is also a boundary for civilians. All villages north of it, if not razed, are deserted. Only military traffic is permitted to cross either of the bridges. The units in reserve are responsible for the security of the nonpopulated area. Roving patrols, referred to as pubic patrols, search through the empty villages and adjacent paths from time to time. The only village near our camp has been burned to the ground. Roving patrols snoop around anyway, hunting for line-jumpers (Korean or Chinese spies that have gotten through our MLR and are trying to cross the river), guerrillas and prostitutes. I had charge of one of these routines the other day, and it turned out to be nothing more than a strenuous but very pleasant walk. We left at 8 in the morning and climbed the mountain behind us. Near the summit we found a large emblem of painted white stones, arranged to form the letter "A," enclosed in a square. It can be seen for some distance. Represents Able company. A similarly arranged "B" and "C" are visible on two mountains across the valley, representing the other two companies of the battalion. There is a somewhat similar custom at Kent school in Connecticut, only they paint the last two numbers of the year upon a large rock on a mountain overlooking the school.

Taking our time, we strolled about those small mountains, enjoying the day, which was beautiful. Deep blue clear sky, and a sharp wind that sifted snow dust around us. On days like this I'll get rhapsodical as hell if given the chance, but thank God I didn't allow myself to recite the only poem I know, which I was reminded of all day. Called "Winter Milk" by Carl Sandburg.

> There are dreams in your eyes, Helga.
> Tall reaches of wind sweep the clear blue.
> The winter is young yet, so young.
> Only a cupful of winter has touched your lips.

Thank you. All sorts of thoughts storm around in the mind when one is standing watch. Food, I imagine, is a most common subject. I spend considerable time creating a breakfast-in-bed menu, often taking an hour or two to work it out. It usually turns out to be the same thing each time: a large glass of fresh orange juice, small dish of canned figs, eggs Benedict, coffee, milk, English toast, buttered w/marmalade. A pretty high-class breakfast but there it is. The other night-watch fantasies usually revolve around Rockland county, New York.

February 17th, 1953

There is a secondary main line of resistance called the Kansas line, which is being completed at the present time. One section of the Kansas line lies within five hundred yards of this tent, not far from the letter "A" of white stones. This particular mountain is an outpost of the Kansas line, and is referred to as OP-2. The Kansas line is not manned; it will be used if the Chinese break through our present MLR. Able company is responsible for the excavation of OP-2, which we completed several days ago, a prodigious feat.

Beginning at 8 o'clock on a Wednesday morning, we worked until 10 o'clock the following morning, without once returning to the area. At noon a jeep climbed the steep fire trail, bringing us sandwiches and coffee. We continued digging all that night, working, fantastic as it sounds, by candlelight. More than a hundred candles were passed out. We stuck them into little crevasses in the ground and managed to get work done under the dim light.

OP-2 is located right next to the Imjim, which flows south at this point. From the top of OP-2, the river is far, far below. Many miles of terrain are visible and the most intriguing sight of all is the Chinese MLR. All Chinese-occupied hills are conspicuous because they are almost always devoid of vegetation; the result of our air strikes and months of bombardment. Their color is usually reddish brown, that is, the exposed earth, as opposed to the greenish brown shrub-covered hills elsewhere. From OP-2 the terrain, looking north, is something like this:

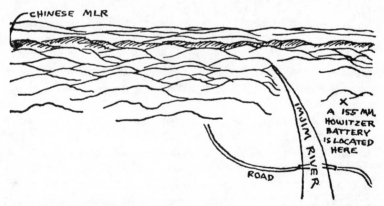

This is a copy of a drawing made on the back of a carton while atop OP-2. One can see from the drawing that OP-2 is lofty as hell. Should the Kansas line ever be used, this will be a key outpost.

The 1st Engineers are building another bridge across the

107

Imjim, about a mile north of OP-2. It looks like it will be a modern citylike bridge, made of concrete. From Camp Rose, we can hear the sound of their air hammers, bulldozers and other heavy equipment. When we worked all day and all night on OP-2, so did they. But in shifts, not like us gibbons. A number of searchlights illuminated their working area and it was, for some reason, a very striking sight. What they saw in our direction must have stoned them; the hundreds of candles way up on the mountain. Which way is the grotto, kind sir? Could that light be seen from the Chinese lines? Possibly. They say that a match is visible at night for seven miles.

So we dug all night. From about three o'clock we were like zombies. The remarkable thing is that when we climbed up at eight o'clock to start work, OP-2 was virgin ground. By ten o'clock the following morning we had built one hell of an outpost. A circular trench, five feet deep, three feet wide, and at least three hundred yards in diameter. Complete with BAR and machine-gun emplacements, fighting-holes and bunny-holes. A company outpost. The roughest part was the beginning: the ground was frozen. It was first necessary to dig thin little holes, at six foot intervals, in which sticks of TNT were placed. Once the turf was blasted loose, the pick & shovel work took care of itself—with a bit of help from 200 men. Such concentrated labor was probably a regular occurrence on Guadalcanal or Anzio, but for us soft ones it was unusual. Not rough as hell, but unusual.

And why was all the rapid digging necessary? The high echelon, probably S-2, got the idea that the Chinese were going to launch a massive offensive on Chinese New Year's and so all units in reserve had to dig like maniacs to prepare the Kansas line for use by—Thursday evening, I think. As far as we heard, the only major action that night was a heavy probe on one of the outposts in the 7th Marines' sector.

It is typical of Marine Corps logic that we were not allowed to hit the sack after we had finished the job. Instead we went through the normal schedule for the rest of the day, which included a field problem that afternoon.

One of the machine gunners uncovered a yellow skull, minus mandible. Another found a long bone, possibly a femur. They found them during the digging session.

There is so much activity in this camp that I couldn't begin to cover it. The discipline approaches that of boot camp. On the second day here, all the barbers and semibarbers were gathered together in the recreation tent. In short, we (the entire battalion) were shaved, short. My mane at the present time is no longer than three fourths of an inch. These maniacal carryings-on bothered everyone tremendously, especially the men that are about to go home. The only thing that bothered me was the so-called haircut itself. This big, crummy bastard came at me with a pair of shrub clippers, and took several probably unintentional nips at my skull. No scissors were used, only these wire cutters. Now everyone wears a hat, all the time. To bed. At least I do.

The training schedule is fantasmagoriatum. Reveille at 5 A.M. —a terrible little man dashing in and out of the tents, ringing a huge bell and blowing a police whistle at the same time. We dress at top speed and stampede outside for fifteen minutes of glorious calisthenics. Every cold, black morning. It's great. GREAT. I love it, I say. I tell you it's all quite grand and I LOVE it. The rest of the day is filled with a wide variety of interesting projects: policing the area (picking up cigarette butts, scraps of paper, etc.), rifle inspection, troop and stomp (drill, marching, etc.), personnel and tent inspection, classes, hikes, training problems, night problems. This is what is called "harassing the troops." It is suggested that we take out our resentment on the Chinese later. One thousand men with persecution complexes.

I have a vivid picture of what my room at home will look like after discharge. I am going to collect all the wastebaskets, ash trays and garbage pails in the house and carry them up to my room, dumping them all in the middle of the floor. Thereafter all garbage and trash will be deposited there. Anyone who tries to remove the collection will be smashed. I will not shave nor bathe nor get a haircut for an entire year. Food and comic books and screen magazines will be brought to me. Breakfast will be served at noon; a mixture of orange rinds, coffee grounds, burnt toast and diluted barley mash. Should anyone speak to me without adding the word "Sir," they will be destroyed at once. If possible I should like to have a brand-new M-1 rifle at my disposal. I will pee in its bore.

February 18th, 1953

I'm feeling better now, but I swear I'd rather be on the MLR than here.

Each infantry battalion rates a bugler or "field musik." In the old days, according to Dad, field musiks were unusually tough youngsters, who were between the ages of twelve and sixteen. Now, they are part of the headquarters section. They blow reveille, chow call, recall (to work), chow call, call to morning colors, morning colors, assembly, church call on Sunday, chow call, recall, chow call, call to evening colors, evening colors, movie call, tattoo, taps. Night colors are sounded a half an hour after sundown. Troops out of doors come to attention, facing the general direction of the post flag, and salute while the call is being sounded. Troops in vehicles dismount and do the same. The phrases of night colors are lovely and some buglers tend to overplay them, stoning themselves out of their head, but sounding like a maturaphone. The battalion guard lowers the flag during the call.

I got some great birthday cards this week. A tiny music box from Jane Owens that wails "Happy Birthday" when the handle is turned. Tonic-tonic-tonic-tonic-tonic.

Been on a destruction rampage during the past few days. There used to be a sign, representing Able company, located beside the supply route that runs through the middle of camp. This sign was a definite discredit to the company. It measured 5′ by 5′ and was a hideous-looking thing.

The god-damned sign nearly drove me crazy every time I saw it. One night I crept out there—about one hundred yards away was the guardhouse—and ripped it out of the ground, cracking the posts. I carried it several hundred yards into the woods and split it into many little pieces with a pickax.

110

STABLE ABLE COMPANY
"THE FINEST OF THE FIGHTIN' FIRST"

The newest addition to the obstacle course is a series of mock windows. We practice throwing grenades through the windows. I destroyed them all. With a bit of encouragement, I would gladly lay low the entire obstacle course. In fact . . .

February 20th, 1953

Tim finally made contact. After commendable persistence in trying to break through the maddeningly complex network of Eighth Army switchboards, regimental switchboard finally "gave" Lt. Russ the Able Company command post, and I was summoned to the wire.

The command post was noisy. Being a miserable, supplicating peon, I dared not ask the officers to lower their Homeric voices so that I might hear my brother's words from halfway across the peninsula. The sound box rested on the operations bench, and I took the phone underneath the table, hovering over it down there in a shadow.

"Hello," I said, and was immediately embarrassed—not because of my incongruous position, but because it didn't seem natural for a corporal to pick up a field telephone in Korea and say hello. No one has said hello to me since November; a strictly civilian word. Over here it's "Russ on" for hello and "Russ out" for goodbye.

The vibrations at the other end said,

"Vangph . . . ? Ivph vphaph vhpg . . . ?" Having had some experience with bad connections on East Berlin and the Burgundy, I had a working knowledge of this language. He had said "Yellow Fang . . . ? Is that you?"

"Yes, my son! How the hell are you?" I shouted back. But the lieutenant was being very businesslike. No doubt he was calling from a command post, and he was probably in the company of senior officers. It occurred to me that he might be defeating his purpose by saying, "Yellow Fang" into the phone, with a straight face.

"Pwv iph yphv skaphuph? Thvph vph hph hphav kphv nuvph." ("What is your status? That's all I want to know.")

My status? Perhaps he wants to know if I've been wounded.

"I'm perfectly all right, Tiwi. In good health. How about you?"

"Nv-v, nv-v!" said the vibrations. "Yphv SKAPHUPH, Yvphov Vangph!" ("No, no! Your STATUS, Yellow Fang!")

"Oh! Well, I'm still a corporal if that's what you mean."

The garbled vibrations became so loud that I had to hold the phone away. After regaining his composure, he said this to me, in a slow-burn voice: "Martin—I may be able to come over to see you next Friday, but first I must know your *status*." He was worried about the guerrillas that sometimes tap the wires. I finally understood that by status he meant location; whether we were in a combat situation or in reserve. Naturally he wouldn't want to visit me on line. In answering him I used a code of my own. "Ah!" said I, finally getting the point. "We punchie-punchie hav-a-no," which is a Korean's way of saying "We are not on the MLR at the present time." Tim understood. He knew the name of our outfit but didn't want to mention it over the phone. He said that he would find the camp with no trouble, and to expect him on Friday afternoon.

I said, "Great, man. Come on over. We'll have a ball." Tim replied, very seriously: "Goodbye, Yellow Fang."

Friday afternoon! I felt like a Southern belle who has a gentleman caller coming in two days—barely enough time to get ready!

As any fool knows, there is a world of difference between the Marine Corps and the U. S. Army, but the difference is not so apparent when we are in reserve. Tim is an infantryman himself. We hear that their reserve periods are pretty rigorous, too. I had to think of a way to impress him. I took the problem to the other members of the squad. We discussed the situation for some time, seated around the potbellied stove. Our deliberations resulted in a temporary change in command. Sgt. Barefield offered to let me act as squad leader while my brother was in the area, a magnanimous gesture. Fortunately there is (usually) no way that a man's rank may be determined by his uniform over here. Since we are given fresh clothes each time we go to the showers, it is not unusual to see a private wearing a jacket with master sergeant's stripes stenciled on the sleeves. For inspections only, each man is required to wear a metal insignia of rank on his cap.

The way in which the other men co-operated was most gratifying, and slightly fantastic. Pugnacci lent me a set of dungarees that he wears only for important inspections. They were very salty, meaning that they had been scrubbed so much that they were bluish white. (Some of the old-timers, especially the drill instructors at Parris Island and San Diego, have been known to soak their dungarees in brine, turning them almost white with a tinge of blue.) By Friday afternoon all eight of those surly bastards looked like models for a recruiting poster. Our tent was in perfect shape. The gear under each man's rack had been uniformly arranged, as well as the racks themselves. It was as though General Shepherd himself were expected. But here is the clincher: There are ordinarily three BARs in a marine squad. The rest of the men carry M-1s. By Friday afternoon every man in the ——— squad had a BAR. A certain amount of temporary trading had been carried on with members of the other two squads. I intended to borrow one of the Thompson submachine guns from the command post, but Barefield said that there would be hell to pay if the captain found out that any of us had traded weapons.

It was agreed that we would snap to attention like kangaroos when Tim walked in—that is, if we were inside when he arrived. Barefield reminded us that no one must slip and address him (Barefield) as "Sarge."

I was excused by the first sergeant from the afternoon field problem. When the men returned at 4:30, Tim had still not arrived. At 5:00 we were lying around waiting for chow call. Footsteps on the gravel outside, then a voice: "This is Corporal Russ's tent, sir."

I muttered "Stand by," and we hurriedly collected ourselves. I was very nervous (Amanda Wingfield). The tent flaps parted and in strode Tiwi.

"Ah-ten-SSHUT!" somebody shouted. Eight Doric columns shot up.

"Rest!" said the lieutenant.

The first thing that occurred to me was that Tim might be embarrassed by a wild brotherly greeting, such as I felt coming on. So I ushered him outside without a word. All he managed to say was "Yellow Fang!" The last time we had seen each other was the autumn of '51 at, of all ridiculous places, the Biltmore. In back of the tent we halted and I turned him around so that the late afternoon sunshine was glaring directly in his eyes. We studied each other. He was lean and had bags under his eyes. He was wearing a Mongolian-type headpiece; his lieutenant's bar was centered in the upturned brim. I reached up and removed the headpiece, staring brutally at his hairline. At the Biltmore that fall afternoon he had spoken gloomily of the alarming rate at which his hair was falling. He would be out of luck at the Bachelor's Cotillion next year, he said. I scrutinized his noble cranium for a moment and then replaced his cap, saying "Hmm." Back inside the tent, the men were introduced to him and they did their best to act like combat veterans.

Chow call sounded and everyone, save the brothers, rose and collected their weapons—it being mandatory to carry one's weapon when outside. I was disappointed that Tim had apparently not noticed the array of elephant guns that had just paraded by. But, when the men had left, he said "Fong, you know, I was just thinking about an ambush that I took out last month. There were seventeen of us. I had a carbine; two other men had BARs. The rest carried M-1s."

I produced the fifth of Canadian Club that I had bought for fifteen dollars in Seoul, and we got down to business with two canteen cups. Tim played it cool; I don't think he even got a buzz on. On the other hand—*loadatum ero*. Not particularly fond of booze, I drink specifically to get clobbered. By the time the men returned from chow, I was roaring. Tim was relaxed and happy.

There was no night problem that night (thank God) and the remainder of the evening is something of a haze. Only isolated things:

Tim questioned several of the man concerning marine modus operandi. He took a liking to Barefield and Higgins. The men were most polite and friendly with him. No one did any bragging. At one point in the evening I was seated on the ground, spreading peanut butter on crackers with my fingers and demanding that the men eat what I had prepared. The most dangerous part of the evening came when I catapulted over to the command post, entered and announced that I must visit my brother's reserve area immediately. I'm not sure who was in the CP at the time, but I don't believe the captain was there. I seem to remember Lt. Buell and the 1st Sergeant smiling at me as though they could hardly keep from laughing. I departed as

115

abruptly as I had entered, having been told to come back in the morning. Tim had followed and was listening outside. He commented that my behavior had been not quite military.

By this time the little Korean driver (Tim's driver) had loosened up and was nodding agreeably to everything that was said, like Dickens's Aged One.

Finally Tim had to go. He said goodbye to the men and walked out to the jeep. We said good luck to each other. He got in the jeep and they drove off, down the dirt road that connects our reserve area with the main supply route, about three hundred yards across the rice paddy. When they were halfway across, I decided to run to the intersection so that I could wave as they went by. Taking off like a great, clumsy bird, I swooped across the ice, lost what balance there was left, sprawled on my ass, and sat there waving weakly at the disappearing headlights.

What I wanted then was more crackers. Instinct told me that if I didn't eat some more crackers, I would become sick. I raced at top speed to the officers' mess hall and entered it—a dangerous thing for even a sober enlisted man. A group of officers were there, watching a movie. I stood in the back and tried to focus, but couldn't. Then, rummaging around the shelves, I found a box of crackers and departed before anyone could question me.

Shortly thereafter the bottom fell out. I passed out somewhere near the guardhouse, right in the middle of the wide path leading to the chow hall. I was revived by some anonymous marine, who half carried me back across the paddy, a most understanding fellow.

We like to think that we impressed Tim.

February 21st, 1953

Pfc. Lester Higgins has a transoceanic radio, a real luxury. He bought it for $50 from a guy who is going home. Who needs a radio at home? Most of the programs piped to us—from Japan or from the States through Japan—are damn good. There are two pop records that have taken the squad's fancy; "Till I Waltz

116

Again with You," Teresa Brewer, and "You Better Go Now," Jeri Sothern. This record and a record of one of Alec's tunes ("Give Me Time") are the only things I've heard of hers, but she is a real gasser, my favorite. She's tremendo. In the feces-kicking world, Hank Williams is very popular around here. He's about the only hillbilly singer that I believe. Listening to that radio is usually disturbing as hell, if one is lying in the sleeping bag dreaming of peppermint-stick women.

Noise of a fierce battle up forward yesterday morning, and later many helicopters flew by, bearing long black bundles underneath, the wounded. Lt. Casimetti told us today that a company of marines from the 7th regiment had raided a hill called Gentry. Here is the score:

Marines—
    16 K.I.A. (killed in action)
    70 W.I.A. (wounded)
    2 flame-thrower tanks destroyed.
Chinese—
    An estimated 200 killed or wounded.

We scoffed at the estimate of Chinese casualties. From the little experience I've had in raids and from the stories I've heard of other raids, I'll bet the Chinese suffered half the number of casualties that we had. When we raid the Chinese, we get clobbered. When the Chinese raid the marines, they get clobbered worse. But they are a bit more intelligent about it; they don't make raids very often.

Three enemy soldiers were captured during the action. A detail of men were assigned to escort the prisoners back to our MLR. No doubt a flash report of this news was sent to division headquarters, causing much excitement. Prisoners in this war are as rare as thirty-day leaves, at least in the marine sector since the fighting became static—that is, with fixed MLRs on both sides. Any man who captures a prisoner these days is promised a five-day Rest & Rehabilitation breather in Japan. Prisoners have been taken in the past few months, but they never seemed to reach the MLR alive. Yesterday morning, as these prisoners were being escorted to the rear, one of the marines got shook and cut them down with a burst from his weapon. It must be true; Lt. Casimetti wouldn't have made it up.

Pfc. Dudley Hogg, from Vallejo, California, is an amazing man. He was recently married—on his last leave. He broods a good deal because his wife does not write him very often. Hogg is extremely well built, of medium height. He has a large leonine head and strong features. He is twenty-five. We had a bitter encounter yesterday.

We were having a company field day, as it is laughingly called; a super-cleaning of everything—tents, outside area, weapons, selves, etc. These productions are always unbelievably morbid. The sky was overcast and everyone was pretty grouchy anyway. I am a fire-team leader now and Dudley is one of the members of the team. I gave him some work to do and he was unusually truculent. He is ordinarily quite gentle but that day he was bugged about something, probably the silence of his wife among other things. He virtually refused to do what I told him. Being a new fire-team leader, I felt that if Hogg didn't "obey" me, since this was literally the first order I had given in that capacity, no one else would. This was sound enough, but I flipped. I called him a son of a bitch and warned him that he had better get to work before I busted him to private. Then he flipped. I was seated on the ground. He came over and cocked his fist threateningly. We would have stormed it up had not Sgt. Barefield interceded. I didn't realize it at the time, but Dudley was in bad shape—one of those surges of homesickness that can't be assuaged no matter what the man does. But I had blown out the back myself; loss of dignity, etc. and I went into a pitch of the most shameful kind.

Standing there, I proceeded to harass him verbally, in the most sadistic possible way, saying things like this, and repeating them over and over again, in a low, grimy voice: "Big, brave stupid Hogg. Gonna mess around with a corporal. Gonna get himself put in the brig. Gonna get the livin' ass kicked out of him for messin' around with a corporal. Poor Hogg, miserable fool.

118

Won't do any work. Won't hold up his end. Thinks he doesn't belong in the Marine Corps. Thinks he should be home. He's homesick. Oh, I pity him. Poor miserable Hogg. Homesick. Feelin' awful sorry for himself. Lost his little temper at a corporal. Almost slugged a corporal. Almost got his poor homesick ass kicked in by a corporal. Miserable, miserable man."

This went on for some time, but it wasn't the least bit funny. The other men stood around, not saying a word. They probably expected to see a murder. Finally someone said, "Come on, Russ. Knock it off." But I was too far gone and continued, speaking slowly but hardly pausing for breath. Dudley, instead of smashing me as he should have, sat down on a couple of sandbags and put his face in his hands. The longer I continued the more broken he became. Corpsman Danny Keppard came up to me and said, "Come on, Russo. This is very bad. Leave the man alone. He's shot." In the middle of my charming soliloquy, a whistle blew outside, summoning us to a company meeting, a class on machine guns. We walked outside and I followed Hogg, close behind, saying something like this: "Corporal Russ is going to watch Pfc. Hogg like a hawk from now on. Pfc. Hogg had better wise up because Cpl. Russ is just waiting for an excuse to run Pfc. Hogg up with the morning colors." I couldn't see Hogg's face but he looked like an old man from the rear. Danny Keppard was walking next to me and he insisted that I stop the routine, or else. I was emotional as hell and I grabbed Danny by the arm and dragged him back into the tent, trying to explain how I felt. At that time, I felt completely in the right. As I think back, the only justification I can offer for this lousy behavior is that I was subconsciously getting revenge on all those guys that had, in my imagination, bullied me when I was a kid. But that's ridiculous and I know it.

Danny finally dragged me to the outdoor class. We were late but no one noticed. We stood behind the last row, where there were several benches. Dudley was there, seated on one of them. When he saw me, he attracted my attention and motioned me over, to sit next to him in the space he had saved.

119

February 22nd, 1953

Danny Keppard, hospital corpsman second class, is a bit hard to describe. He is from Winona, West Virginia. First of all, he is my best friend around here. Physically he is a remarkable-looking man. He is as tall as myself but perfectly proportioned; also graceful of movement but very powerful. He is extremely intelligent and articulate, and his humor is inclined to be offbeat although he works hard at being a conservative young man. The outstanding feature of his character is his conception of privacy. He'd listen to a man talk all night about himself, and be interested, and yet would never intrude upon another man who doesn't care to talk about himself. In other ways, he strikes me as being an almost ideal Christian cat. One more compliment; he looks like a model for a statue of Apollo—a colored Apollo. (Get—in—*the* car . . . *Put*—your—left—earlobe—*directly* alongside the end—of—my LARGE—toe . . . WHEREUPON I—will execute—a—half-gainer—thereby—positioning—*my*—glorious—tessatura—*directly*—adjacent—to—*your*—stately—donicker).

Run for the hills and man the life boats; it's camping time.

There are two corpsmen attached to each platoon. Danny is one of ours, and lives in this tent, fortunately right next to me. These corpsmen are not marines; they are in the Navy, but trained by both units. The Navy gives them extensive medical training, the Corps trains them for combat. They all take a great deal of ribbing. We for instance pretend to resent the fact that a "swabbie" is living in the tent with us. They are also referred to as "chanchre mechanics." But corpsmen are dedicated folk, and have an admirable reputation among marines. During patrols, raids, probes, etc., they assume staggering responsibilities and are completely dependable. The training these men receive is considerably more extensive than the training the Army gives their medics. This deal has excited Danny so much that he intends to study medicine after he is discharged. Although he considers himself strictly a sailor, he acts more like a marine all the time.

120

He doesn't swear but is certainly far from righteous. As a matter of fact, he does swear, but in a strange way. He substitutes biological terms for all scatology, sometimes going way out to avoid using the word itself. The results are unbelievably complicated.

He had a bad experience yesterday. He opened up his B-1 unit—his medical bag—to check his supplies and found that the morphine was missing. This is very bad indeed. He called the squad together and asked that the person who took it replace it as soon as possible. He left the B-1 unit out all night, but the morphine was not returned. He reported the loss to the company commander. A few minutes later, the battalion medical officer and a CID (counterintelligence) man were questioning everyone in the squad. The impression they gave was that the corpsman was at fault. They didn't find out anything.

Dan is the first man I've met in this outfit with whom I can talk freely. I trust him. Through him, I've climbed out of the ivory tower and have begun to make friends with the rest of the squad. Not that we were enemies before, but I didn't go out of my way to make it with them.

I learned at prep school that a kid can impress others by simply keeping his mouth shut. My first year at South Kent I was a yold; a nonentity, except at night, when I used to turn on the "Poco-moco-Slow-ly-I-turn-step-by-step" routine which fractured the roommates. I was unaware of the importance of gaining what prep-school boys call "respect." Asinine as it may be, this is what the South Kent boy seemed to want most. Not self-respect, but respect from the others. At the end of that first year I was being treated like a congenital idiot, possibly because I acted like one. It seemed that the boys who were the most respected were the quiet ones. So, the following fall I returned to school wearing a continual slight frown and remained almost mute. Before Christmas vacation I was elected president of the third form. As soon as this happened, I resorted to yoldom once more, with venom. I was no more suited to be a leader than I am now, and I knew it then. There was a boy in the form ahead of me who was just plain dumb, a real empty-head. But he never said a word, and he made the football team, and he was made sub-prefect his senior year.

When I arrived at college, I tried it again; strode about the campus wearing a red beanie cap (which almost ruined the act) and a slight frown. Never uttered a sound. Elected to student council immediately. The point I'm hammering at is that I pulled the same act when I joined this squad, but for slightly different reasons. I felt that the authority of a corporal should be respected, and I wanted to be left alone. But to hell with it. I'm no Pericles, and these guys know which end is up anyway. So now, thanks mostly to Dan Keppard, I'm my own cretinous self and having a ball.

February 25th, 1953

Before the battalion returns to the line, it is hoped that every man will have had the liberty of a day in Seoul. A small group is transported there every day and brought back the same night. Tony Colia and I had the honor last week. Here is an account of that wild day.

Colia is a fearless little pfc. He has a Purple Heart and partly because of it he is incorrigible as hell. By the standards of the Marine Corps he is a good marine: arrogant, tough, ignorant and loyal. He is the kind who will ultimately spend his Christmas Eves drinking beer in some grubby little liberty town, like Jacksonville, North Carolina, and whose Sunday afternoons will be spent near a dusty bus depot, waiting for the bus back to Camp Lejeune. But he is where he needs to be. The all-inclusive parent, the United States Marine Corps, protects him from hunger and exposure, and he pays his keep with a BAR.

On patrol, he is as dependable as his weapon. On liberty—on his own—he is likely to find himself in the custody of the military police. Most company commanders, I suspect, are secretly proud whenever the Army MPs deliver some riotous marine back to his area. Captain Krupp, our new commander, collared me the morning we left and told me to stay close to

122

Colia, saying that if he were brought back by MPs, he—the captain—would have Colia thrown in the brig and that he would punish me in some way. He was half serious.

After breakfast we stood about in the darkness while the captain gave the set speech. Something or other about venereal diseases and conduct yourselves accordingly as befits United States Marines. We boarded the truck and took off, ten of us.

Camp Rose is located about twenty-five miles north of Seoul. We huddled together in the back of the open truck, waiting for the sun to warm the air. Having boarded the truck with clean dungarees, smooth chins, and scrubbed bodies, we were covered with dust by the time we reached Uijonbu, halfway to Seoul.

The sun appeared not long after we left Uijonbu, its rays sneaked across the craggy ridges and the huge shadow covering the vast rice paddies gradually drew off; kinda makes a man choke up, don't it? Wisps of smoke rose from most of the thatched huts in the valley and on the mountain slopes. Quiet and peaceful down there. Only a few miles north, the rumble of artillery and mortar fire causes the earth to shudder.

The capitol city appeared, as out of nowhere. The road becomes a precipitous mountain pass and then, abruptly, there is Seoul. I tried to describe Inchon, but I won't even bother with Seoul, which, in the early morning is indescribable. It is beautiful, ugly, breath-taking; the most intriguing, moving sight I've ever seen. It's farnsgaldo and krunsdrass and ponoriferous. At once!

We came to a stop in the military parking lot and an officer appeared at the tail gate. He held us at seated attention and delivered another conduct yourselves accordingly speech. And we would have to be back, he said, in the truck, at 5 P.M. We catapulted over the tail gate.

Two ferocious South Korean policemen, in tan uniforms, white gloves, and white barracks caps, about five feet tall, guarded the parking lot gate, outside of which mingled a phalanx of wild children, armed to the teeth with chewing gum, shoeshine kits and other more curious wares. The ten of us passed into the street and were assaulted from all directions, each kid screaming his particular pathetic pitch. The two police-men waded into them, screaming at the top of their lungs. They were ignored. The policemen began shoving them, trying to get them away from us. There must have been more than twenty-five kids. When the cops began to get a little rough, Colia lost his temper and stormed in among the miniature throng, trying to get at the cops. I followed. He shouted terrible insults at them, in Korean. Colia, who, it is said, has emptied an entire magazine into the body of a Chinese, jumped at the chance to be chivalrous. But I caught him and steered him the other way.

The ten marines were spread out by then, each surrounded by kids. All of them shouted at once. A filthy little boy dressed in a ragged utility coat with sergeant stripes on the sleeves was hanging onto my sleeve crying, "Sheba-sheba (whore) hav-a-yes, sahji (sergeant). Sheba-sheba number huckin' *one* hav-a-yes! You come!" I don't mean he was a "horrid little boy," I mean that he was filthy, but most of them were. Dirt, soot.

A small girl with bangs, and her brother, scuttled around my feet as we shuffled along, pleading to give a shoeshine. Colia and I were quite miserable. Would this last all day?

"No, no, no, no!" we said, wading through the shallow hu-man wave. By the time we reached an alley, we resembled walk-ing trees. Kids were climbing all over us. My legs were enveloped by them; it required the strength of a gibbon to move forward. Quite a bit like one of those nightmares. The other walking tree disappeared into the alley and when I reached the corner, I found Colia standing on tiptoes, removing his .45 from its hol-ster and wielding it—a last resort. The children scattered in all directions. Colia guffawed and shouted like he was driving a team of work horses. The children, frightened, then became spiteful and obscene. We two brave marines stood together in the alley, regarding the small faces that peered out at us from corners of buildings and shacks, ash cans and wooden crates. A thin brown arm lashed out and a pebble struck Colia on the chest. More pebbles flew through the air, a veritable barrage. Colia and I

124

knew we were beaten, so we ran down the alley, and came out into the open air of another street. Safe. I discovered that the top of my boots were covered with bright red dye. The little one with bangs must have applied this for spite, because I ignored her.

It is difficult to find a place to sit down in Seoul, for less than three dollars. The only place to go is the immense post exchange, which looks like it used to be an office building. We did not buy anything except food, but walked around the floors observing pretty Korean salesgirls, and the uniforms of soldiers of different countries.

We left and walked around the streets, perfectly satisfied with sight-seeing at first. We were always accompanied or followed by children, some remarkably attractive, others remarkably ugly. All selling something—whiskey, beer, chewing gum, pornography, shoeshines, shoelaces, leather holsters, emblems, shoulder patches, whores. Many were just begging.

Seoul is surprisingly modern, and ancient buildings and temples often appear huddled between office buildings. There is a large bank, on the same block as the post exchange, that is comparable to some Western banks. No Hellenic columns, but something vaguely like an early Greek temple minus columns. The streets are lined with open-air vending places and much traffic, including weird streetcars passing along the wider boulevards. Quite a few trees around, which helps. It is a melancholy city. It never was a great city, but it's utterly fascinating. It is laid out in a valley, surrounded by lofty mountains, much higher than any mountains in our sector of the MLR. Well over a thousand feet in elevation. That's a guess. High Tor, in Rockland County, is over eight hundred feet tall, and these great hills are much higher than that.

We eventually came upon a rickety wooden door, on which was painted, in green: No. 1 PICTURE YOU SEND HOME

No. 1

We decided to go in so that we could at least sit down for a while. The four walls inside were close together, made of old

U. S. Army crates, pasteboard and oiled paper. The logistical markings on the crates were well faded. There was no ceiling, and the enclosure was well lit by sunlight.

An elderly Korean entered from the rear of the place, and greeted us in the usual obeisant manner. He was small and very thin. His suit was made of fine herringbone tweed, but he had probably owned it for a number of years; it was ragged and patched in various places with G. I. utility cloth. He wore a matching grey vest and slippers. His hair was long, but he was clean shaven and his face and attitude were quite distinguished. And he was rather elegant, I thought, despite, etc. It would by no means stretch the imagination to picture him as a one-time professor at the University of Seoul.

He operated this pathetic enterprise with his daughter. The girl was a living doll. She wore a grey sweater, over a blue shirt, and a G.I. scarf. Like her father, she wore slippers, the rubber Korean kind. There was a small scar on her right cheek, close to the eye, and the eye was half closed. Nevertheless she was a lovely girl, too young to have taken on the characteristic obeisance of her father, and too young. Her attitude was not unlike that of an American schoolgirl.

The father bowed, smiling. "Good morning, soldiers," he said.

"We ain't soldiers, ace," replied Colia.

"Of course. Forgive! Please take seat, marines."

While Colia primped himself for a photograph, I studied the many unframed photographs on the wall: pictures of soldiers of many nations. The girl watched me and said hello in Korean, something of a surprise.

I said, "*Ania has-imnika*," another greeting.

She asked me how I was feeling. I hunched down, sitting like a Korean farmer, and we tried to talk. This was the first girl I had talked to in a long time and I'm not ashamed to admit that I was immediately STONED by her—immediately *infatuo ero*. I learned that she was fifteen. She brought a Korean propaganda comic book and we looked at it. Very crude drawings, uncolored, showing fat Communist warlords beating children, handsome young South Korean soldiers to the rescue, etc. Oh, man, was I stoned by her. I'm afraid she caught me giving her the agate-eyed stare. She knew all about it though and played along, putting a silk scarf around my neck when my turn came to pose. It was a garish yellow scarf with several marine emblems hand-painted on it. I attempted feebly to remove it but was "forced." The backdrop was a painted Oriental pastoral scene with a temple in the middle.

The picture was not bad. We paid and left, and walked around the crooked alleys, accosted occasionally by old beggars and a few children.

We were being followed by a natty young pimp in a black leather jacket. We walked along a miniature Wall of China, in a residential section of town. On the other side of the wall was a well-spaced row of ancient, angular houses with overgrown gardens. The gates to each were closed, but I climbed the wall once and looked over. Give me one of those houses any time. We followed the narrow, paved road, turning gradual corners, meeting no one. The wall ended and we walked under an archway of tree limbs that continued for a hundred yards or more, at the end of which we came upon a whorehouse. The young man took Colia inside, but I waited outside. Later I went inside and found someone willing to find me some beer. Colia yelled from upstairs to come up. The door to his room was a sliding one, lightwood frames covered with oiled paper. There were two beds in the room, and I lay down on one. There was an iron brazier in the middle of the floor, coals or charcoal glowed in it, warming the room. Colia's gal was fairly attractive. I don't know how well she'd make out on the corner of Broadway and Forty-second, but over here anything looks good. We talked for a while.

The boy returned with two quarts of Asahi beer, a Japanese brand, and we drank them. Two girls came in and sat on the edge of the bed. No, thank you. The name of the joint was, believe it or not, the Sin Fin Hotel.

There was a commotion downstairs, and the girls, all three of them, were panicked. Among other things, we heard them whisper, "MP!" They hid, cramped together, in a sort of cubbyhole behind a knee-high sliding panel in one of the walls. One was naked, the other two wore bathrobes. Colia dressed hurriedly. I was fully dressed and lay still on the bed. Alan Ladd-like, I unholstered my .45 and placed it on my chest.

If Colia hadn't been along, I would have trouble convincing anyone that what happened next really happened. A fist came crashing through the pasteboard wall, less than two feet from my face. I sat up like a shot and peered through the jagged aperture, and met a pair of eyes, which disappeared at once. A moment later, the sliding door to our room opened and a small, middle-aged Korean woman entered the den of iniquity. She stood still and looked about. She was hatless, and wore a black wool coat and a pair of dark slacks. By some unheard-of process of thought, I believed this to be the madame of the establishment, merely checking on her cuties. It hadn't occurred to me that she was the one who tried to knock the wall over. Helpfully, I pointed to the little closet in which the blue jades were hiding. The woman went over, parted the panels, and ordered the girls out. I was completely confused, and tried to find out from the woman what it was all about. She handed me a card to look at. It bore her photograph, her name, and an explanation—in Korean and English—concerning her authority as a policewoman; a member of a women's detention unit. The girls were angry as hell, of course, but fortunately were not aware that I had unknowingly turned them in. Colia and I got out of there.

Later I went back to the U.N. post exchange and bought some things for the girl in the photo shop.

February 27th, 1953

One of the men in another squad brought a booklet back from Seoul, which I borrowed, to make some notes.

Korea—called "Chosen" by the Japanese—means "Land of the Morning Calm." Haw! The history of Korea is traced back to 57 B.C., but its founder is listed as the Chinese philosopher Kija, who lived at the time of the Trojan War (beginning of the twelfth century B.C.). Chinese influence was always predominant, although the Japanese have conquered and lost Korea

128

many times. One of the agreements of the treaty ending the Sino-Japanese war was that China recognize the full independence of Korea. This was in 1895. Fifteen years later the Japanese annexed Korea to its empire.

The principal crop is rice. We have seen the Korean farmers beating rice shoots with long flails. On a windy day, the grain is thrown into the air; the heavier rice falls on a mat and the husks are carried away by the wind.

Fishing, fishing, fishing. And this pamphlet states that Korean lobsters are the best in the world. The chief crops then are rice, barley, wheat, beans and grain. Good cattle. Some silkworm raising. Gold, copper and iron are abundant. Gold? The principal imports are cotton and silk goods, machinery, kerosene oil, grass cloth, sugar and coal.

Granite mountains surround Seoul. In ancient times, the city was enclosed by a wall, pierced at eight points by magnificent gates. The Gate of Elevated Humanity was one. The Gate of Bright Amiability was another. Great! There was an inner wall within the city, parts of which remain, which enclosed the royal palace. This may have been the wall Colia and I saw the other day.

The Koreans like "kimshee," a combination of turnips and sauerkraut. They also eat a kind of seaweed, cooked in oil and occasionally dog flesh, seasoned with a peppery relish. The more wealthy drink honey, flavored with orange peel and ginger. I'm positive an American wrote this pamphlet, patronizing ass. How quaint and picturesque he found these Koreans to be.

Koreans are taller than the Japanese, but have oval faces, high cheek bones, narrow eyes. The Koreans I've seen have beautiful complexions and marvelous teeth. The common apparel is a plain white cotton robe. Korean girls wear little navel-high white vests until puberty. Their hair is usually cut in severe bangs. After puberty, it is long but drawn back in a tight bun. But lots of teen-age girls in pigtails—I *think*.

Yours for better deportment,
Thelma Theopompus,
your fashion editor.

According to this odious pamphlet, no needle and thread are used over here. Glue. That is what the man says. Clothes are glued together. When washed, the parts are merely glued together again. (But I don't believe a god-damn word of it . . . Herodotus, book 7.)

Women marry very young and do not speak to their husbands for several days. Male children are a big deal. Female children are immediately impaled. Women are often spoken of as "the mother of so-and-so." Quotes we doubt ever got quoted. I better put this thing away. There's one part that particularly interests me:

The Koreans believe that the air is full of good and evil spirits. Even stones and trees are reverenced as the abode of spirits. This is called animism: the belief that natural objects have souls. Hills and mountains are looked upon as gods. I can understand this. The hills and mountains here are severe, grotesque, sometimes beautiful, always startling, each with a personality or characteristic of its own. In order to appease the hill and mountain gods, votive offerings are carried up to them. Trees are often covered with colored strips of paper or rags, gifts to the tree spirits. We have seen these during field problems. Noise scares away the evil spirits—hence firecrackers, gongs, etc. Obviously the gods have evacuated No Man's Land.

"The Korean tiger, a magnificent beast, is almost extinct." Almost? He is considered to be a great wizard. Certain animals are supposed to be good or evil spirits.

Confucianism, Buddhism, and animism are declining in popularity, giving way to Christianity.

Someone discovered that my MOS (military occupation specialty) is in the ordnance field, so I was asked to give a lecture on the functioning, disassembly, and cleaning of the carbine. This kind of thing isn't at all unusual. People are often being asked to give lectures on something they know: weapons, hygiene, fire-team tactics, etc. The entire company was present; I made grotesque faces and double-talked myself through it. Much guffawing and tittering from the bleachers.

February 28th, 1953

The news of Stalin's death was a shocker, but most of us are aware that someone else, not far removed from Stalin in policy, will take over. They're after our blood and are in no hurry. The night after his death, the Chinese and North Koreans sent up multicolored flares and star clusters. Also, each man fired his weapon in the air at approximately the same time, at sundown. Farewell salute. It must have been an awesome thing. The Chinese are so quiet. Never a sound from their lines, only occasionally one hears digging from the paddies in front of their positions. They never test-fire their weapons, as we always do before going out into No Man's Land. Never shouting, never talking. On the other hand, we are constantly yelling for kicks, or shooting blindly at the hills during the day. Several times, at 76-Alley, I went up to the trench and fired bursts at hill 139 just for the hell of it. Maybe I wanted to communicate; let somebody over there know somebody over here was awake. The most effective bit of psychological warfare that the Chinese employ is their total silence. And we *never* see them during the daytime. We are forever poking our heads up for a look.

Spring is coming and I don't like that. I avoided thinking about it until today. We are having a premature spring and it is fairly warm. Walking back from chow this evening, I smelled the exhaust from a truck roaring down the road, and at the same time saw some rivulets of water from the melting ice and snow in the ditch. Nostalgia followed like a flood, why I can't say. Fortunately there are no chicks around. This is the best place to be in springtime; I've been infatuated every spring since I was eight. Listening to the radio doesn't help. Higgins turned it on last night, sometime after midnight. Heard two of Alec's pieces, "Slow Dance" and "Air for Oboe." The latter record used to have an odd effect on my sister Kate. She got me interested, and we would work out improvisations while listening to the record. She was about ten then, I was fifteen. The imagery suggested by the music was tremendous, and this is so in all his work. Of all the American composers, he is the one that I am certain will be played a hundred years from now, when his music will have been given the respect it deserves.

We hear good jazz sometimes on overseas broadcasts. I think Lee Konitz is the greatest improviser around. Sometimes what he's trying to do doesn't come off, but it's marvelous to hear him make the attempt. "No Figs" is his finest solo. The two high priests, Gillespie and Bird Parker are erratic, but when they're not being cute or obscure they are unbeatable. There is a trumpet man from the West Coast named Chet Baker, who is someone to watch. As soon as he gets control of the instrument, he'll cut everyone cold. Thelonius Monk, one of the early experimenters at Minton's, sounds as though he doesn't have the vaguest notion as to what jazz is all about. But I've only heard a couple of his sides. Plays like a troglodyte on those two. And Dave Brubeck. Oi! He's in the wrong business. Studied with Milhaud, eh? Not long enough, dad. Sounds like John Cage trying to play Dixieland. A lot of the cats think he's great, but they should listen more closely. He doesn't seem to have the feel of jazz and plays as though he invented counterpoint. No beat, corny ideas, pretentious. Takes himself too seriously in general. Barbaroi. I have spoken.

I wrote to Alec, asking him to obtain the address of a new daydream image, Sheila Bond—prompted not so much by infatuation as by the coming of spring, which, despite this unlikely setting, has conjured enough of the profoundly disturbing nostalgia connected with the writing of mash notes, to keep me in a state of mute logorrhea during most of the day. Terrible time of the year. Got the itchy-foot. But where can one go? Kaesong? I've been taking long walks after evening chow, up into the hills and the big draws of the Kansas line. Just for the hell of it I've been practicing moving silently through the brush. The night birds make real weird sounds up there. This reminds me of the time I climbed the mountain behind the training camp at Pendleton, once at dusk. Very late dusk, only a bit of light in the west. I saw a huge bird, like an eagle, on the skyline. He just sat there, moving his head once in a while. Scared the hell out of me when he suddenly beat his wings and soared away. There was a USO show going on far below. I could see the lights and faintly hear the music. June Christy was part of the show, and I had decided that it would be perversely bad for my morale if I saw that show—which is exactly why I climbed the mountain. But I changed my mind after I got up there and thundered down the mountainside in time to catch several of her numbers.

March 1st, 1953

These notes have been conspicuously unpeopled. It is because the squad complement is fluid. Men either go home, are transferred, or become casualties. There are only four men in the third squad that were here when I joined it. Dudley Hogg and Dan Keppard will be here as long as I will, which is why I wrote down a bit about them.

Although its members change, the squad retains an inherent spirit, a combination of intense, but unspoken, pride, and intense, but definitely voiced, discontent. We are all *crying* to go back on line. I've never encountered a more bitter group of men. It's the same old cornball story: they claim to loathe the Corps and all it represents, and yet they turned in that performance when Tim came over, and when they get home none of them would hesitate to take a poke at anyone who speaks disparagingly of the outfit.

The Marine Corps is the most colossal example of inefficiency, incongruity, wasted talent, and organized confusion that I know of. "The difficult we can accomplish immediately; the impossible takes a little longer." An arrogant slogan—but thank God for the arrogance. Marines have the reputation of doing things the hard way, which is rough on the legions. Possibly the fact that the men of the Corps are the most skillful killers in the world compensates for the sometimes inane rigidity of its senior officers. The point that I should mention here, before I forget it, is that I have no regrets as to choice of service. And I'll go so

133

far as to say that my morale is exceptionally high, thanks in part to the compulsion of keeping these ragged notes.

When they let me go in November, I think I might go immediately to Seal Beach, and walk directly into the water in full uniform—shined shoes, pressed greens, ribbons, barracks cap, gloves, scarf and overcoat—and just keep walking until I'm completely immersed. Then I'll wade back to shore, remove the entire uniform, bury it in the sand, and walk naked to the nearest men's clothing store, where I'll buy a zoot suit.

GROUP SIX

Camp Myers

March 3rd, 1953

It's cold again. Much better.

The 1st Battalion has moved to another location called Camp Myers, about ten miles from Camp Rose. Myers is more compact; the tents are set up on a series of little round hills. We are closer to the MLR than at Rose.

Captain Nathan Krupp, from Oklahoma, took over the command of Able company while we were at Rose. He is an Old Corps man, a good C. O., but rough. The men are awed by him —he's irascible as hell. He's about thirty-five and large. We don't know much about him yet.

Another member of the —— squad will be around as long as Hogg, Keppard and myself (conjecturally speaking). He is Carl Pugnacci from Lac de Flambeau, Wisconsin, and he is referred to as "Pugnacious." Over six feet, average build, stringy muscles like a farmer—he is a farmer—very homely, almost a comical face. He quit school at the seventh grade and feels very bad about it. Because I am often scribbling in this notebook (he thinks I'm writing a novel), Pugnacious acts as though I'm a scholar. He is always questioning me on various subjects. Most of the time I don't know any more about the particular subject than he does. He wants to hear all about New York, music, history, flowers, sex, how to dress, how to mix drinks, arithmetic, sailing, etc.

135

Last night he began questioning me concerning the origins of Christianity; it turned out that I knew less than he did. But there was one point when we were discussing the life of Christ, sitting comfortably around the stove. I told him about the Sanhedrin and that crowd. Pugnacious suddenly interrupted me; his big hands were stretched out, batting the air. He was trying to remember something. "Wait a minute," he said, "let me think. . . . Now, who was that feller that—that condemned Christ? No, don't tell me! 'Cause I know. . . . Ah—oh! I got 'er. It was Pontiac Pluto! Right?"

March 4th.

Dan Keppard and I have reworked the following manuscript several times within the past few days. Yesterday we submitted it to S/sgt. Rohas for confidential criticism. Here is a copy of it. Dan calls it "a testimony of madness."

PLAN FOR PROSPECTIVE TWO-MAN AMBUSH

1) Information is incomplete, due to lack of knowledge of the next position that the second platoon of Able company will occupy.

2) Mission is to ambush and destroy the personnel of an enemy patrol, using a predetermined section of the path which will have been reconnoitered by a previous patrol.

3) A two-man unit, A and B, leaves the MLR under cover of early evening darkness, and proceeds to the ambush area. B advances approximately twenty yards further, *i.e.*, toward the enemy MLR, and acts as a listening post. A prepares the ambush by burying two satchel charges in the mud adjacent to the raised path or dike, at a distance of approx. fifty yards from each other. After burying the charges, A will string the wires, *i.e.*, the wire leading from each charge, seventy-five yards in length, perpendicularly away from the ambush path, in such a manner that the two wires will meet at their ends:

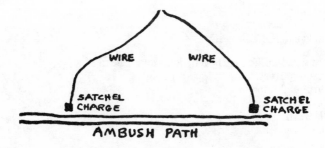

The ends of the wires must be brought together in preparation for their attachment to a magneto. Having made certain that the satchel charges and the wires emanating from them are well concealed, A retrieves B by joining him at his forward position and tapping him on the ankle, whereupon A and B withdraw to the point at which the two wires have been drawn together. The two men will lie five or ten yards from each other. A will remain with the wires. He will connect both wire ends with the poles of the magneto.

A must have a clear view of the ambush path, and the magneto should be in an accessible position. Both men should occupy well-covered positions in order to avoid the concussive effects of the explosions.

When and if an enemy column appears, A will wait until the main body of the column is contained within the boundaries of the buried charges before twisting the handle of the magneto. Manipulation of the handle creates a current which flows along the wires into the electric blasting caps of both charges, thus setting off both explosions. A and B will then return to the MLR.

4)   A will carry out the following equipment:

> one satchel charge
> one electric blasting cap
> 75 yards of double-strand power wire
> a light automatic weapon w/ammunition
> two fragmentation grenades
> magneto

entrenching tool
USMC knife

A will wear the following:

camouflage helmet cover, tied around head
armored vest
armored shorts
utility coat and trousers
Korean rubber slippers
wrist watch

B will carry the following equipment:

one satchel charge
one electric blasting cap
75 yards of double-strand power wire
light automatic weapon w/ammunition
two fragmentation grenades
pyrotechnic pistol w/green flare

B will wear the following:

camouflage helmet cover, tied around head
armored vest
armored shorts
utility coat and trousers
Korean rubber slippers
wrist watch

A and B will blacken their exposed skin.

The seventy-five-foot wires will have been attached to each of the electric blasting caps before the unit leaves the MLR. To promote ease in carrying, each wire will have been rolled into a spool and secured to the charge. The only wiring necessary during the actual ambush preparation is the unwinding of the spools, the insertion of the blasting caps into the satchel charges, and the attachment of their ends to the poles of the magneto.

A is the ambush leader, and A leads all movement in column.

5) Communication: B carries a pyrotechnic pistol. Discharge of the green flare indicates that the ambush unit is approach-

ing the friendly outpost, or listening post, or MLR. Neither sound-power nor radio would be necessary.

Submitted for official approval by

Martin F. Russ, cpl., 1216432

Danny L. Keppard, corpsman second class.

Sgt. Rohas continues to study it. His first comment was that more men would be needed, possibly a fire team, for cover during the withdrawal. In time he will present the plan to Lt. Buell. If it is refused, we'll submit another plan concerned with planting trip-wire booby traps on paths leading from the Chinese MLR. If this is refused, we'll submit still another plan, for sniping at enemy trenches with a single-shot BAR (with bipod) from a forward position in No Man's Land during the day.

I also intend to suggest the use of lay-outs: A patrol escorts a man—or two men—to a point as near an enemy position as possible, where he—they—are left in a camouflaged hole. The escort returns to the friendly MLR before sunrise. The lay-out observes enemy activity during the day, drawing pictures of the terrain in front of him, indicating paths, barbed wire, fortified bunkers, defilade areas, etc. Another escort would retrieve the lay-out after sunset. If there was a volunteer available, there's no reason why a company shouldn't utilize a lay-out. He could obtain valuable information regarding, for instance, a position on which a raid was planned, by recording in detail the lay of the land ordinarily photographed from high in the air. Dan and I made it perfectly clear to Rohas that we drew up that plan with ourselves in mind, as A and B.

March 5th, 1953

Sgt. Rohas has given the plan to the lieutenant, who spoke to me about it today. To my surprise, he considers it a "sensible idea" and believes that we will eventually be allowed to put it into effect. He spoke of one or two changes, including the use of a covering force during the withdrawal—the same suggestion that Rohas made. The lieutenant said he'd think upon't some more.

One of our night problems last night consisted of listening to individual men, at various distances, successively clicking the bolts of their weapons, or whispering, or digging, or smoking, or crawling, or walking. We were asked to guess what each man was doing. We learned that noises carry for a considerable distance when it is quiet at night.

We had a competition yesterday to see who could disassemble a BAR most rapidly, blindfolded. I won the squad race in one minute, 43 seconds; the platoon race in one minute 37 seconds, but lost to a member of the ———— platoon in that race.

Cpl. Cal Tibbels, from Caribou, Maine, and I are good friends. Except for a scarred, parboiled type face, and the fact that he has been a marine for seven years, Tibbels resembles what might be called a typical Princeton man. He is eccentric as hell, as are most of the members of this squad, it turns out. He and I have developed a curious game. I hesitate to say what we look like when playing it. According to the new rules, we may pinch, scratch, or slug. If blood is drawn, it counts as a K.I.A., or killed in action. It is a simulated war game, very complicated. For some reason, no one else will join us. Only one mode of attack is allowed per game; the pinching one is most popular.

Tibbels's girl sent him a Howard Johnson menu and it is carefully studied by a different member of the squad each night.

March 6, 1953

Some time or other, every NCO (noncommissioned officer) is required to attend NCO school, a four-week grind.

Two days ago M/sgt. Schiff, our new "top" or first sergeant, called me up to the CP (command post) tent and said that my turn had come, that I would leave the following morning. This was like a kick in the face. The battalion is moving up on line soon, and I couldn't stand the idea of being frozen somewhere in the rear while the rest of the outfit draws combat pay. He told me to report to the supply tent, in order to pick up the necessary equipment.

S/sgt. Connant—the leader of that patrol that scouted the Cork—is the company supply sergeant now. He is referred to as Mother Connant, but not to his face. His fastidious concern over the company equipment is a community joke. In his usual manner, he gave me a hard time, chewing me out for each piece of gear that I had lost; articles like sunglasses, a tent peg, a lip-chap stick. Being discouraged over the prospect of losing out on line time, I was unusually surly with Connant, who finished our business with these words: "Bitter, corporal?" Confused, I muttered something vague. He replied, "Speak up; I can't hear you." I repeated whatever it was. He said, "Stand up when you're talking to me." I stood up, with cow eyes. "Maybe a little NCO school is just what you need, corporal." I started to answer but he broke in. "Get out," he said. You learn early not to get wise with superiors in this outfit. This is exactly as it should be. Marines are always appalled at the way Army men are allowed to address superiors, and I'll go along with that, too. But if I ever run into Connant in the dark, I'll take his head off his shoulders.

My next commitment was to lay out all my gear on the cot. The tent was deserted, or so it appeared. Actually Dan Keppard was lying on his cot in a dark corner. Lt. Casimetti came around to inspect the gear. After he had made the inspection and was about to leave, I asked if he would hear a complaint. He sat down on the edge of the cot and pulled out a cigarette. Casimetti is a tall, slender man, from New Rochelle; probably a graduate of an Ivy League school. He is the executive officer of Able company. I said something like this to him:

"Sir; I know that NCO school is a good setup and the truth is, I actually want to go. But not now. See (sir), if I leave tomorrow, I'll probably miss out on two or three weeks of line time. Could it possibly be postponed?"

The lieutenant was against it. So I let loose a neat little bomb. I explained to him how much trouble I had gone to in order to get into a line company, and told him how gung ho I was without making it sound too ridiculous, and in doing so became rather animated.

His answer was a variation of the usual spiel: It was my duty to, the order had already gone in, I was expected to report the following morning, etc. I had another bomb ready. Said something like this:

"Sir; I didn't buck for corporal; as a matter of fact I'm lousy at it. I'm not a leader of men, never have been. I'm a natural follower, always have been. (Sir) . . . And I'm willing to take a bust in order to get out of it, so that I can be with the platoon on line. As a pfc. I can't very well be sent to NCO school."

I was dead serious, and would gladly have accepted a reduction in rank. Lt. Casimetti scoffed at all this melodrama but finally acknowledged the apparent urgency. It was disconcerting though when he began to go into the same spiel. I could hear that he was leading up to ". . . so, Russ, I'm afraid there's nothing more to be said about it. You'll have to go tomorrow as scheduled." But I interrupted him with my old friend, *request mast*. At this time, I would have requested mast on up to the commanding general, so fervent was my aversion to NCO school by now. The lieutenant told me to report to the captain's tent in an hour.

When he departed, Dan sat up, which was startling. He had been listening, unseen. He suggested that I find someone as a replacement; that this would be in my favor when I talked to the captain.

I found out, through M/sgt. Schiff, that Cpl. Cal Tibbels was due for NCO school soon. I found Cal and had no difficulty convincing him how important the matter was. Also, he is not particularly anxious to go back to the MLR. He agreed to the substitution.

When the time came, I climbed the hill to the captain's tent, resolute as hell but nervous. Pvt. Jesse Aduce was outside, cleaning the captain's stove. We talked awhile before Captain Krupp called me in. Lt. Casimetti was there. The captain was shaving. The lieutenant summarized the situation for the captain, but in an informal, negative manner. Sergeants Connant and Schiff had both stated that my name had already been submitted, and the captain added casually that it would take an act of God to remove it from the records, etc. The captain being a chicken-feces officer, I was held at attention throughout the conversation. The captain seemed as adamant as Casimetti. He was about to dismiss me when I reached way down in the bottom of the barrel. I told him about the plans for the two-man ambush unit, and that Lt. Buell was already interested in them, and that it would be decidedly advantageous for us to be attached to the forward party which usually precedes the main body of troops to the MLR. The captain was now squatting on the ground before a pocket mirror on his cot, applying shaving lotion to his shiny puss. I went on and on—even mentioned that my father had been a marine in WW-one. I was positively raving. The clincher came when I mentioned that I had found a substitute, Cpl. Tibbels.

The captain immediately called the battalion executive officer, and I was in business. He was put through to Lt. Col. Mac-Duff, at regimental headquarters. He went through the entire story for the colonel, even exaggerating certain points for clarity and effect. One of his sentences was: "He's a real hot-blooded, gung-ho marine, colonel." Haw! The colonel's decision was affirmative and my name was taken off the lists, Tibbels's inserted.

With a great leer, I returned the gear to Mother Connant, who said, "Played a nice trick on Tibbels, didn't you, corporal?" But Cal didn't mind. I magnanimously helped him lay out his gear for Casimetti's inspection, and felt better than I've felt for a long while.

March 7th, 1953

We have been standing "clutch duty" lately, which means that we are on call as reinforcements or replacements for the front-line troops. Several times, both here and at Camp Rose, we have been called out in the middle of the night, issued ammunition and grenades, and led—by forced march—to a number of secondary MLR positions. Apparently life is pretty hectic up there now. The other night we watched a Chinese probe on a hill in the Bunker Hill sector. We were approximately four hundred yards behind the MLR, but we could see lines of tracers and the impact areas of the enemy mortar barrage, after the withdrawal. Three stray rounds exploded in our vicinity. After the fire fight a group of heavy, propeller-driven planes flew overhead and dropped a string of flares, extremely bright. The parachutes from which the flares are hung are about half as large as the ordinary bail-out chute. They descend quite slowly. One of them landed near our position, atop the mountain, and half the platoon went scrambling after it.

The word is that we will be in reserve for at least two more weeks, a morbid thought.

Instead of arbitrarily calling out a unit for clutch duty, a provisional clutch platoon has been formed, composed of volunteers. Pugnacci, Keppard and I, thinking that this was the only way to get on the MLR, volunteered. It was a terrible mistake. Fortunately Keppard, being a corpsman, was turned down. But Pugnacci and I are stuck in the crummy outfit for a while. There are forty-five of us. We built an entirely new camp area, out of virgin ground. Although we occupy only three tents, we are isolated from the rest of the battalion, except for chow. The officer, Lt. Klinge—Kringe we call him—fancies himself the leader of a suicide brigade, and runs us ragged with meaningless inspections and calisthenics. The inspections are ostensibly designed to maintain readiness of gear and personnel, but the gear and personnel are an utter shambles. The men are so harassed that most of them resort to the old devices comparable to sweeping dirt under the carpet. It is essential, absolutely essential, to leave enlisted men alone from time to time, subject only to regularly scheduled inspections, but Kringe—incidentally fresh out of Quantico—hasn't found this out. Yesterday, for example, we were called outside for inspection at 8 A.M., 9 A.M., 1 P.M., and 3:30 P.M.

Every night we ride up to the MLR and merely go to sleep on the floor of several bunkers at the bottom of the reverse slope, about 300 yards behind the main trenchline. We never know where we are and lack the energy to climb the slope to find out. We are at least available in case of an emergency. Whenever one of the companies on line sends out a large patrol or a raiding party, there is a gap in the MLR, and it is our function to fill that gap, or at least be ready and in a position to fill it.

Lt. Buell, whose name is Virgil, called me up to his tent the other day and gave me a warning. "You better get squared away," he said, adding that he would be forced to bust me if I didn't calm down. I've been gibboning it up lately and he knows it.

Sgt. Henion, our platoon guide, held an inspection the other evening—a punitive inspection. Sgt. Henion is a good man, but he carries a portable wailing wall around with him and is inclined to be bothersome. Out of pure prickishness, I conned the entire ———— squad into groaning, making horrible faces, and waving their arms as soon as he called us to attention. It was a grand sight, but I got extra police duty for it and was, of course, reported to Lt. Buell. But Ol' Virgil, he knows I'm a hot-blooded gung-ho marine, and he let me off. Just the same, I got to cool it.

And I hate to start kvetching again, but there is a definite strain involved in keeping these shambicular notes. It becomes more difficult all the time, and I find it necessary to make compromises as an NCO. I have skipped classes and missed out on sleep and my back aches constantly because of the odd positions I assume while scribbling. Poor struggling artist-corporal. Incidentally, it would be most unfortunate if some chicken-feces person, especially an officer, were to discover this notebook. It is strictly against the rules; in fact, it was mentioned during a lecture at Camp Rose that not even diaries are permitted. If a Communist sympathizer ever got hold of this, he would be awarded the Soviet Victory Medal.

Pfc. Dunbar Bloomfeld, from Calumet, Illinois, is a twenty-year man, who loves the Crotch, as we call it. He is a gentle soul, very naïve. It has become a mild sport in the tent to refer to him by a series of extemporaneous nicknames, prompted by the fact that he loves to talk about his former duty stations and that he is obsessed with the ordnance world. He also has a gigantic head.

145

"O, Double Sasebo Subic Anti-Tank Sangley Point Satchel Charge Double Hanghead!" someone is likely to say, in endearing tones. Or "O, Sasebo Energa Subic Grenade Recoilless Sangley M41 Trip Flare Quadruple Hanghead!" To our perverted minds, the farcical possibilities of using deadly weapons as terms of endearment are unlimited and side-splitting.

An accidental discharge in one of the tents today. A short BAR burst. Two men hit; one through the leg, the other got a flesh wound in one side of the back.

GROUP SEVEN

Bunker Hill Outpost

March 9th or 10th, about 10 P.M.

We were pulled out of reserve abruptly. We haven't actually taken over the new sector yet, but we will have by morning. The 7th Marines are getting ready to move out. I'm writing in one corner of a large supply bunker. Almost the entire platoon is crammed in here, trying to sleep on the floor or write letters. This is a very lofty and wide hill, with a tank road running parallel to the ridgeline, about twenty or thirty feet behind the main trenchline.

Some time tonight—after the moon goes down—we, the ——— platoon of Able company, will sneak out to Bunker Hill outpost, en masse. We will relieve the 7th Marines who are out there now.

We walked up here from Camp Myers and reached the MLR this afternoon. After we unsaddled, Pugnacci and I went up to the main trench for a look. Dutchy, who has been up here for a week with the forward party, showed us the way. An unbelievable sight. The general color of the terrain is unique, something like the Painted Desert. It is grey, white, yellow, and red, and looks almost like sand. The difference between the terrain south of the MLR in this sector and the terrain north of it is fantastic. There seems to be no connection between the two. No Man's

Land here is a vast piece of ground; one can see for miles and miles.

Bunker Hill looks like a city dump, but spooky as hell. It is a nondescript shape, a low, sprawling knoll. The spiderlike trenches were visible from our vantage point.

Our company mortars are located less than one hundred yards behind the MLR. The hill mass to our rear is immense but too far back to accommodate the relatively short range of the 60mm. tubes. The battalion 81mm. mortars are located at the bottom of the slope, only five or six hundred yards behind. Walking by this afternoon, we recognized this as the spot where some of us sacked out while "on watch" with that screwy provisional clutch platoon, which has now been disbanded. Two "quad-fifties"—four .50-calibre machine guns on a single mount; two of these units—are set up on that hill mass behind us. They fire intermittently over the top of our MLR, into enemy territory. One of the quads is firing right now, a wicked racket.

It is a great relief for some of us to be here. But I don't think I've really been scared yet. The Little Rock probe wasn't exactly an outing, but I didn't reach the panic stage. The word is that the Chinese are very active in this sector.

3rd day on New Bunker

We were told that the Chinese have been known to send recon and ambush patrols to the area between New Bunker and the MLR, which kept us twitching on the way out.

Sgt. Mark Van Horn, of Monongahela, Pennsylvania, met us at the outpost gate. Van Horn is a member of Able company; he had been on New Bunker for two days as part of the forward party. According to him, Kostis and I occupy the most undesirable, and possibly the most important segment of the outpost trench. I lost my sense of direction as soon as we got here, but I know that our position covers the right flank of the outpost, and is the closest to enemy-held territory. Old Bunker—

the original Bunker Hill—is not more than three hundred yards in front of us. From our position, it looks like a gloomy mass of low sand dunes. The men whom we relieved three nights ago put the fear of God into us by a warning that this had been "a hot spot" for them, and that they had already spotted figures out there that night.

The position is called Burgundy-One, or simply B-1. It is the right flank listening post of New Bunker. There are four others: B-2, B-3, B-4, and "Lorretta," but God knows where they are located. From listening to their voices on the phone at night, we know that Pugnacci and Hogg man B-2, Van Horn and Bloomfeld help man Lorretta. Lo Castro is on B-3 with somebody else. The other thirty-odd men are spread out among machine-gun bunkers and fighting-holes. Sgt. Paul Barefield, our squad leader, is in charge of this end of the outpost and he stands watch with us in the B-1 bunker. The bunker itself looks like this:

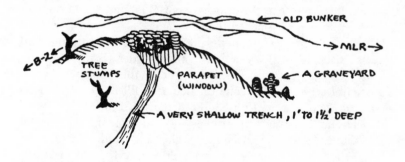

The rear of the little bunker is wide open, and the parapet is somewhat larger than shown. There must be forty or fifty grenades lying around the immediate area: inside, outside, on top, on either side of the feeder trench.

Most of us left our cold-weather gear with Mother Connant. This, it turns out, was a mistake. The position we occupy is relatively high ground, with no surrounding ridges to block the chilling wind that sweeps down from Manchuria. It is strongest and most cold just before dawn. Fortunately, the 7th Marines left two blankets in the bunker.

The shallow trench shown in the drawing runs down the slope to a machine-gun bunker called Gun-One. It is twenty-five yards behind B-1, and is manned by Pfc. Barrows and Pfc. Nordstrum. The trench becomes deeper as it runs by Gun-One. There are two bunkers further on. Barefield and Virgin live in one; Pugnacci, Hogg and myself in the other. These living-bunkers are slightly larger than B-1. Roughly 5′ by 5′. Very crowded. The first morning here I slept with feet and ankles protruding in order to stretch out. One of these Chinese idiots fired three shots at them. We had no idea where they came from. We had been warned that New Bunker is practically surrounded by snipers, but we hardly expected to be bothered by them while sleeping. So now I'm forced to sleep folded up. We're all stiff as hell, but we'll get used to it. Dirt sifts down on our faces from the mortar explosions that occasionally rock the outpost. We have a little kerosene stove to heat our C-rations.

Here is what happened the first night:

We arrived close to midnight. I brought out the following items: sleeping bag, tooth brush and powder, BAR, magazine belt, canteen cup, mechanical pencil, this notebook. Fortunately I sent the other one to Alec. It is filled up, and I don't want to leave it around for Mother Connant to find.

The outfit we relieved was the ——— platoon of Fox company, 7th Marines. As Sgt. Van Horn was showing us our new position, B-1, he mentioned that we might "get a little trigger-time in tonight." He was referring to the fact that the men we relieved had seen figures in front of them shortly before. Andy Kostis and I took over the watch, very tense and alert.

At 1 a.m., Lt. Buell, accompanied by Cpl. Lauroesch, came up to B-1, crouching low. The lieutenant inspected the area as well as he could, spoke to us in whispers for a minute or two—trying to find out what we knew about the terrain in front of us —then departed. The trench leading down to Gun-One is quite shallow. They must not have crouched low enough; two burp guns opened up, several short bursts. The area between B-1 and Gun-One was sprayed. The gunners were located somewhere along the gradual slope north of the outpost, that is, somewhere between B-1 and B-2. There are a group of tree stumps down there; they probably found cover by them. It is hard to believe that the lieutenant and Lauroesch were the targets, but they obviously were. We heard Lauroesch yell, "I'm hit!" in a sonorous but not panicked voice. He said it as though he were telling the burp gunners, "All right, you got me. You can stop now." Neither of us in B-1 saw the muzzle blasts, and we were unable to estimate, even by the sound, how far away the two Chinese were. The lieutenant helped Lauroesch down the trench to the command post cave, where Dan Keppard patched him up. He had been hit near the ankle, a flesh wound in the rear of the ankle.

Actually the first thing the lieutenant did was to crawl down to Gun-One, call the CP (command post) and instruct whoever was there to call the MLR and request the "box" for the right flank of the outpost. Our 60mm. and 81mm. mortar crews are on call throughout the night and their tubes are zeroed-in in such a way that they can send out a concentrated barrage and thus block off any two sides of the outpost, in order to squelch an incipient probe. And the lieutenant believed this to be a probe. So did everyone on the outpost. Within a very short time, mortar projectiles were rocketing into the slopes in front of B-1 in sort of a half-moon impact area. Thus we were "boxed in" with a supposedly impenetrable wall of fire.

In the meantime—as we learned later over the phone—Pugnacci and Hogg had both seen the muzzle blasts and had fired back at them. Pugnacci has a BAR, Hogg a carbine. We were all warned by phone that the right-flank box was on the way. Kostis and myself scrambled down to the Gun-One bunker and sat it out there.

At 4:30 a dense fog rolled in across the rice paddies between New Bunker and the MLR, and all the surrounding low ground. Our view of Old Bunker was obscured, making everyone quite nervous. At 6:40 we were ordered to withdraw.

This is what happened the second night:

Kostis, who is from the Bronx—a real cool cat—and I assumed nighttime security at 7:30 (*i.e.*, we occupied B-1 at 7:30). At 10 P.M., outpost Hedy received a heavy Chinese mortar barrage. We could easily hear the THUNK noise as each round left the tube, but we saw no muzzle blasts. They came from the direction of 64-Able. New Bunker was alerted for a probe, as well as outpost Hedy.

Near midnight we spotted a dim green light, definitely on Old Bunker. It disappeared, and a minute or so after we lost sight of it, we saw the muzzle blast of a mortar tube—a sharp, thin tongue of white flame—in the same area that we had seen the dim green light. The mortar tube itself was situated on a reverse slope but apparently near the skyline; near enough to it for us to see at least the tail end of the muzzle blast. They fired four rounds, which landed back on the MLR—the vast bulk of hills that loom up three hundred yards behind us.

We got Lt. Buell on the phone at once and reported that we had seen the muzzle blast. He in turn called the 60mm. crews on the MLR and told them to send out one round in the direction of Old Bunker, so that we could correct it. In a couple of minutes a round exploded about 150 yards to the left of that area where we had seen the muzzle blast. This was reported to the lieutenant. He relayed it to our mortar crew. They adjusted their tube accordingly and sent out another round. It landed almost exactly in line with our direct line of sight, that is, directly between B-1 and the target. But it appeared to have overshot the mark. I managed to keep sight of the spot by holding my head perfectly still and sighting along one corner of the parapet and a little rise of earth in front of the bunker. Needless to say, one's judgment of distance goes all to pot at night, but we thought we had it pretty close. We told the lieutenant, "About twenty yards more toward us (sir)." The third round *appeared* to be right on target. I said, "On target, sir," into the phone, and heard the lieutenant repeat "On target," into his phone—the wire to the mortar crews—and add, "Fire for effect." Five consecutive rounds exploded in the target area, within a space of about 20 yards by 20 yards. But the Chinese mortar crew had probably moved out. They at least knew that they had been seen.

Near 2 A.M a loudspeaker, located somewhere near or on the Yolk, began blaring forth. It was windy, but the gist of the monologue was "Welcome, Marines of the 1st Battalion, First Regiment." It didn't require any brilliant undercover work to discover that a battalion of marines had replaced another battalion of marines on the line, but how in hell did they find out the designation of our outfit? As far as I know, we are not informed as to the name of their outfit. No one in the squad knows it. Possibly they do at S-2. The man who was speaking was either reading from a paper or making it up; it couldn't have been a record. He stumbled over several words. To be honest, neither Andy nor myself actually heard a word he said, but the men on Hedy did. Lt. Buell heard them talking about it over the phone with Captain Krupp; that is, he heard the captain's end of the conversation. He told us about it later.

At 3 A.M. the same Chinese mortar tube (that we saw supposedly liquidated) began pooping out a series of rounds, the target again the MLR. Kostis was on the phone at the time and reported this to the lieutenant. In less than one minute, five WP (white phosphorous) rounds exploded within the same concentrated area that we had established before. A WP explosion resembles a brilliant Roman candle, a shower of white-hot sparks.

Half an hour later the men on B-2 and B-3 spotted the muzzle blast of another mortar tube, firing from several hundred yards in front of them; somewhere along that immense plateau out there. They went through the same procedure of calling in our own mortars on the target. This seems to be a routine procedure.

It is fascinating to spot the muzzle blast of an enemy mortar tube; to know that a group of Chinese are close by it, and for us to be in a position to direct a counterbarrage from Burgundy-One.

At about the same time that the men on B-2 and B-3 spotted the mortar, a lone burp gunner aimed a long blast at Lorretta, the left-flank listening post—way over on the other side of the outpost. We heard Bloomfeld call in and report that the gunner was firing from Sniper Ridge. The end of this ridge lies within thirty or forty yards from Lorretta. Bloomfeld was down in his hole but said that several rounds skidded by near the position. After an interval of about a minute, the Chinese fired again, but the noise was muffled. He was probably firing from the other side of the ridge then, target unknown.

The fog rolled in, and the moon went down, disappearing neatly behind Old Bunker.

Outpost Hedy received a relatively heavy probe between 4:30 and 5 A.M. Hedy is located approx. seven hundred yards away, due west. Although Sniper Ridge obstructs our view of it, we nevertheless heard the encounter. The raid was preceded by the most eerie sounds I've ever heard IN MY LIFE. Rooster, crow, cat and wolf calls. They echoed back from the steep slopes of the MLR. A most unhappy sound. This is apparently the way in which the Chinese prepare themselves for a raid. Although it is much more terrifying than corny, it stupidly announces the fact that Chinese are in the vicinity and that an attack is about to be made. This entire sector of the line—including outposts New Bunker and Ingrid (on the other side of Hedy)—was alerted, expecting a sector-type enemy thrust, it not being unusual for the Chinese to attack in more than one place within a sector.

Someone fired a flare pistol out there—the POP was clearly audible—and presently a small but intense green light appeared in the sky; a little parachute flare having been the signal—the Chinese launched their attack. As the burning green flare began its lazy, oscillating descent, a chorus of burp guns opened up almost simultaneously, followed then by a variety of noises: machine guns, rifles, carbines, phosphorous and fragmentation grenades and whining ricochets. The flare cast weird moving shadows along the landscape. It was extinguished before the parachute disappeared behind the ridge. Frequently stray tracer rounds would appear above the ridge and one could follow their trajectory until they burned out in the air. Each time a phosphorous grenade detonated, the skyline of the ridge looked as though a small sun were about to rise from behind it, such was the intensity of the bright sparks.

The fire fight lasted for four or five minutes. In accordance with the way things are set up over here now, this is a pretty heavy action. It is especially dangerous for any unit to announce its position, as the Chinese attacking force did last night. In this stationary type of fighting, our mortars and artillery are capable of bombarding a remarkably tight area if necessary. This is why the fire fight was so brief. The Chinese had to get the hell out of there before our mortar crews could send out a barrage. Our shells began landing shortly after the last burp gun was heard.

We learned this morning that the attacking force was of platoon strength—about 40 men. Several of them reached the crest of the slope, and four or five of the more intrepid ones actually entered the Hedy trenchline, causing little damage but considerable terror. A phosphorous grenade was thrown inside one of our bunkers; that is, one of the bunkers on Hedy—a machine-gun bunker. The three occupants were severely burned.

All things equal, it is usually easier to defend a well-fortified position (*i.e.*, East Berlin), than to attack it. In the case of last night's probe on Hedy, however, and any probe on Hedy in the future, the Chinese had and will have the advantage. This is entirely due to Hedy's reverse slope location. I haven't actually seen Hedy but have heard it described. It has a reputation for being practically undefendable. Being situated as it is on a reverse slope, it is therefore out of sight of Chinese lines, and the enemy is able to approach it without being detected.

Two marines were killed. Five were evacuated with wounds. Two Chinese bodies were found. The late mortar barrage may have picked off some more of them.

Hedy is situated close to the MLR. It is merely a terrain finger jutting out from the MLR hill mass. The point is that it is on a level with the MLR trenches, indicating that if the Chinese overran Hedy they would have an unobstructed path of attack to the MLR. Incidentally, there is a trench connecting Hedy with the MLR.

155

At 6:15 the sky began to lighten. Not as much fog this morning, but some. The four listening posts are withdrawn only when the artillery forward observer—located far behind us, on the MLR—is able to see the terrain north of us from his high position. In this way, he and his reliefs stand watch for us during the daylight hours. There is a live, or open wire running from the New Bunker command post to the artillery observer's bunker. Someone in both bunkers is always awake, so that, should the artillery observer spot an enemy force approaching our outpost, he would be able to alert us immediately.

The difficult part of it is that by the time the artillery observer is able to see the terrain surrounding us, it is quite far into daylight. And when we get the word to pull back the listening posts, we must crawl rapidly along the shallow trench to the deeper cover near Gun-One. This trench is twenty yards long, and completely exposed to view from Sniper Ridge. Also the rear of the B-1 bunker, being open as it is, the men inside are also exposed. So for about fifteen minutes—as the sky begins to lighten—Andy and I get pretty nervous.

The main trenches of the outpost are generally deep enough so that men can pass through them without being observed. There is, however, a fifteen-yard stretch between Gun-One and Gun-Two which is wide open. From any point within this short segment of trenchline, Sniper Ridge is visible. According to Lt. Buell, four men of the unit we relieved were made casualties by a sniper, or snipers, on the ridge. One of these was a lieutenant, who died.

We know that at least one sniper is up there now. He is a patient and dedicated man. He fires at anyone who scrambles through that fifteen-yard stretch which rises and dips like a roller coaster. We have been warned to stay inside during the day, but it often becomes necessary to run to another bunker to pick up rations or borrow rifle oil or something. I'm afraid that no one will respect that sniper until he hits somebody. No one so far; but everyone is careless. Sniper Ridge is about two hundred yards from that exposed part of the trench. It was probably that sniper, or his relief, that fired at my feet and ankles.

I stole a BAR from the 7th Marines before they pulled out. It happened while we were waiting to move out to New Bunker. The weapon was leaning against a deserted fighting-hole. I picked it up and carried it down a steep slope, where I hid it under a piece of tarpaulin. A half an hour later, Pugnacci was crying out that someone had stolen his BAR. I told him to quiet down, that I had it. When I brought it back to him he said, "This ain't mine!" Soon a lieutenant from the 7th Marines appeared, accompanied by Lt. Buell. The 7th Marine lieutenant said, "Listen up, you people. One of you 1st Marines stole a BAR that belongs to us. It was leaning up against that fighting-hole over there. In retaliation, one of my men has stolen one of your BARs. Now let's changee-changee and get this foolishness squared away." I hesitated, because I wanted Hogg to have a more powerful weapon than that dinky little carbine. Lt. Buell spoke up. "The thief will not be punished," he said. So I handed the BAR to some sulking gentleman and Pugnacious retrieved his.

Fourth day, New Bunker
This is what happened the third night:

Because of the phosphorous grenade casualties on Hedy the other night, all of the parapets of our machine-gun bunkers, as well as those on Hedy, have been covered with chicken wire. There are four machine guns on this outpost.

Andy and I assumed night watch at about 7:30. From now on I'll do away with the word "about" when talking about time, even though whatever time I say it was is only approximate. The same with distance. I'll just go ahead and guess. We realize now that the view from the B-1 parapet is unsatisfactory, in fact lousy. A shelf of earth borders the listening-post area and partly obstructs our view. Looking out of the opening, we can see Old Bunker, but we cannot see the lowland in between, which means that someone could approach us without being seen.

There is a partial defilade area between the little hump in front of us and the bunker itself. On the third night, I crawled around the bunker and lay huddled up within that defilade, while

157

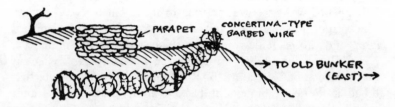

PARAPET   CONCERTINA-TYPE
           BARBED WIRE

→ TO OLD BUNKER
  (EAST) →

Andy crawled on top of the bunker to cover me with his carbine. When I got enough nerve, I stuck my head above the knoll and looked down the slope. It was a bit startling at first: a neat pile of sandbags, fifteen yards down the slope, on the other side of the barbed wire. A small, semi-square shelter. Much against Andy's will, I crawled, on my back, underneath the concertina roll. Technically, I was in No Man's Land at this point. In daylight or even bright moonlight, that would have been the end of John Wayne II, but it was very dark. I went down to the pile of sandbags and lay near it for a minute, pointing the BAR in that direction. No movement or noises. It was an open, isolated supply point, built in a conspicuous spot. How it was built—without the builders being shot down from Old Bunker—or why it was built, is a mystery. It looks like this.

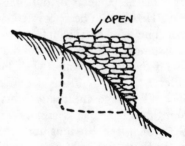

OPEN

There are several empty machine-gun ammo boxes in it, and an old grenade box. This is why I believe that it was a supply point of some kind. I climbed in it and stood up. The view was spectacular. The terrain is wide open to view. But there is little cover there; the top sandbag came up to my elbows. Looking around, I made a fascinating but morbid discovery. There is a trench out there. It runs right by the bottom of the slope—about fifty feet below the B-1 bunker—and appears to continue on toward B-2. We talked to Pugnacci and Hogg about it later over the phone. They said that there is a trench in front of them. It ends fifteen yards from their bunker. That's cheerful. They said that they watch this trench most of the night; it would be a likely avenue of approach for an enemy probe. From where I saw it, that mysterious trench appears to head toward Old Bunker. Perhaps it runs into Old Bunker. If so, it would be logical to suppose that the Chinese have a listening post stationed somewhere along it.

I didn't stay out there long; it would have been a bad place to get caught. Anywhere on the other side of the wire is a bad place to get caught, because it takes so damn long to pass under or over the wire. The only way to get through it, without standing up and climbing over, is to lie on one's back and inch along, using shoulders and elbows to propel oneself. Even then, clothing gets snagged. . . . When I did get back, Andy was pissed off.

Near dawn we sat through a 76 barrage, about ten rounds. They make a very strange sound when they arrive, like pf-f-f-f CRACK! The impact area was between B-3 and Lorretta. Segments of the trenchline caved in from two or three well-placed rounds. They were immediately cleared. No one was hurt from the barrage, but there was a casualty a half an hour later. One of those wily snipers went to work just as the men on B-3 were withdrawing. The time was 6:45. Pvt. Uris, a machine gunner who was helping to man B-3, was shot through the groin; in through the front, out through the back. *Non emasculatatum est.* For some reason Uris had tarried behind after receiving the word to pull back, and it had gotten light on him, light enough for a sniper on the ridge to pick him off. Van Horn crawled up and brought him back. They were both fired at again but not hit. Uris screamed loud enough to be heard miles away. The sound was so terrible that everyone started to go up and get him, but Van Horn was nearest. He had just left B-3 himself and was waiting at the junction of the trenches for Uris. The lieutenant called the company CP and requested a smoke-screen mortar barrage, in order to obscure Sniper Ridge. Uris was alive but had to be evacuated as soon as possible. When the smoke barrage was laid down, four volunteers carried Uris down the gradual southern slope of New Bunker, across the narrow paddy, and up the treacherous mountainside, into the MLR.

I went for a rather constricted stroll last night and got the general layout of the outpost. In doing so, I was vigorously challenged by practically everyone. Here is a diagram of New Bunker, not very accurate.

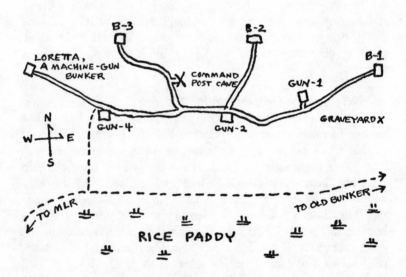

Fifth day, New Bunker. March 1953
Writing as usual in the sleeping-bunker. Pugnacious and Hogg are sound asleep. It is noon.

160

Much excitement this morning. We got the word to withdraw at 6:30; comparatively early. I told Andy to go ahead back to his bunker and sack out. He went, and took the phone and the wire with him, the usual procedure. I remained inside B-1, alone. By way of preparation (for this foolhardy experiment) I spent two hours, from 1 A.M. to 3 A.M., filling sandbags with sand and dirt. With Andy's help, I built up a fourth wall to the bunker, as a daylight protection against sniper fire from the Ridge. The rear of the bunker is no longer open. Nineteen sandbags were needed to complete the wall. The entrance is only large enough to crawl through on hands and knees.

I squirmed around, getting comfortable in the cramped space, reluctant to peer out of the aperture in broad daylight. The rays of the sun had begun to filter through the fog, which was dispersing rapidly. I decided to wait until the fog cleared, and then see what there was to see.

In the meantime, a man coughed. He was somewhere out in front of the bunker, on the other side of the little knoll. I had a very strange reaction to that sound. Got deathly cold all of a sudden, and seemed to catch a severe chill. The cough was abrupt but distinct. It was no different than the kind of cough one might hear in the audience of a theatre, but I nearly dropped my load. I sat as rigid as an axle spring. My damned imagination conjured up the picture of a Chinaman or two, lying not twenty feet from the bunker. Despite the violent cold fit, I took a ferret-look through the aperture and huddled quickly down in the hole, having seen nearly what I had imagined. The head and shoulders of a man. He was at least seventy yards away, directly between B-1 and Old Bunker. I looked again. You couldn't miss him—a dark silhouette against the light sandy shale of the surrounding terrain, which is entirely devoid of vegetation due to months of intermittent bombardment. The excitement of seeing a Chinese soldier for the first time was enormous, and that is an understatement.

I managed to make note of the following details: His uniform was of an indeterminate color. He wears a headpiece of some kind, also indescribable—possibly the Mongol type winter

161

issue of cotton or wool. His features at this distance were at least definable enough to show that he is a thick-featured man with a broad head and swarthy skin, almost olive-colored. He was engaged in some task; looking downward and moving slightly back and forth. Excited as hell, more excited than I can remember having been, I made the mistake of firing a long burst at him, without really aiming. It would have been simple to have picked him off with a single aimed shot, but I think I was afraid he would disappear.

He returned fire almost immediately. Three rounds; one of which slammed into a sandbag on top of the bunker. My ears rang with the crack of each report, which is a sound you never hear unless a rifle is being fired at you. On the rifle ranges of Parris Island, Camp Lejeune, and Pendleton—when I was working in the butts, pulling targets—I could always tell when the target I was tending was being fired upon, even from five hundred yards away. One's ears ring.

I remained huddled below the parapet, quaking with the chill. Judging from the rapidity of shots, he uses a semiautomatic weapon, probably a Seminov, possibly an American Garand.

Now the feces hit the fan. The characteristic THUNK of a mortar tube, discharging a projectile. The sound came from behind Old Bunker. Seconds later: S-S-S-SS-SHHH-VA-RUMPH! The projectile exploded somewhere off to the left, between B-1 and B-2. Looking again, I saw the Chinese peer over the rim of his hole for a second and then disappear. It seems fairly obvious that he functions not only as a sniper, but as a forward observer for a 60mm. mortar crew on Old Bunker. He must have a phone or a radio out there. He was at that moment directing or calling in consecutive mortar shells in such a manner that Burgundy-One will be zeroed-in for future reference. In the same manner that Kostis and I tried to zero-in the muzzle blasts we spotted the other night. But my interest in military matters does not include a desire to be zeroed-in, and I scrambled down the trench before the second projectile landed.

Barrows, one of the machine gunners on Gun-One, met me at the entrance of his bunker and said, "Are you hit?" I wanted to tell him about the sniper, but the third projectile landed so close that both of us went our separate ways; he hopped through the entrance to his bunker, I sprinted over to ours.

Hogg, squatting anxiously in the bunker entrance, was literally flattened when I catapulted inside. We lit a pile of heat tablets near the entrance—the fumes are nauseating—and boiled water for coffee. Meanwhile, the sniper called in more projectiles, correcting the elevation & traverse of the tube on Old Bunker. The process ceased after the fourth or fifth round.

Later in the day, I went over to Andy's small cave and told him about the sniper. He is wildly excited at the prospect of seeing the enemy, this sniper being the first one seen in daylight since we occupied New Bunker. He expressed his impatience to man the listening post at sunset, despite the fact the enemy mortar crew probably knows our exact position, having plotted it by co-ordinates this morning.

Sixth day, New Bunker outpost

Last night:

Kostis and I were both a bit squeamish about sauntering up to B-1 as usual. Instead, as soon as it was dark, I crawled up the shallow trench on all fours; Andy covered from the rear.

At 9 P.M., Bloomfeld, who is on Lorretta, the left-flank listening post, called the CP cave (this is a party-line; everyone with a phone can hear what everyone else who has a phone says, and there is a phone in almost all of the bunkers). Bloomfeld said he heard noises. The lieutenant said, "Play it cool." Five minutes later Bloomfeld called in again. He whispered, in an unmistakably quaking voice, "Sir; I smell garlic." The Chinese are said to season all their food with garlic, and there is always someone around who will tell you that he has been so close to a Chinese ambush that he actually smelled the garlic fumes, which permeate clothing. No one really believed this until Bloomfeld said he smelled garlic last night. The lieutenant answered, "Are you sure it's garlic, Bloomfeld, and not a dead rat or something?" Bloomfeld whispered back, faintly, "Garlic, god-dammit." The lieutenant didn't hesitate; he called the company CP and asked for the left-flank 81mm. box. In a short time, the boundaries of the left flank were being bombarded. But before the 81mm. projectiles arrived, Lo Castro, on B-3, reported that he, too, had heard noises. We all heard a grenade explode in that direction and then the 81s landed. When the barrage was lifted, five minutes later, Lo Castro told the lieutenant that someone had thrown a grenade at the B-3 bunker; it had exploded five or ten yards from the parapet. Lo Castro and his companion Ankers had begun heaving grenades out in front of them, at the same time that the barrage had commenced. There is little doubt that there was somebody roaring about out there, between B-3 and Lorretta, but they didn't bother us again.

I went down to the CP (command post) for the first time just now, to pick up the squad rations. The CP is a small cave, shaped like a T. It goes back about ten yards and five to either side. Ceiling is low; four feet or so. Poet 'n don' know it. Lt. Buell, Sgt. Kovacs (machine-gun section leader), Dan Keppard (corpsman), and Pfc. Engvick (the platoon guide in charge of supplies) live down there. It is quite a cheerful place somehow. I hadn't seen Danny boy for a while, so we talked animatedly— we talked about nothing but the past few days on the outpost. He, too, was fascinated by that idea that we had a sniper up near B-1. He made me a cup of hot cocoa, and Lt. Buell told me to stick around for a while, that is until the supply column arrived from the MLR—they bring rations to us. The lieutenant and I talked a bit. Out here, the chicken-feces attitude isn't so important and he was informal, not familiar, but certainly relaxed. I asked him where he had gone to college. "Princeton, sort of," he answered. He is rather shy for a marine officer, he doesn't like to look into people's eyes. He is thin, his face is drawn, high cheekbones, bags under the eyes. A nice-looking gent, about twenty-six, but always looks a bit dissipated, as after a bawdy weekend in Trenton or Atlantic City. No one has bothered to shave out here, including the lieutenant.

In general most of us are in pretty good shape, but I would say our senses are markedly dulled. About the most interesting stimulus is the occasional chocolate-chip cookie we sometimes find in our assault rations. There is also an obscene putrescence in one of the cans which is labeled "Ham & Eggs." Most of the men are tired but not exhausted. The usual flow of crude humor, with infrequent exceptions, is dormant. We sleep in the morning.

Back to last night: The supply train, arriving at 10:30 P.M., was retained in order to help deepen the finger trenches leading to the various listening posts. The supply column, or "yo-bo train" as it is called, is usually composed of ten members of the Korean Service Corps (yo-bos) escorted by a fire team of marines, that is, four marines. Burgundy-One, being the most accessible of our positions to the enemy, was loaned four Koreans with three shovels and a pick. These men are civilians, either too old for combat service or lacking in health. Most of them seem to be tough as nails, but they also seem content to be treated exactly as slaves. We led them out to the shallow trench and put them to work.

The amount of digging they accomplished was almost unbelievable, in spite of the fact that they were obviously unhappy with their nearness to enemy lines. Dan Keppard, who is apparently a fan of Kipling, had said earlier, "It's lucky they don't know how close they are to their little yellow brothers out there. We'd never get any work out of 'em—the 'eathen beggars." We allowed them to rest at midnight. They crouched together in the bottom of the trench, which they had already deepened considerably, and smoked their shredded-compost cigarettes. In the meantime, Andy and I took turns at digging. One of us would work while the other maintained watch inside the bunker. It is still quite cold these nights and unusually windy. The exercise warmed us so that we removed our gloves and parkas.

Kostis told me later that one of the Koreans crawled into the bunker with him, while he was looking through the aperture. Not having removed his gaze from the opening, he took it for granted that it was myself entering the bunker. When he spoke to the figure and received no answer, he took a look at the creature huddled in the dark corner, and, according to him, nearly passed out. A leering Oriental face. Andy emphasized the word "leering." It wouldn't have been unlike him to have shot the man down, but he allowed the Korean to stay for a minute or two. He gazed through the aperture several times, as though he were studying the terrain in front of the listening post. Kostis is therefore convinced that the man is a spy. As a matter of fact, this is not at all improbable. Pugnacci told us today that one of the Koreans who was working in the finger trench of B-2 last night climbed up on the skyline and lit a cigarette. Pugnacious reported that he dragged the man down to the lieutenant. What better opportunity for spy work than to join the Korean Service Corps?

The yo-bos brought a pack of sandbags with them, and I had another extra-curricular inspiration. At 12:30 I crawled around the side of the bunker, armed with Andy's carbine, two phosphorous grenades, and carrying an entrenching tool and ten sandbags. Andy covered with the BAR. Hiding within the defilade area just this side of the concertina wire, I began digging, in order to deepen that defilade. Over a period of a couple of nights I intended to build a small shelter out there, to be used as a listening post for B-1. As I mentioned before, the view from the aperture of B-1 is limited, being obstructed by the little knoll in front. From where this new shelter would be built, however, the view is wide open, although the person on watch there would have to peer over the rim of the knoll. As it stood before, we had to crawl on top of the bunker in order to see down the slope.

At any rate, with myself digging and the four yo-bos digging further back, there was a fair amount of noise coming from the B-1 area. The sniper was certainly aware of the activity. The moon was not up yet, but it was not extremely dark, and Burgundy-One, from the sniper's vantage point, is on the skyline. I stopped digging for a moment and sat up to survey the forward slopes for any sign of life. Immediately the sniper—either having seen me sit up, or just firing blindly at the noises he heard—opened fire. The several muzzle blasts of his rifle were easily discernible because he was firing at us. I immediately returned fire with an entire hysterical magazine. Andy had slid off the top of the bunker and was cranking away with the BAR. Altogether we must have given that poor sniper white hair. BAR makes one hell of a racket. I don't know about Andy, but I was definitely shaken when I began to think not about the proximity of the sniper but about his amazing nerve. Not that marines are immortal, but, if the madman is willing to fire at us with a high-powered rifle, he will surely have courage enough to call in a mortar barrage. So I returned to the bunker. We told the yo-bos to lie down in the trench. We couldn't see them; they probably were prone anyway. We could hear them whispering frantically to each other, obviously scared to death. But no barrage came.

The Koreans were recalled at 2 A.M., and the supply column returned to the MLR. We spent the remaining dark hours reinforcing the bunker, in case a barrage did come. In its original condition the bunker would not have withstood a direct hit by a 60mm. shell. During the next two hours Kostis and I filled nearly twenty sandbags and lay down two more rows of them upon the overhead, a total of four layers. The sandbags are supported by a uniform layer of 2″ by 6″ planks, set horizontally side by side and embedded in the hard earth on either side of the emplacement. All this constitutes the ceiling, which is in turn supported by four vertical planks, one in each corner. The vertical planks are approx. 4″ by 8″. We feel that the structure is now extremely solid. Kostis believes that it will withstand a direct hit by an 81mm. shell, which I am inclined to doubt.

Before dawn, Andy went over to B-3 and borrowed Lo Castro's #400 field glasses. We were given the word to withdraw at 6:30 or thereabouts, and Andy took the phone and wire down to Gun-One, informing Barrows and Nordstrum that we intended to stay up there, on B-1, for a while, so that they would know where to find us in case something happened. Pallas also borrowed Nordstrum's M-1 rifle.

Meanwhile, I was peering out of the aperture, wielding the BAR in hope of a target as soon as the mist rolled away. In a few minutes, I saw him. It may not look like much, but here is a

167

fairly accurate drawing of his position and the terrain around him. The dunes in the distance represent as much as we can see of Old Bunker, the coloring of which is a startling white.

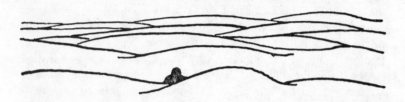

He saw us too. He disappeared, came up again, thrust his rifle over the rim of his chest-high hole, and fired one round. The small puff of smoke from the muzzle blast was visible, which means that I didn't duck very fast. Despite the drawing, he is not conspicuous at all when he stands up. He is surrounded by little rises and dips in the ground, as well as considerable military debris that is strewn all over the area between New Bunker and Old Bunker: canteens, belts, helmets, C-rations, boxes, etc., and several small tree stumps. The gradations in the terrain are so slight that the only way in which I can relocate his position each time is to look for a certain tree stump, and then mark off a known distance below and to the right of that stump.

The area between Burgundy-One and the sniper's hole is a sort of miniature desert. We look down upon it from where we are, and so does the sniper, but we two are on a level with each other. What we see is an expanse of white-grey-yellow sand shale —the miniature desert—extending perhaps fifty yards toward Old Bunker, at the end of which rise a series of small, barely noticeable dunes. The skyline of Old Bunker is strange-looking; the white coloring and the fact that, even though it is a low hill mass, it gives the impression of looming above the dunes to the foreground. The history behind the taking and losing of that hill by marines over a year ago adds to the imposing quality of it. This isn't my feeling alone. When we came up to the line last week, the first thing everyone wanted to see was Bunker Hill.

The sniper's hole isn't actually visible, although its location is known to us. When I saw him, it looked as though he were planted into the sand up to his chest.

It was therefore almost impossible to orient Kostis as to the exact location of the sniper by means of description alone. What I did was to place the binoculars on the parapet and focus them on the spot. Andy moved up and sat cross-legged behind them. I smoked.

Then he moved so fast I had difficulty seeing him. He had grabbed the M-1, shoved it through the aperture, and emptied an entire clip of eight rounds, rapid fire. He proceeded to jam a second clip into the open, smoking receiver, while I frantically collected all the grenades at hand, having decided that we were being overrun by at least a platoon of Chinese. But there was nothing to be seen through the vague haze of gunsmoke. Not being overrun in the least. At all. This had merely been Andy Kostis's reaction to his first sight of the enemy. When we calmed down, and found our nerve again, Andy crawled through the entrance and stood erect behind the bunker, waving his arms in the direction of the sniper. He drew fire immediately. One of the rounds slapped into a sandbag *inside* of the bunker, and I shrieked at him to come inside. He tumbled in and we hugged the ground and laughed like a couple of idiots. We laughed, I suppose, because there was ACTUALLY A MAN OUT THERE WHO WAS TRYING TO *kill* US, and the incongruity occurred to us at the same time, evidently. Big joke indeed.

We heard a muffled THUNK from Old Bunker and stopped laughing. Seconds later a mortar explosion rocked the rafters and showered dirt upon us. Not bothering to consult each other, reacting purely by instinct, we scrambled out of the entrance and flew down the trench like two rapid turtles. Four consecutive explosions jarred the hillside, but Kostis and I were hiding in the crabhole near Gun-One, laughing again. For some reason we found this absolutely sidesplitting.

Andy said that he had gotten a good look at the sniper and suggested that he resembles Thomas Blackwater, an Indian boy in

169

the ———— squad of the ———— platoon, from Prescott, Arizona. His nickname, oddly enough, is Chief—as men from Texas are invariably called Tex, blond men are called Whitey, thin men are called Slim, Polish men are called Ski, and so on. Now that Andy has mentioned it, there *is* a resemblance between the two men, Blackwater and the sniper. We refer to the sniper now as Chief.

During the day, a marine 75mm. recoilless rifle crew fired a mission from the MLR. The target was Old Bunker.

Seventh day, New Bunker. March, 1953

Sgt. Barefield, who is from Dayton, Ohio, came up with us last night as he sometimes does. Being the squad leader, he divides his watches among the three posts within his domain: B-1, B-2 and Gun-One. Shortly after we had set in, Andy whistled at Chief—a loud whistle, the kind you hear used sometimes when a person is calling a dog. To our delight, the Chinese answered the whistle, approximating the sound Andy had made. We three rolled in the aisles over this, rather in the bottom of the bunker, and Barefield called the lieutenant and told him about it. We whistled again, all three of us, but received no response, even after trying again several times. Maybe it made the sniper nervous to find out that there were so many of us there. On the other hand, maybe he isn't alone himself.

Sgt. Barefield, whose name is Paul, is obsessed with grenade launchers. He has one, and has been itching for an excuse to use it. A grenade launcher is a cylindrical piece of metal which fits firmly into the muzzle of an M-1 or a carbine. The rifle grenade itself, that is, the projectile, looks like this.

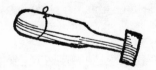

It is fitted onto the adapter. A special cartridge is used; there is no slug, and the open end has been crimped, or squeezed evenly together.

The metal ring shown around the front end of the projectile is the safety mechanism. When the band is unfastened, the projectile is then in an "armed" condition and will explode if dropped on the ground. Barefield, as I started to say, brought the assembly with him last night and set it up at eight o'clock. We got behind him and corrected his elevation and traverse as well as we could. He fired. The thing has a rough kick to it; that's why it is usually mounted on hard earth before being fired.

We didn't hear a sound for several seconds—the projectile was arching across the miniature desert. Whapf! It landed and we saw the flash. We didn't expect a direct hit but knew that it would be close enough to shake up Chief a bit. The projectile Barefield fired was an anti-tank grenade. No more from Jazzbo for the rest of the night. Except for the deal with the grenade launcher, it was a quiet night—for us. God knows what happened elsewhere along the lines. We saw a fierce fire fight, in the eastern section far to our right. A distant mortar barrage is a real gasser to watch; like a group of fireflies, followed by little muffled thumps that are the reports. Tracer trajectories were also visible. We learned today that Fox company had made a raid on the Chinese hill called "Siberia." Able company raided this hill last fall, with heavy casualties. Colia, my companion in Seoul, was one.

At dawn Kostis and I decided to withdraw like normal folk; partly because Sgt. Barefield said he frowned heavily on our staying up there in daylight, and partly because the bunker is zeroed-in. Instead of going to sleep, I sat in the bottom of the trench outside of our living-bunker and talked with Lt. Buell. He wanted to hear the details concerning Chief. I told him everything except the fact that an enemy mortar tube is registered on the B-1 bunker. He might not permit us to go up there in daylight; something I intend doing this afternoon.

This is being written in the crabhole next to Gun-One, at five o'clock in the afternoon, same day. I awoke at 2 P.M. and had some chow before going up. I went up on my stomach. No pun. The finger trench is much deeper than it was before, but parts of it are still exposed to Sniper Ridge. Incidentally, Sgt. Van Horn is obsessed with the idea of getting that sniper on the Ridge. This is not Chief; this one is working from the other flank of the outpost.

Van Horn told Barefield that he intends to sit up all morning and see if he can locate that sniper's hole. He is a brave man, that Chinese on the Ridge. He is actually nearer to the marine MLR than we are. The nearest he is to friendly territory is Old Bunker, and we (New Bunker) are in between both. We all wonder where the hell he comes from. The most popular guess is that he lives out there. Poor bastard. Van Horn, an obstinate young man, will probably put an end to him and his troubles. I sat in the bunker for some time and studied the area around Chief's humble abode through the field glasses. No sign of life. Later, I crawled outside and slithered around the bunker into that defilade area, in which I'd been digging the other night. In that position, between the front of the bunker and the roll of concertina wire, I was under observation from the MLR which rises to the south, but not under observation from Sniper Ridge (the B-1 bunker covers me) and not visible from any of the Chinese positions.

I'll try to describe the geography of this entire sector. Picture two parallel ranges of hills—my dear—with a long, narrow rice paddy in between. The hill range to the south is the MLR. The smaller hill range, three hundred yards to the north, is that range on which the following positions are located: Hedy, Sniper Ridge, New Bunker, Old Bunker. Although this northernmost hill range is a sprawling one, the positions named are almost in a line with each other, running west-east in the order named. The over-all ridge is approx. one mile long, with Old Bunker on the eastern end and Hedy on the western end. New Bunker and Sniper Ridge are in the middle. The whole mess then is one big geological formation. And now let us gaze still further north, my child. We will see that the terrain descends on a gradual plane, for two or three miles. There is a huge rice paddy down there, dried up of course. Several white-yellow hills jut up above the paddy. These are Chinese hills; 64-Able, Yolk, etc. Although they are lofty, distinct hills, and are situated far down that gradual incline, their summits are generally on a level with this ridge on which we are located. Looking sideways at a sand table of this sector, it might look something like this.

The distance between New Bunker and the Yolk is more than a mile. The distance between the MLR and Tae Dok-San, the Red Bastion (to quote a news broadcast) is more than three miles. It's all wide open to view out there. With field glasses, we can study the terrain all the way across. By daylight it is breathtaking, and at night it looks like somewhere in the bottom of the sea. Wide, deep trenches are clearly visible on 64-Able and the Yolk and also many, many feeder trenches that cut across the hundreds of paddies down there. During all the time I watched, there was not a soul to be seen. I'd hate to know how many Chinese there actually are in that area.

What I was most interested in was the terrain between Chief's hole and Burgundy-One. As I mentioned, it is strewn with much military gear. It is generally flat. In daylight, I was able to follow the course of that deserted trench, the one that ends so close to B-2. It meanders toward Old Bunker and disappears from sight not far to the left of Chief's hole. I got the idea then that Chief does not work from a hole; that he merely occupies a fighting-hole or an indentation in a trench emanating from Old Bunker itself. This seems fairly logical; it would be extremely dangerous for a man to remain in an isolated hole so close to a marine outpost and under direct observation from the

173

MLR, without having some sort of covered exit, *i.e.*, a trench, by which to withdraw into the nearest main fortification—Old Bunker. Well, what about that unfortunate *enfant perdu* on Sniper Ridge? The only possible explanation is that he is stark raving mad. I suspect that whatever trench Chief occupies is connected with that meandering, supposedly deserted trench running near B-2. Pugnacci and Hogg have reported noises in front of them on several occasions. There is probably a listening post somewhere along that meandering trench. The Meander is a river in Asia Minor which in ancient times meandered. This trench would be a wonderful spot for a listening post.

Lt. Buell crawled up later in the afternoon. He said he'd been looking for me. I expected to get hell, but he merely asked what I'd seen. I gave him the glasses and he settled down for a while. By the time he arrived, I knew the terrain between B-1 and Chief's hole like the back of my hand, including the meandering trench. Another morbid inspiration, but I'll mull it over before I tell anyone.

At 3:30 P.M. there was an air strike. Lt. and I had ringside seats. The objective was Old Bunker, our neighbors. First a Corsair would drop down and fire a barrage of 5″ rockets from beneath the wings, then a blue-black Panther jet would plummet down and drop its charming load. We made a very interesting discovery during the air strike. There are at least two heavy machine guns on this flank of Old Bunker, that is, the flank nearest B-1. We saw cumulative puffs of smoke at two points within the dunes. We couldn't hear them because of the diving planes, but they were certainly machine guns. This discovery, and the fact that there is a 60mm. mortar crew and tube over there, suggests that Old Bunker is occupied by at least a company. When we saw this, the lieutenant scrambled down to Gun-One. I presume he called the CP cave and told someone there to contact Capt. Krupp and request a mortar barrage, target Old Bunker. At any rate this is what happened, although the barrage arrived some time after the air strike had ceased, and the machine-gun crews had probably hidden themselves long before then. The air strike was a very violent affair. It's slightly fantastic to watch a neat, compact hunk of metal—the aircraft—slip through the air in such a maneuverable manner, and come so close to the ground. The Panther jets looked like flying manta rays.

I don't know the history of Bunker Hill as thoroughly as I'd like to. As I understand it, Bunker Hill was finally captured by the marines after many days of fierce fighting, during which at least two battalions were used. But because of the tremendous casualty rate even during our occupation of it (the Chinese were dug in literally on the other side of the slope, close enough to throw grenades), and because of the fact that the place was littered with Chinese corpses which presented a health problem, Bunker Hill was evacuated. The Chinese, of course, moved right in. New Bunker was then fortified by marines.

Eighth day, New Bunker outpost

Last night: Much excitement. We whistled at Chief as we occupied B-1, shortly after sundown. Our new friend whistled back this time. But the fool also fired blindly at us, after he whistled.

The result of Lt. Buell's visit the other afternoon was that the supply train brought out several compressed rolls of concertina wire, at his request. This was an extremely intelligent and timely move on his part, and something of a coincidence. It happened that the enemy made a probe on New Bunker the same night that we decided to reinforce our barbed-wire entanglements. I'll attempt to relate the incidents of last night in order, and with as much detail as I have energy for.

The supply train arrived at eleven o'clock. By midnight, three KSCs were helping us lay down a new roll of wire in front of the original roll of concertina. There is a kid's toy called a "Slinky" which descends stairs, plays out from one hand to another, etc. Compressed concertina wire comes something like this. Two men, each wearing thick gloves especially made for barbed-wire details, grasp each end of the roll and gradually work

175

it apart, until it resembles the wire in the drawing [on page 158]. It is then secured by iron or steel stakes driven into the ground. Barbed wire is not designed to stop the enemy, but to slow him down. We were therefore very, very nervous working in front of an already secured roll of wire—the one that was there when we arrived. Naturally as we worked on the B-1 side of the new roll that we were laying in, we were still obstructed from free passage to the bunker by the original roll.

We were, of course, as quiet as possible. Barefield and Kostis were lying side by side on top of the bunker. Barefield covered us with a carbine; Kostis with my own BAR. His carbine was slung across my shoulders as I worked with the yo-bos. I had four grenades in my pockets. The Koreans were unarmed as always and, to put it mildly, terrified. They knew at least that they were in front of a listening post which was in front of an outpost which was in front of the MLR. Had they known how close Chief was, and Old Bunker, they probably would not have worked. I am surprised that they agreed even to go into No Man's Land.

The moon was not out. Nobody would have worked if it had been. It was almost pitch-black. We worked either in a prone position or crouched. Sgt. Barefield constantly surveyed the terrain in front of us, down the slope, through the field glasses. At the same time, Pugnacci, Hogg and Ankers, plus another group of KSCs, were laying wire in front of Burgundy-Two. We worked quickly; in less than ten minutes the roll was stretched out and we were about to hammer the first stake into the hard ground with an entrenching tool. This was by far the worst part of the job. The *clang! clang! clang!* noise resounded for some distance, and echoed back from the steep slopes of the MLR. The Koreans' faces, near enough to see, were taut with suspense, but I dare say they weren't half as worried as we three were, with the knowledge that B-1 was zeroed-in.

Then things began happening. What will take probably a page to describe occurred in less than half a minute. Some of the details I picked up later, so I'll include them as though I knew they were happening at the time.

As we drove in the stakes, Barefield spotted movement in front of us—off to the right, down the slope in front of the little graveyard. The three yo-bos and myself were ten yards in front of Barefield and Kostis, and they hesitated to call out. They should have; we were making a great racket driving in the stakes. Instead they threw small stones at me. I looked around and saw them, Barefield and Kostis, both making constrained movements with their arms—they didn't want to attract more attention by waving violently. Both of them had climbed off the top of the bunker. Andy was leaning against it, crouched down, Barefield was on his side, next to the bunker. I didn't catch on. I moved over and peered curiously at Barefield through the barbed wire. He was muttering terrible sounds under his breath, all conso- nants, and moving one arm back and forth in a jerky motion. The Koreans had stopped driving in the stakes. I caught on, and my heart began jumping. I didn't dare glance toward Old Bunker. If I had, I probably would have panicked. The yo-bos knew some- thing was wrong; I shoved them violently toward the wire and they picked their way, agonizingly slow, through it. They were naturally in a desperate hurry but couldn't help getting hung up on the wire. In the meantime, Andy—the cool one—took the phone a few feet down the trench and called the CP, explaining in whispers what was happening. Barefield collected all the gre- nades he could find. As soon as the lieutenant got the word, he called Capt. Krupp and requested the 81mm. box, on the double.

I'd like to describe exactly where we were when the Chinese opened fire: Two of the yo-bos were already in the finger trench. The last yo-bo was just disentangling himself from the wire. He was poised over Barefield, who was crouched next to the bunker. I was directly behind this yo-bo—actually to his right rear—and almost out of the wire.

From this point on, things were confused and my memory of the sequence is hazy, mostly because I definitely did panic. When the firing commenced, the Korean—the last one—slumped over. He was free from the wire, but wounded. I ripped myself loose, tearing a gash in my thigh doing so (you can be sure I didn't know it at the time). I grabbed the Korean around the neck with both hands and hauled him around the bunker, knocking against Barefield, who fell over. Andy, bless his little butt, returned fire immediately with the blunderbuss. The path of the burst was close to my head, the muzzle blast was blinding, but he probably saved our lives. As soon as I got past him, Barefield began firing, spitting out that rapid chatter of the carbine. I'm not ashamed to admit that I dropped Andy's carbine among the wire. I had taken it off my shoulder as soon as those pebbles hit me, but in stepping through the wire—after the firing had begun —the weapon became snagged and I let it go. I dropped something else, too, although I didn't know it until a minute or so later. All I could do was start chucking grenades, any kind that came under my hand.

None of us had any real idea how many Chinese there were, or how far away. One's judgment at night is always lousy. From the muzzle blasts, they seemed to be very close. One of the grenades I threw was a white phosphorous and when it exploded into a shower of sparks, the attacking force—or part of it—was exposed in the light for a second or two.

They were spread out along a shelf of earth in front of the graveyard; we could see four or five of them. The grenade exploded on the other side of the shelf; there may have been more of them down there, out of sight. Since the detonation was behind and below them, the four or five figures were only black silhouettes. We could make out the shape of their weapons. They were all lying down, except one who was scooting down the slope. We could see his upper body moving back and forth as he ran the other way. They were between twenty-five and thirty yards away. We continued firing and throwing grenades. They had stopped firing almost immediately. Then Barefield's carbine jammed and he began heaving grenades. I found myself yelling at the top of my voice, and noticed that Barefield and Kostis were yelling too, but I don't know what any of us were saying. Shortly thereafter, when Andy had stopped firing into the dark, we heard an ear-piercing whistle high up in the air, and the 81mm. box arrived. We scrambled into the bunker and sat it out.

The Korean was lying there where I had left him, beside the

bunker. We had neglected to drag him in, but he was in a fairly well-covered position. He was silent, but breathing. I leaned down and said hello in Korean—at the moment I couldn't recall how to ask him how he was. He said something in Korean, which none of us understood. I saw that he was a fairly old man, not a *papa-san*, but getting on in years. I said something like, "O.K. you? O.K. yo-bo? Huh?" He answered, "Me number-one, sah-gee." Andy said, "Number-one, my ass. He's number-ten. Better get him down to Danny." We carried the old man down to the CP and Dan worked on him out in the trench. He had a slug in his back. The yo-bos were collected and Dan put the wounded (dying) one on a stretcher, gave him morphine, and they moved out. The lieutenant sent a couple of men up to B-1 and allowed us to take a break. After changing trousers, I went back to the CP and had some cocoa and cigarettes. The lieutenant was complimentary to us.

Barefield is unhappy over the fact that his carbine jammed. I would be. I'd throw the god-damned thing away. He said he had cleaned it that afternoon.

When we returned to B-1, at 4:30, the moon was out. Nevertheless, I felt obligated to retrieve Andy's carbine. Barefield, Kostis, and the other two temporary replacements provided cover and I stomached out and picked it off the wire.

We wonder why Chief didn't call in mortars on us last night while we were laying the wire. I didn't go up on B-1 today.

Ninth day, New Bunker. March, 1953

Last night: We whistled at Chief but got no answer; perhaps he isn't there any more.

The lieutenant, making his rounds last night, rationed my daylight time on B-1 to thirty minutes. I'm surprised he allows me to go up there at all in daylight. Only one thing of real interest occurred last night. Someone on the MLR called for parachute flares at about nine o'clock. The terrain between us and the MLR was illuminated and we saw that two bodies were lying on the earth shelf near the graveyard. We call it an earth shelf;

179

it is a momentary lessening of the angle of the slope. One of the bodies is almost out of sight, the other is crumpled up beside a group of bushes. (There is quite a bit of vegetation on this side of the outpost, grass and small bushes, all leafless. At the bottom of the MLR range—across the paddy—there is a good-sized woods.) One man's headpiece was lying nearby, and his weapon next to an outstretched arm. I mentioned the presence of vegetation in this area because this is the only reason I can think of as to why the artillery forward observer, or someone else on the MLR, failed to see the bodies during the day. Barefield and Kostis were inside the bunker, looking out the aperture. They could not see the bodies from that angle. I was standing up, peering over the top when the first flare started burning. I decided not to tell Barefield about it, for two reasons. First I wanted to go out and get the dead man's weapon; second, I was curious to know whether or not the Chinese do come back after their dead as we always do. If I had told Barefield he would not have allowed me to go out there, and he would have reported the discovery of the bodies to the lieutenant, who in turn would organize a detail of marines to bring the bodies in. So I waited until Barefield went down to his bunker for a spell, to get warm —we all do this every couple of hours, one at a time. I followed him down a minute or so later, and went into the Gun-One bunker, found Barrows and told him to come up to B-1 with me. Kostis and Barrows lay on top of the bunker and I crawled out in front again, cutting around the southern end of the concertina roll and descending the slope past the graveyard. The rim of this slope obstructs the view of anyone who might be watching from Chief's area. Also it was another dark night. In a couple of minutes I was beyond the graveyard. Things look a great deal different from down there, although I wasn't exactly studying the lay of the land at that moment. When I came across the body it was something of a shock; why I don't know. It was too dark to see what kind of shape he was in. I grabbed the weapon and ran back up the slope.

It is a pp-S, a Chinese burp gun. There is a star on top of

the receiver, cut into the metal—just the outline of a star, and also four Chinese characters. We are led to believe that all Chinese weapons are Russian-made, but apparently this one is not. This is a recoil-operated sub-machine gun. It is very cheaply made, and easily disassembled. There are only five parts, one of which is a little black rubber pad which fits over the end of the long spring. The pad helps reduce the recoil. A 35-round magazine was in the weapon. I removed the remaining rounds and found that he had fired 17 of them. The burp gun is extremely inaccurate, and the Chinese have never had a reputation for marksmanship. Also it was dark. Also, what difference does it make to him? Maybe it was he who hit the old yo-bo. The burp gun fires approx. 900 rounds a minute, much faster than our carbine. It's stopping power is poor. The slugs are a fraction of an inch wider than our own (.31 calibre, or 9.72mm.) but they are very short and the powder charge is small.

There is an oil & thong compartment in the butt plate, but it is empty. The weapon was lightly lubricated with an ill-smelling kind of oil.

The 11th Marines fire artillery missions once in a while. I should say, they fire missions all the time, but only occasionally in this immediate sector. They fire various types of projectiles, one of which is called "V-T." I think this means variable time. Even though I did a hitch with the 10th Marines, an artillery outfit at Lejeune, I never ran across this type of shell, so my description of it will probably be incorrect. The fuse on this shell is set so that after it leaves the gun it will detonate itself by radar. That is, as soon as the shell comes within a certain number of yards of the ground—immediately before impact—it will explode. By exploding in the air, the shrapnel sprays the ground below, which is deadly to men in trenches. It sounds almost exactly like a gigantic freight train when one of them passes, usually quite low, overhead. We are always alerted whenever a V-T mission is to be fired on a target anywhere nearby, and we huddle in the bottom of the bunker, in case one of the shells hap-

181

pens to explode prematurely. The point is that one did just that last night, causing such a noise, and with such a concussive effect, that we were deaf for several seconds.

While watching enemy hills in daylight, during an artillery mission, we see the sand ripple like water as the shell (not V-T) buries itself. Then, seconds later, the shell detonates and a great cloud of sand is thrown into the air. White phosphorous shells are an extraordinary sight; a hundred times more powerful and more deadly than a WP grenade. Incidentally, in the account of the Little Rock raid, I mentioned a strange smell as we crossed that paddy below Texas Ridge. The other night, smelling the same odor, I questioned Barefield about it. He said that it was the odor of the white phosphorous grenade that I had thrown. During the regimental T.O.T., before the Little Rock raid, white phosphorous had been used.

Near dawn, Hedy was probed. It didn't sound like much of an encounter but we learned today that a couple of Chinese had entered the trench. Major Pennock, a former lawyer, was inspecting the outpost at the time and surely got the hell scared out of his well-protected life. No marine casualties. The word is being passed around that one of the Chinese—must have been an arrogant soul—stood on top of one of the machine-gun bunkers of Hedy and sprayed the area with burp-gun slugs, aiming at nothing in particular and hitting no one. Just his one-man war against us rotten capitalist warmongers. The machine-gun crew, so the story goes, were inside the bunker at the time. There were no Chinese casualties either. A great big ol' Hallowe'en party; ever'-body scarin' hell outen ever'body else an' nobody a-gitten hurt.

The yo-bo train brought out a monstrosity last night called a snooper-scope. It is mounted on an M-1 carbine; that is, a semi-automatic carbine. We worked with it at Camp Rose one night during a field problem; looking into the scope, you see a dull green light and, if a man is within fifty feet of the thing, he—or rather his shape—can be seen. The men on Lorretta were given this one. More about it later.

182

Tenth day, New Bunker

Two nights ago, shortly after I picked up the burp gun, the lieutenant passed around the word that a "Rolls-Royce," the code name of a body-snatching team, would be working near our outpost within an hour. They would come close to B-1 we were told. This was, of course, a precautionary measure, so that we would not fire on them. In a few minutes a group of marines appeared, creeping along the slope by the graveyard. They loaded the Chinese bodies on the stretchers—it turned out that there were three bodies—and carried them silently back to the MLR. So obviously they were spotted during the day, from the MLR. The bodies will be turned over to the CIC (counter-intelligence corps).

Over on Hedy, private John Riley of Columbus, Ohio, was killed by a sniper. It happened shortly after the sun came up. He was hit in the head. Lt. Buell passed the word around. His friend, Lt. Knight, is the officer in charge of Hedy and they talk to each other frequently by radio, using their own peculiar code. In this way we are made aware of news on Hedy and vice versa.

Last night: Chief answered our whistle, just once. The man has taken on a personality, as far as we are concerned; the result of an incredible incident:

As soon as Chief whistled back, Andy stood up and yelled every Chinese obscenity he knows. Something about "spawn of a turtle turd," one of the more innocent ones. "*Nee wamba toosa molika pee*" it sounded like. And "*goonya*"—girl, according to Andy. "*Ee bey shway*"—bring me some of your water. "*Neeta sety*"—you're crazy. "*Nee sola jeeba*"—unprintable. Plus two others, the sound of which I can't remember. No response of course. I joined him outside and screamed, "Mao-Tse Tung, Ding boo hao." Mao, very bad. The most violent Chinese I know—the *only* Chinese, except gung ho. Then Andy had a great inspiration. He shouted, in a very sonorous voice, "Gung ho!" the phrase eventually known to all marines as a cynical battle

cry meaning "work together." Then the wondrous thing occurred. His cry was still echoing about the hills, causing, I am
sure, a certain amount of confusion among a few marines and
Chinese, when the sound of one clear, evenly pitched voice
reached our ears, from the direction of Old Bunker, out of the
darkness. One word: "Okay."

We made a resolution on the spot not to fire at Chief again
and to attempt communicating with him at dawn.

The phonograph blared forth last night, but as usual we
couldn't hear the words. At one point we were certain that a girl
was talking. Today we learned from the lieutenant, who had got
it from outpost Hedy, who had got it from outpost Ingrid, who
had got it from Thucydides, that a girl had indeed spoken, in
English, and that the gist of her speech was that if any of us put
down our arms and came over to the Chinese lines, we would be
escorted safely to her and "shown a good time." And a good time
was had by all. And I wish to thank Mrs. Pubitch and the other
ladies of the congregation who so generously devoted their time
and service to bake us that tasty collection of pastries and goodies and various assorted foodies. Har! Naïve fools.

I probably use the word "fascinating" too much, but something fascinating happened last night beside that colossal word
that Chief said. After midnight, a distinct green light appeared,
directly north from Burgundy-One. Pugnacci and Hogg saw it
from B-2. It was between 150 and 200 yards away, down the gradual incline. Studying it through field glasses, it resembled the
kind of deck light that you might see on a luxurious cabin
cruiser. The glass appears to be neatly corrugated.

All that we could see of course were subtle gradations in
the light itself. Two or three times something passed in front
of the light, blotting it out for a second. We had seen the same
kind of light on Old Bunker, immediately preceding the mortar
muzzle blast we spotted. It occurred to us that perhaps this was
the light attached to an aiming stake, which is used whenever a
mortar tube or an artillery piece is being set into position. Kostis
called the CP and told the lieutenant about the strange phe-

nomenon. The lieutenant told Kostis to put me on the wire. He
said, "Russ, if you get it into your head to climb over the wire
and go down there to take a look, you won't come back. And if
you do come back, I'll have you court-martialed. Clear?" "Aye-
aye, sir." Evidently he heard about the business of picking up
the burp gun the other night. He later called back and explained
— O, omnipotent one!—that this kind of thing is an old, tired
ruse of the Chinese. They hope that some fool will leave his position to see what the light is. The curious one will walk into
an ambush set up around the light. I wouldn't have ventured
that far away, but I certainly considered it; my curiosity was extreme.

The moon rises a bit earlier each night. It rises now at about
2:30 A.M. Still very cold at night, not too uncomfortable during
the day.

When we were told to withdraw, Kostis again took the
phone down and returned. The air cleared of mist, we whistled
and waited, then yelled and waited. We had hoped that Chief
would appear so that we might wave benignly at each other
across the narrow strip of No Man's Land, like a trio of idiots.
As far as we are concerned, this strip of land is neutral territory.
But our olive-skinned friend did not show himself.

Eleventh day, New Bunker
Our incongruous friendship came to an abrupt end last
night. At 11 P.M. I crawled around in front of the bunker, armed
with BAR and two WP grenades, and carrying an entrenching
tool. Andy lay on top of the bunker with the phone, carbine
ready. It started out casually; we knew that Chief at least
wouldn't bother us. Before I forget it—Pugnacci, Hogg and I,
talking in the living-bunker yesterday morning before we went
to sleep, worked out a message that we'd like to send Chief. The
trouble was that no one on the outpost knows enough Chinese
to write characters. We would like to have made a large sign to
put up for Chief to read:

Comrade:
Leave your position and run over to this sign.
We will cover you with our weapons as you come.
We will guide you into our trench quickly.
You will be escorted safely to our lines.

We are presumptuous in assuming that any of those cats want to come to our side, in the same way that they with their asinine propaganda are presumptuous. But we felt that Chief was with it. By this time everyone in Able company, on the MLR and on Hedy, knows about Burgundy-One and the sniper. Kostis and I keep the others posted because everyone is fascinated by the thing.

I began digging in front of the bunker, deepening the defilade area and filling sandbags to form a hidden parapet. No attempt was made to muffle the sound of the shovel against the hard earth. I had worked for ten or fifteen minutes when the mortar crew on Old Bunker sent off a round. I recall telling myself that there was nothing to worry about, that Chief wouldn't do that to me, that the round was intended probably for the MLR. In the meantime, another round had shot out of the distant tube, then another. There was a sharp whistle high above us, rapidly increasing in intensity, and then a horrible, hoarse roar as the first round plummeted down, exploding ten or fifteen yards to the left of the bunker. Andy was knocked off the bunker by this first round, and received splinters of shrapnel in his arm. The second round exploded. Then another; altogether six projectiles of 60mm. variety rocked the earth around B-1, landing in the same ordered interval of time with which they had been discharged, about three seconds apart. During the barrage, I tried to draw my entire body within my helmet, like a fetus, and I was frightened to tears. A second before each round landed I thought: "This one is going to land right on top of me"; and I believed that each one would. Every one of them sounded that way. In the space of one second or less the roar would become louder and louder until it seemed obvious that each round would land right on my head. Keep a tight sphincter muscle, they say, and I did just that. And after each round exploded, I wondered why I was still alive. No prayers; I was simply amazed.

Not one of these projectiles landed within the defilade area in which I lay, and the only damage I suffered was a severe headache which had lasted all day, and a few seconds of complete helpless terror.

Andy is hurt, but not badly. His left forearm is cut up a bit. He had retained enough presence of mind to crawl into the bunker before the second round arrived. He was the one who got hurt, but our conversation as soon as the barrage lifted was pretty interesting.

"Russ?"

No answer.

"Russ?"

No answer.

"Well, Jesus Christ, Son of a bitch . . . RUSS!"

"What do you want?"

"Well, where did they get you?"

"I don't know."

"Where does it hurt?" No answer.

"Well, where does it hurt, you ass?"

"I'm not hit."

"Well, I am. Get your miserable ass in here."

Our phone wires were severed during the barrage, which means that one of the rounds had landed within the finger trench. Andy walked down to the CP by himself and Dan patched him up. He was told to stay in his living-cave for a while. The lieutenant questioned us but was not severe. He could justifiably have punished us for assuming unnecessary risks. He did say that he intended to call the captain and request that the position of B-1 be altered.

Barefield and I dug two indentations in the finger trench close to Gun-One and stood watch from these temporary fighting-holes until dawn. When we were withdrawn I went down to the CP and told the lieutenant the idea I've been considering for two or three days. I feel that a small raiding party can find their way to Chief's position without being discovered:

Five men—Barefield, Hogg, Pugnacci, Keppard and myself—
would leave the outpost at B-2 and enter that deserted trench
which peters out a few feet in front of that listening post, and
which wanders toward Old Bunker. I have referred to this trench
as the meandering one. I would be willing to take the point of
the column, since I know that area better than anyone, having
studied it during the day. But whoever the point man be, I suggested that he carry only a .45 or possibly two .45s.

This trench is visible for about fifty yards. It disappears
from sight twenty or twenty-five yards north of Chief's position.
As I mentioned somewhere else, we believe that Chief occupies
a trench rather than a hole; probably a long finger trench that
leads all the way back into the main fortifications of Old Bunker.
This meandering trench probably forms a junction with the finger trench somewhere near Chief's position. By guess only, this
is what the layout might look like.

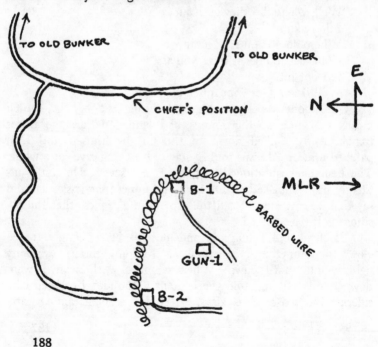

We would enter the Meander and move along it until we reached the junction. Once there, the men would deploy in the following manner:

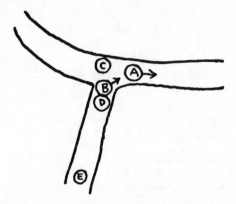

The man marked A would move toward Chief's hole, accompanied by B. C would guard the approach from the north, accompanied by D. E would remain a few yards from the junction. In case the mission became a total shambles, he at least would be able to get back to report what happened. As soon as Chief is captured or killed, or a grenade thrown into his cave—if he has one—the five men would meet at the junction and return to the outpost. If the Meander is used as a listening post, we at least would find out for certain. There is also the possibility that the Meander peters out at the other end also, as it does in front of B-2. If so, we would find out for certain, and the mission will have been an informative reconnaissance patrol. I've talked with the other four men and they are all willing to go—the brazen fools. Dan said that he would act as B. The lieutenant said he'd think upon't. I wish he'd stop taking these plans of mine seriously. I'm merely trying to make buck sergeant by devious methods. God knows what I'd do if he said, "O.K., Russ. You can do it. Tonight."

I went up to B-2 this morning at 8 o'clock. It is not dangerous. The finger trench is well covered and the bunker strong.

The view is magnifico. From B-2 the terrain, the gradual descent and everything else is laid out to view far below. There are the scanty ruins of a village two hundred yards down the slope, directly north. No huts remain, only several foundations. This is possibly where we saw the curious green light. It was one of those mornings when the sun keeps trying to break through the fog. At 8:30 the heavier fog dispersed, but a string of mist hung low over the paddies below and a breeze wafted them in and out of the draws and over the small ridges.

I have left out so many things. Every single night we have called in a mortar barrage on some enemy mortar crew. It's a routine procedure. Almost everyone on the outpost has done it. Chinese mortar crews are working all through the night. It looks as though they fire a mission from one position, then pull up stakes before our counterbarrage arrives, and move quickly into another position some distance away, and fire another mission. We have undergone several bombardments on New Bunker. None of them have had any effect other than to chew up the lip of certain trenches. At dusk the Chinese almost always bombard the MLR.

Sgt. Barefield, who is not renowned for his gigantic intellect, calls in more missions than all of us put together. It has become an outpost joke. During the day he will often sit up on B-2 or B-3 and keep the sleepy phone watch in the CP busy calling the mortar crews behind the MLR, usually waking them up. Yesterday morning he called in a series of missions on what he believed to be an enemy tube. Sgt. Kovacs, the machine-gun leader, was on the CP phone at the time. Barefield reported the tube as "roving"; firing a round here, then moving and firing another round over there, and so on. This went on for some time, until Kovacs got bored and told our mortarmen to go back to sleep, that they would not be bothered again that morning. Barefield of course continued calling in rounds. Kovacs would say, "On the way!" signifying that the mortar crews had told him over the wire that a projectile had been discharged and was headed for the target.

190

Barefield, to the amazement of Sgt. Kovacs, called in and described where the "round" had landed, and proceeded to correct the elevation & traverse, saying something like: "The next one should be fifty yards more to the left, and twenty-five yards further out. Tell 'em to send another round, Kovacs." "O.K., Barefield," and Kovacs would pause for the interval it usually takes to relay the information to the mortar crews who by this time were sound asleep. Then "On the way!" over the other phone to Barefield. In a few seconds, Barefield called back and said, "Right on target! Tell 'em good work, Kovacs; well done." I quote Sgt. Kovacs, who wouldn't keep it to himself but has told everyone on the outpost. No one has any idea what Barefield saw. He obviously saw nothing but didn't want to admit to Kovacs that he had not seen the explosions. Lt. Buell might well consider the possibility of sending Sgt. Barefield to the rear for a little rest.

Riley was killed while crawling out in front of his position, called "Charlie-hole," in broad daylight, in order to pick up a burp-gun magazine that one of the enemy probing party had dropped.

Twelfth day
Last night: the Hour of Charm. The atmosphere on New Bunker today is saturated with profound uneasiness because of the terrible events of last night.

A Diesel, the code name for a combat patrol, was scheduled to go out. The general mission of any combat patrol is to make contact with the enemy. The objective of this patrol was to be Old Bunker. Sgt. Kovacs, at the request of the lieutenant, asked to be escorted up to B-1 during the afternoon so that he could register a mortar concentration on Old Bunker; specifically, to zero-in that area where we believe the mortar crew to operate. Within four rounds the area was registered and labeled concentration "X-ray." Before this, it had been labeled concentration

"10-Able, fifty left." I think that the original concentration was more accurate but Kovacs doubted it, since the original was established at night and X-ray during the daylight. It was Kovacs who told me about the Diesel, and that the new concentration would be used during the withdrawal, if needed. I found Lt. Buell and told him that I wanted to go along, even though the Diesel was originating from the MLR. In the first place, I know the character of the terrain around Old Bunker, having studied it from B-1 during the day. Second, I knew exactly where Chief was, and could inform the point man as to his location so that the column would avoid him. Third, I felt that they were up against lousy odds. Evidently none of the high-echelon people believe that Old Bunker is well fortified, or they would have sent out more than a Diesel; they would have staged a full-scale raid. From the scanty evidence that I had gathered with my eyes, I believed that there was a company of Chinese on Old Bunker, *i.e.*, the two machine guns that we spotted during the air strike, and the fact that there is a mortar tube there. Now—today—we know that there is a company of Chinese on Old Bunker. I haven't said, "I told you so" out loud, but I've got to put it down here. I TOLD YOU SO, YOU STUPID BASTARDS. The assaulting unit was *thirteen* men strong.

The lieutenant said no, I couldn't go along; thereby saving my precious skin. His main point was that I had already missed the briefing, which was held on the MLR.

Toward dusk, a machine-gun crew on the MLR began firing tracers into the forward slopes of Old Bunker, zeroing-in the weapon so that it could be used as cover during the withdrawal. This was an asinine thing to do, a real blunder. It must have been obvious to the Chinese that something was going to happen, otherwise why would a U.S. machine gun be registered so carefully on their forward slopes? Also, no machine gun had ever fired tracers at them during the day.

At 9:30 the men on all listening posts were informed that the Diesel—about thirty men—had left the MLR and would be passing close by New Bunker in a few minutes. It was another dark night and they were admirably silent. We neither heard nor saw them as they passed below us, along the rice paddy between us and the MLR hill mass. In the meantime I had asked the lieutenant if we could move the machine gun in the Gun-One bunker up to Burgundy-One, in order to provide cover during the withdrawal. His answer was correct; he said that the machine gun and crew would not have sufficient cover if moved to B-1 and that, in its present position, the gun has a direct line of fire to the skyline of Old Bunker. He told us to keep our eyes on the objective during the action so that we could call in for concentration X-ray if the Chinese mortars began working; later on, however, he got Hogg on the phone and said to forget about the concentration, and to keep our heads down. Kostis has been transferred to B-2, trading places with Hogg.

At 10:30 the feces hit the fan. A chorus of burp guns opened up, almost in unison. The fire fight began, an intense one. BARs, carbines, burp guns, Maxims and grenades. We could see none of this from B-1, surprisingly enough, meaning that the encounter was taking place on the other side of Old Bunker. The point to note is that the burp guns opened fire initially; that is the first sound we heard. Obviously the approach of the Diesel had been detected. Lt. McGinnis, a good friend of Buell's, was the patrol leader.

The fire fight lasted for at least five minutes—a hell of a prolonged encounter for this type of situation. Lt. McGinnis began withdrawing his men. Here I'll make an insertion; facts we learned later that night: Thirteen men had made the assault. Seven of these men were hit, almost at once. This means that the assault squad must have gotten quite close to the enemy trench before being fired upon. Although it sounds too good to be true, the word is that none of the seven were killed. All of the marine shooting thereafter took the form of covering fire, while the wounded were being brought off the hill. Before the unit returned to the MLR, twelve of the thirteen men had been hit; two missing in action.

As McGinnis's outfit approached New Bunker, during the withdrawal, the enemy fire was directed our way. At this point we (on B-1) could see muzzle blasts from Old Bunker. Stray slugs were whizzing over our bunker and we huddled in the bottom of it. The enemy mortar crews went to work, as did every other mortar crew in the vicinity, Chinese and marine. From here on, my recollections are disconnected. Within the description, I'll interpolate facts that we learned later.

It is beyond my power to describe adequately the mortar barrage which the enemy sent out. Concerning the actual number of projectiles sent out by them, there have been estimates from 500 to 1000; and there were surely more than 500. This is precisely why the fighting in Korea—in this so-called static phase —is so very tricky. The accurate mortar concentrations. It is probable that the enemy used artillery during the bombardment, or at least 120mm. mortars. We have learned to distinguish between 60mm. and 82mm. rounds, and much of the gear last night was considerably more powerful. There was nothing for us to do except remain within the bunker and keep near the phone. Then stray projectiles began to land in our vicinity.

B-3 reported that burp-gun fire was being directed on them, from only a short distance in front of them. They returned fire and grenades.

B-2 reported that 82mm. rounds were walking up on their position, one at a time. They were close to hysteria. The lieutenant shouted, "Pull out!" into the phone, and B-2 was evacuated.

An 82mm. round exploded somewhere between Chief's hole and B-1, closely followed by another, and another. We realized— it was a slow take—that each round was getting closer; that we were being walked in on. Hogg and I were glaring at Sgt. Barefield, who is known for his slow takes. Poor Barefield was stupefied. I yelled into the phone "B-1 withdrawing!" An 82 landed quite near; the concussion was terrific. Hogg pushed Barefield out of the entrance as another projectile screamed downward, exploding close to the lip of the finger trench. Barefield screamed, "I'm hit!" Another round exploded, I think right in the trench, but further down. The concussive effect reached us with a smack, and all three of us were knocked off our feet. I understood what "seeing stars" meant. Hogg crumpled loosely in the bottom of the trench, wounded. Barefield was on his feet in a second. We were, to put it mildly, in a hurry to get out of there. Barefield was out of his mind; he half shoved and half kicked Hogg down the finger trench until he was out of Barefield's way—he was yelling at the top of his lungs but I couldn't understand a word—and then disappeared into the main trench. I dragged Hogg into the small cave near the Gun-One bunker. Barrows and Nordstrum were busy firing their machine gun toward Old Bunker.

Hogg's cheek was laid open and a piece of shrapnel was lodged in the front part of his thigh. The first thing he said was, "There's a pack of matches in my hip pocket." By the light of the matches, I found the wounds but neither of us had our first-aid packets. I scrambled up to the Gun-One bunker and borrowed Nordstrum's and at the same time had the arrogance to order both gunners to get down in the cave. Both of them have been in the Corps three times as long as I have, but pieces of shrapnel were flying through the air around the bunker and one might have come through the parapet, in front of which they were standing. They weren't accomplishing much by firing the gun anyway. Nordstrum was hit in the hand by a piece of shrapnel, but I haven't been able to find out when it happened.

We did our best to bandage Hogg. He muttered something like, "I guess I'll never see Jeanne again." Barrows blew up. Following a long string of obscenities, he added, "Men are dying out there in the paddy and you sit here wailing because you got *cut* in two places."

The CP cave and the main trenches of the outpost had become crowded by this time; with stretchers and wounded men of the raiding party. Dan Keppard was working like a demon to stop the flow of blood. Lt. McGinnis was dying. A chunk of shrapnel had caught him in the anus and he lost a number of things, not that it made any difference.

It had become an emergency situation. Men were called down from the MLR to help. M/Sgt. Schiff—a dark, stocky little man who resembles a Hollywood actor named Gary Merrill —co-ordinated the traffic; leading the stretcher-bearers into the trenches of New Bunker. The bombardment slackened momen-

195

tarily, and Barrows and I took Hogg down to the CP, getting the shock of our lives. It would take an Ambrose Bierce to describe the shadows and sounds and faces down there. Lt. Guyol was there, weeping. He had been out in the paddy bringing people in. We didn't hang around. The barrage resumed its former intensity, as Barrows and I made our way back to the right flank of the outpost. Barefield, despite his cry, had not been wounded and was huddling in one of the fighting-holes near Gun-One. He reported that burp-gun fire was being directed intermittently on the B-1 knoll, suggesting the possibility of a probe. This sounded incongruous at the time, but he was not mistaken. We were forced to find shelter in the cave, probe or no probe.

The barrage continued. Our own mortar and artillery crews were retaliating with a counterbarrage, and the din was unbelievable. As far as I remember, no thoughts entered my head during this period. I think we all had alternate surges of panic and control. Melodramatic as it may seem, a melody ran through my mind, over and over, a fragment of a melody. I don't recall such a song, or such words but this is what it was:

When the barrage lifted, a long time later, and gradually died out, we sat numb and silent and wondered how many casualties there were.

Today we learned the number, and it is appalling. Nine dead. Twenty-seven wounded. Two men were missing. An estimated twenty Chinese casualties; but that is pure guesswork.

The combat patrol-turned-raid was a complete failure. The thing that is most disturbing of all is the fact that two men are missing. One of them is known to be dead. His name is Peter Waldron. He was from Kentucky, a white-faced little guy who used to read horse-racing magazines that his folks sent him from home. He was a member of that ridiculous provisional clutch platoon back at Camp Myers. He was being carried in a stretcher during the withdrawal, when a piece of shrapnel caught one of the stretcher-bearers. Waldron, already dead, was rolled off the stretcher and the other man loaded on. Some of the men said that a group of Chinese were following the withdrawal at a distance, hoping to capture any wounded. This is hard to believe, but it is true that grenades were thrown at several of our men from a short distance. At any rate this is the excuse given for the fact that nobody went back to get Waldron's body.

No word has been passed around as to the condition or circumstance of the other M.I.A (missing in action). His name is Sidney Carlough. Barrows knew him well; they had served together on Guam.

Nordstrum was evacuated. A shrapnel wound in the hand. Dan said that he might lose a finger. Hogg was evacuated; he will be all right. Nate Bell, a new member of our squad who had remained on the MLR, was hit in the butt and evacuated. He had come down into the paddy as a stretcher-bearer. We have been unable to find out any more about him, his condition. Vincent Dell-Aquila, who was the clown of the ——— platoon, was killed. He was a member of the supporting group. Two of the K.I.A.s were flame thrower men. I don't know whether or not they had a chance to use the weapon. Throughout the remaining hours of the night we could hear the drone of helicopters coming in to pick up the wounded as they were brought in. The helicopter strip is located behind the MLR. Besides Hogg and Nordstrum, the other men on this outpost who got hit were: Bull Goldstein, wounded in the nose; Alan Sisco, received a concussion; and Savario Marano, wounded in the legs. These men were all evacuated except Goldstein.

Lt. Buell met me in the trench later and said, "Sorry you didn't go along?" When it began to get light, the men on B-3 reported that there are two straw mats lying across the concertina wire in front of them, and possibly a body, but they aren't certain. This makes it quite clear that a unit of Chinese had at' tempted to probe B-3. It is likely that whoever they were, they were not sent from Old Bunker.

The final touch to the evening was this. Several minutes after the barrage died out, we all heard a strange, dreamlike sound. We came outside and listened to it. From high above us, somewhere along the crest of the lofty MLR range, a powerful voice was calling. Each word echoed, and is still echoing within the minds of some of us.

"THIS—IS—LIEUTENANT—CASIMETTI. ARE—THERE—ANY—MORE—MARINES—OUT—THERE? . . . THIS—IS—CASIMETTI. IS—THERE—ANYONE—ELSE—OUT—THERE . . . ?"

Thirteenth day, New Bunker outpost. It is still March, I believe

Shortly after I stopped writing yesterday Pugnacci awoke from a fitful nap and we talked about it. The ill feeling of the night before still hung in the air. It was very quiet, which wasn't helpful. Intermittent machine-gun fire or distant mortar explosions are somehow cheerful. Pugnacci was sullen, brooding. I wasn't exactly scintillating myself. We began talking about different things, all having to do with home. It wasn't mawkish, but he moved me deeply when he began talking about what his farm is like. I told him about the summers I've spent working on farms in Wyoming County, New York. He asked me to come stay at his farm for a while when I get discharged. But it wasn't a mawkish thing. It began to grow dark outside and the Coleman stove on which we were boiling water made less morbid the feeling one usually has at dusk. Pugnacci began talking faster, the rhapsodical quality was gone; he was trying to avoid thinking about the fact that we would soon have to go out and man the listening posts, places neither of us cared to see again. Lt. Buell appeared in the entrance, out of breath.

"Either of you want to volunteer to go out and bring back Carlough?" he asked, adding that he had already found three others who would go. Pugnacci climbed out of his sleeping bag and we went out into the cold evening wind, carrying our weapons, helmets, armored jackets and ammunition. The briefing, held by Lt. Buell outside the CP, went something like this:

"There's no time for a thorough briefing. We've got to get out there before it gets dark. Listen up: Captain Krupp called me this morning and said that Carlough can be seen from the MLR. He's lying beside the path between Old Bunker and here. The goonies have probably spotted him, too; so we'll have to get to him before they do. Sgt. Van Horn will take the point. I'll be behind him. Russ and Tumbleweed will be behind me. Then Lo Castro and Ankers. Clark, you bring up the rear. Russ, I want you to carry the prc-6 (radio). Tumbleweed, you carry the stretcher. Van Horn, as soon as you see the body, motion to us and we'll lay down and cover you. I want you to examine it carefully for booby traps. Roll it over. When you've done that, motion to us again. I'll join you and we'll move further on a few feet and lie down there, facing Old Bunker. Then, Russ and Tumbleweed, you two move up and load the body on the stretcher. Move out immediately—we'll follow you. Russ, keep the radio on but turn the volume way down. Nobody's going to call us out there. If anything happens, call Lt. Knight on Hedy. He'll be standing by. Any questions? . . . Let's go."

As we passed through the Gun-Four gate I contacted Lt. Knight at Buell's request. The message was: "Rolls-Royce is leaving the Champagne." The snatch party is leaving the outpost. He replied, "Tell the boss: Good luck." But we were already in No Man's Land, trotting along at a rapid rate.

We were profoundly uneasy for several reasons. We were covering ground that had been a hellhole the night before. There were craters everywhere. The Chinese might detect us and push the same horrendous panic button. Or a Chinese ambush might be set up around the body, knowing that a snatch party would come, sooner or later. And last of all, Van Horn, Tumblehead and myself were going to handle the body of someone we knew.

We went along the path for a couple of hundred yards, stepping around the craters. Van Horn, up ahead, halted abruptly and raised his hand. We lay down. Van Horn crawled up to it, a dark form beside the path. He examined it and rolled it over. No booby traps. The lieutenant moved ahead, and he and Van Horn lay down, facing the other way, ten yards beyond the corpse. Tumbleweed and I moved up. We lay the stretcher beside Carlough. He was lying on his side, like a fetus. His face was covered with a mask of blood and the blood gave off an odor. Decomposition had progressed enough so that the smell was like that of a dead woodchuck. It occurred to me that the decay of animals and humans are alike in smell. It was faint but unmistakable. Tumbleweed, a less morbid soul than myself, averted his head as we loaded the stretcher. He picked up the lower part and I reached under the armpits to lift. Van Horn had picked up an M-1 rifle that was left out there; he placed it on top of the body. We moved out, retracing our steps. Lt. Buell and Van Horn covered the rear. Clark was now the point man. After moving for several yards, Tumbleweed—whose name is Herbert McMaster —tripped on the edge of one of the shell holes. Carlough toppled out and fell on the ground. We loaded him back on. His arms were bent at the elbows and poised over his chest; he must have died that way. I lifted him by the elbows and they were stiff. I recall that Tumbleweed made a peculiar sound as we loaded Carlough the second time. It was a vocal shudder, and it came from his stomach: "Huh-ugh." The stretcher was extremely heavy, and the BAR and radio were swinging back and forth across my chest and back. We tripped again and Carlough toppled out. Tumbleweed, who is a new replacement, was shook and exhausted; he would not handle the body again. He made that sound again, "Huh-ugh." Ankers was standing nearby; I motioned for him to help me. He shook his head negatively. I groped out and clamped my hand on his bicep and squeezed so hard that he batted me on the shoulder to stop. Together we loaded the stretcher, and moved out once more. The M-1 kept falling off, sliding down from atop the body. Each time it fell we were forced to put down the stretcher to replace it. No one was expected to carry it; there were few enough of us, and two of us already carried extra gear, leaving but five men who were able to use their weapons at once if necessary.

By the time we reached the cut-off trail approaching New Bunker it was dark and Ankers and I were breathing like steam engines. We left the body on the lip of the trench outside Gun-Four. Lt. Buell told everyone to return quickly to his post. I sat down in the trench, not far from the body, and made contact by radio with Lt. Knight on Hedy. "The Rolls-Royce was successful." That was all. He said, "Congratulations." Barrows, a big cowboy from Texas, came along the trench, stepped over me, and went over to look at Carlough. He stood there for some time, staring. Then he went into the Gun-Four bunker, borrowed a poncho and brought it outside, with which he covered the remains. He looked down at the thing for a moment, said "Shit," and went away. So much for Sid Carlough.

My hands are remarkably repulsive. They have not been washed for two weeks, despite the variety of charming things I've handled. It looks as though I'm wearing black gloves—the stain and residue from a number of commodities: tobacco, molasses (from the C-ration beans), jam, rifle oil, bore cleaner and blood, all of which are caked together in the pores. Why not wash? No god-damned water, sez I. The risk involved in carrying out supplies to us is considerable, due to the ominous presence of the snipers, who seem to have formed a perimeter around us. The supply train—ten yo-bos and four marines—cannot be hindered by excess impedimenta, so that we receive a disappointingly small amount of ammunition, food and water. Accordingly water is used primarily for drinking. Few of us retain enough dignity or interest to wash in the dregs of a five-gallon water can. With this ice-cold water, I manage to brush my teeth every night—a luxury most of the men at the Chosin reservoir were deprived of.

No one has shaved. Lt. Buell made the un-lieutenant-like remark that this was what he often looked like at Princeton. As a matter of fact he's beginning to look like a caricature of a starving and consumptive poet.

The rest of the night was normally quiet; not even the loudspeaker.

Fourteenth day, New Bunker. March, 1953

Last night was unusually quiet. I think the Chinese are as reluctant to leave their trenches as we are.

At dusk we whistled at Chief, but he did not answer. Before midnight we noticed a fire, burning somewhere in the vicinity of Hedy. We couldn't actually see the flames, only the reflection against the higher surrounding slopes of the MLR. There is a demolished marine tank in front of Hedy. It was believed that a sniper inhabited it during the day, that possibly it was he who killed Riley. We learned today that it was the tank that was being burned last night. How a tank can be burned is a mystery to me.

Barefield is still shaken. We usually talk together in low voices during the night on B-1; last night he insisted that we whisper.

Fifteenth day, New Bunker

Yesterday afternoon: before crawling into the sleeping bag yesterday morning I had a clear, sudden picture of something that I was going to do. When I awoke at 1:30 p.m. I thought about it some more and then went to work.

Carrying BAR and binoculars, I went up to B-1 and began building a crude stand of sandbags inside of the bunker, having removed them from the new rear wall. The BAR was then placed so that its stock was supported by the stand and so that the muzzle extended roughly toward Chief's hole, resting (that is, the muzzle) within the crotch of two sandbags of the parapet. The magazine contained only one round. Aiming the piece toward Chief's hole, having located the target through the field glasses, I squeezed off one round and observed the strike of the bullet. It landed two or three feet to the left of the target, kicking up a little spray of sand. It was necessary to place sandbags on either side of the stock in order to compensate for the recoil. Firing again from a magazine of one round, the slug skimmed the right flank of the hole. As I mentioned before, his hole is not actually visible, although its exact relative position is. By using this trial and error method, the weapon was within four rounds precisely trained or zeroed-in on Chief. To explain further: That fourth round skimmed the foward lip of the enemy trench, a few inches off the ground above which Chief had appeared on several occasions. This last round buried itself in the sand of the small dune that rises immediately behind the hole, so that Chief, had he appeared in his usual place at that moment, would have been shot through the chest. The object was to lure him into appearing that night. The BAR would be trained on him.

We were not absolutely certain that he stands watch in the same position each night. However, the two times we have seen him, he has occupied exactly the same spot.

Without disturbing the fixed line of aim, I removed the magazine from below, inserted a round of tracer ammunition in it, and replaced the magazine slowly in the weapon. I left it in this condition.

Pugnacci had asserted that Chief probably occupies his position in somewhat the same manner as we occupy Burgundy-One; that is, only at night and sometimes a few minutes after dawn. If this is so, Chief would probably not have been aware of the zeroing-in process described above.

At dusk, Barefield and I occupied B-1. We did not whistle, or make any noise whatever. The night was cool and windless. Some time after midnight the moon rose. This is what we had been waiting for. The moon shone on the vast white terrain, casting jagged shadows, and we knew that our bunker was visible to Chief. Barefield knew about the BAR and was careful not to disturb its position.

Near 2 A.M. Barefield crawled outside and lay beside the bunker. Sitting inside, beside the BAR, I stuck my finger within the trigger guard and waited. Barefield began scraping the hard earth with his entrenching tool, making considerable noise. We gambled; either Chief would see Barefield and fire at him, or he would call in mortars again. In either case, we were both ready to race down the finger trench to Gun-One at a moment's notice. Barefield was gambling on Chief's lack of marksmanship.

Chief did not wait long. He fired one shot, which made a TSING! noise as it whipped overhead. Barefield's ears rang. When Chief fired the second time, I squeezed the trigger. The weapon shuddered and coughed once, and we watched the brilliant burning red trajectory as it streaked across the seventy-five-yard expanse, disappearing into one of the shadows among the low cluster of dunes. I heard Barefield say, "Gung ho, you poor bastard."

He crawled back inside and we sat silently for the rest of the night. We haven't heard from Chief since and doubt that anyone ever will.

Sixteenth day. New Bunker

Tumbleweed heard someone coming along the trench last night, toward his bunker. He challenged the person—we all take this precaution, always—and there was no answer. The person came closer. Tumbleweed shoved his carbine through the bunker entrance and sprayed the trench with an entire magazine, killing a large rat. This speaks well for Tumbleweed, although while telling us about it, he purposely made himself out to be the fool. From now on, people approaching his bunker call out their names, nicknames, make jokes, and wait for a full acknowledgment.

I'm still pretty jumpy myself, I guess. I approached his bunker later on, identified myself, and then came on. When I saw the dead rat, I damn near fainted. Anything dead will do it. Also, I opened up a tin of red raspberry jam this morning and found that it smelled unmistakably like Carlough did when we found him. Pugnacci has, of course, offered me tins of red raspberry jam all through the day, in his slightly sadistic way.

A Chinese patrol was spotted by one of our ambush units on Sniper ridge last night. New Bunker was alerted but no contact was made.

I went up on B-2 this morning shortly after dawn and

watched the mist disperse, and then the strings of fog that hover over the gullies. Very beautiful. Land of the morning calm is right. Despite the occasional rumblings in the distance, early mornings in Korea are almost too much to take.

The marines have a unit called "Charlie rockets." They are 4.5 rockets, and their barrages are referred to as "rocket ripples." The weapon itself is a small cart affair containing 144 tubes. They are fired from behind the MLR, and the back blast is terrific; we (and the Chinese) always know exactly where the weapon is being fired. For this reason, the rocket unit is usually dropped by a helicopter, the mission fired, the unit evacuated by the helicopter immediately to avoid a Chinese counterbarrage. It may be ridiculous to call any barrage beautiful, but if one doesn't think about it too hard, a barrage is beautiful—to watch; especially a rocket ripple. It is the most violent barrage of them all: 144 rockets are released within seconds; they pass overhead almost in formation, and land with a tremendous overlapping of explosions. Each projectile weighs 42 lbs. The range is approx. 5200 yards. The weapon is not accurate, is not used for concentrated targets. The explosions cover several hundred yards of terrain, but God help any Chinese that are not protected by a deep trench at the time of impact.

Captain Krupp has been out here twice. To Barefield and myself he said, "I understand you've been getting some work." I like the idea of this being called work.

GROUP EIGHT

‖‖‖

Hill 229

March 27th, 1953. On the MLR.

We were pulled back to the MLR without warning, a happy trip. Before leaving, we oriented the men who were to replace us; scaring hell out of the men who were taking over B-1 by our warnings and lucid descriptions.

Reaching the lines at 3 P.M.—we accompanied the supply train—we occupied our new positions and stood watch for the rest of the night. The hills of No Man's Land are sprawled out below us now. New Bunker is a low, broad knoll. B-1 is visible, far below, an extraordinary sight. Not exactly nostalgic, but extraordinary. Old Bunker appears to be larger in all respects. The sight of it alone is ghastly.

Our squad sector is three hundred yards long; there is a wide interval between each man. In almost every case we are out of sight of each other. It makes little difference; we are far safer here than on New Bunker.

After a long morning sleep in a bunker with a stove, Pugnacci, Barefield and myself climbed down the long, very steep ravine behind us and found the MESS HALL. It is a large bunker with tables inside. Hot chow is prepared back at battalion headquarters and then brought up to us, reheated. We swaggered in, bearded, filthy and stinking, and played it up to the hilt, like a bunch of asses. Danny Keppard, the black Apollo, joined us in line. He alone is beardless; says he doesn't need to shave. We sat down to a meal of spaghetti, mashed potatoes, lettuce, cake, and two cold cans of Pabst Blue Ribbon beer. Pure bliss. We made all sorts of Homeric sounds. Fartensissimo, Belchitorium. Coughilensis. Spitandum.

After the meal we sat outside in the sun and talked, told sea-stories. Each time a friend arrived—anyone we knew—we greeted each other loudly. Lester Higgins was especially happy to see us. He had remained on the MLR to take charge of the yo-bos. Higgins lay sprawled out in the sunlight, laughing boisterously and insulting us with glee. We were happy to see him. He kept saying things like, "My! You are all so lovely. So delightful. So well-scrubbed and lovely." He told us that Nate Bell was sent to the hospital at Yokasuka, Japan and that he will be back. Dudley Hogg and Lauroesch are at Able Medical Bn., and will be back shortly.

There is a wooden commode near the mess hall which we happily assaulted. Defacendorum superabundorum. Then we went back and had another meal. Later we walked to the showers, some distance away, located behind the secondary MLR. The entire platoon might have been there, including Lt. Buell. Pure delight. We shaved under the stream of hot water. What horrible sights we were when we came out into the sun. Dan handed me his pocket mirror. O, most terrible sight! A long white face covered with blackheads. We are all white, and lolled about in the sun before returning.

Back to business: That night I took out a five-man ambush, or "Mercury" as it is called. This was somewhat startling; the idea that five men were being asked to set up an ambush, with a corporal in charge. The captain was casual during the afternoon briefing. He said to pick out any four men I wished. He pointed out the check points on the map, which were as follows. One: Bunker gate—a large opening in the MLR trench, actually a revetment for a tank, called a "tank slot." Two: The little bridge at the foot of the MLR slope—there is a trail leading from

Bunker gate to the bridge. Three: The base of Hedy-Bunker ridge—on which Sniper ridge is located. We would reach check point three, the one just mentioned, after crossing a narrow rice paddy. Four: The Captain said, "I'll leave that to your discretion." I was to choose a spot that would be a logical avenue of approach for an enemy patrol. We were to keep our eyes open for snipers.

In preparation for the ambush I went down to the supply tent and wangled eight concussion grenades from Mother Connant's clutching hands. These are called "offensive grenades" in the manual; they are simply half-pound blocks of C-3, a fairly new type of explosive which resembles yellow opaque celluloid. The block is bound in cardboard. They are sent to us unfused; we screw regular fragmentation grenade fuses into them ourselves. This is a touchy procedure. The fuses are attached to blasting caps which will detonate if not handled with extreme care. Concussion grenades are not considered deadly; they are designed to stun in order to take prisoners. The Chinese use them extensively. We rarely use them. We had none on New Bunker.

Our briefing was held after dark. I chose Kostis, Pugnacci, Bloomfeld and Higgins. Each man was given two fragmentation

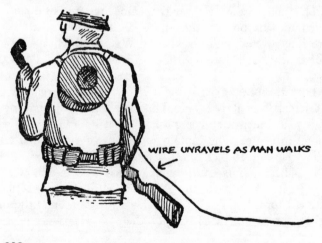

WIRE UNRAVELS AS MAN WALKS

grenades and one concussion. Pugnacci and I carried BARs, the others carbines. Higgins carried the sound-power—a field telephone attached to a spool of wire carried on the back.

We reached the Hedy-Bunker ridge at 9:30. It took us an hour to get there. After some preliminary scouting, we picked out a location and set in. It was near the general junction of Sniper ridge and the Hedy-Bunker ridge. From the air it might look something like this.

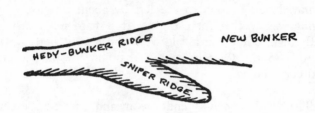

On the other hand, it might not look like that from the air, but the drawing shows the approximate layout. We were set up near where the hyphen is in the drawing, just this side (MLR side) of the skyline. This is how we were deployed.

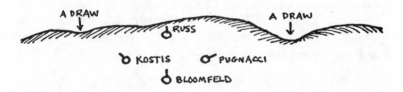

The two flank men, Pugnacious and Kostis, covered the most likely avenues of approach; two small draws, or saddles that run down the northern slopes of the ridge. These draws crossed the skyline for a few yards. This type of terrain feature would provide considerable cover for any unit wishing to cross the skyline. Bloomfeld and myself were in a position to fire quickly in any direction.

After we had been there an hour, I crawled up to the skyline and took a look. There are many bushes and small trees on the Hedy-Bunker ridge and I was well covered. Nothing to be seen except the vast piece of terrain down there. The moon came out and it became colder and windier. By this time Kostis and Higgins were bitching under their breaths. Toward 2 A.M. Andy had a coughing spell, which he couldn't seem to repress. Trying to get rid of it, at all costs, he coughed once loud and hard. I frowned on this and told him so in heated whispers. Any Chinese in the area would have heard that cough. Because of this, we moved our position to the left by about seventy-five yards. Moving was a relief for everyone. It is hard for a man to lie quietly for five hours in a cold wind and remain alert.

At 3:45 the Captain contacted us on the phone and told us to come home.

The words "goonie" and "goonyland" are used exclusively around here. I have never heard the words "Reds" or "Commies" used by anyone but Army men. They are typical of Army lingo. We saw one of their supply trucks at Camp Rose. "KILL THE COMMIE BASTARDS" was painted on the side, in large red letters. "Heartbreak Ridge" is a typical Army name for an outpost. "Operation Killer" and "Operation Smack" are the official names of two Army missions in the past. It's a small point, but the word "goonyland" has a kind of special meaning to us. Like Toyland of a department store, it suggests something innocent and—much as I hate the word—cute.

March 28th, Hill 229
Last night: A new lieutenant took out a combat patrol. Objective—Old Bunker; size of patrol—thirteen men. Lt. Sandler is McGinnis's replacement. It is interesting that the objective of his first patrol was the objective of McGinnis's last patrol. I met Lt. Sandler for the first time yesterday morning. I was a-settin' in one of the phone emplacements in the main trench, writing in this here thang. He came along, big as life, and introduce hisself. He talks with what might be called the accent

of a Virginia aristocrat. Like every marine officer I've ever seen, he is a handsome devil; fairly small, well-proportioned, has short blond hair. He was, of course, very reserved as we talked but that is always to be expected. He asked what I was doing. I said, "This is how I write letters, sir. Easier than lugging around a box of stationery and pen and ink." When I found out about the combat patrol, I found him and asked to go along. He said come back later, he'd have to ask the captain. When I did come back, he said he'd be glad to have me along.

I'll be interrupting myself many times during this narrative. The first is this. In all of these entries I've been careful not to exaggerate. I've been misinformed on many subjects I'm sure, but I have written down only what I believed to be facts. Here is the point. On several occasions I have actually toned down the facts, feeling that the truth would seem incredible to whoever reads this later. And since I intend to send the notes to Kostis, Hogg, Keppard, Lt. Buell and some of the other men when I get home, there's no reason why I should do this. If I'm writing this for anybody, it is for my friends at home. Writing about the liberty in Seoul, for instance, I made it sound as though I didn't get laid, but I did. And Chief didn't merely say "Okay." What he did say sounded so much like a movie script that I left it out. He said, "Okay, marine," and we heard him laugh. There have been other instances which I don't remember now. Not that the events of last night were especially fabulous, but from now on—no more monitoring.

Lt. Sandler briefed us in the following manner. He took a fire team (four men) at a time up to the main trench, and actually showed us the route we would take. This was infinitely more revealing than a map. Then we were gathered together behind the MLR, and he filled in the details. Sgt. Kee was to be in charge of the rescue squad. This patrol originated from the —— Platoon; I was, so to speak, the only outsider. During the patrol, the rescue squad would stand by, armed and with stretchers, in case the patrol was hit badly. We were dismissed; Lt. Sandler told Kee to take the rescue squad into the main trench and show them the route. Instead of taking them up by fire teams, Kee took them up all at once. A Chinese forward observer, an extremely talented one, spotted Kee and his men all huddled together on the skyline, gazing over the edge. One 60mm. round was sent out; the most precise placement of a mortar that I've ever seen or heard about. It exploded smack in the middle of the group. This is the unbelievable I was talking about; and it is even more unbelievable that none of the men were killed. There were eleven men in Kee's squad, all of whom were hit by shrapnel. All but three were evacuated by helicopter. The remaining three were caught by splinters, causing numerous minor cuts. Two of them, however, were so badly shaken that the captain sent them back to the battalion command post for a two-day rest. One of the eleven lost his foot. Two others have shredded legs. Another caught many pieces of shrapnel in the face and neck.

Pfc. Garapedian, who was nearby, described the incident to me. He said that he heard the shell land, that he ran down the trench and found them all lying down, stunned and bloody. He used the word "slaughterhouse." He couldn't give them any immediate help so he sprinted down the tank road, yelling for the corpsman.

The —— platoon has had terrible luck. They were the ones who made the raid on Old Bunker the other night. This makes a grand total of forty-four men that they have lost within the past three weeks. A hard-luck outfit if there ever was one. It occurred to me that maybe I shouldn't offer them my services any more.

The combat patrol was postponed for an hour. No doubt every one of those men were nervous as hell about going near Old Bunker; some of them had been on that raid. No one else has bothered Old Bunker since then, when they retaliated so goddamned viciously. We would be the first.

I found Dan Keppard, old father-confessor, and told him my troubles; how scared I was. He told me that I was an ass to have volunteered, and he gave me a little bottle of codeine. He assured me that it would help.

At 11:30 we filed past Bunker gate. My legs were shaky during the descent but it was due to the codeine, not fear.

The point man was John Cahill, a red-faced, apish man. I had the doubtful honor of following him. Lt. Sandler was third in line. We three had crossed the little bridge at the bottom of the MLR slope and were climbing the small rise to the plateau of the rice paddy, when another piece of bad luck fell on the ———— platoon. A Chinese forward observer, another talented gentleman, who was probably watching us from the Hedy-Bunker ridge, called in a round on the column—an 82mm. projectile. The placement of this round was excellent, except that it landed in the stream bed and almost all of the shrapnel was absorbed or diverted. At any rate, no one was hit although it exploded less than fifteen yards from me, and I believe that we three were the nearest to the explosion. The flash blinded me for a few seconds and the concussion knocked several of us flat. A headache for me, nothing more. Ears ringing loudly, and seeing stars again. We all thought that everyone had been hit. Cahill and the lieutenant ran along the column, checking for wounded. Only Pfc. Garapedian, with a wrenched back. When the shell exploded we were all erect; no one had time to fall down. Had it landed on firm ground there is no doubt that several of us would have been clobbered. The sound it made was Whffump!

We climbed back to the MLR and took a break. More codeine for Old Doctor Trepidation. Ten minutes later, off we went again. No need to comment upon our mental status. Cahill led us across the narrow rice paddy which runs a short way past the little bridge, along the path which skirts the base of the Hedy-Bunker ridge and Sniper Ridge. We passed the southern slopes of New Bunker. Burgundy-One was not visible. We passed over the spot where Carlough had lain. There we were again, right in the middle of that rice paddy, that had been the impact area for Chinese artillery and mortars. We were completely exposed. The only available cover was the craters.

We approached the first broad knoll of Old Bunker hill mass, and heard a whistle from somewhere on the skyline. We halted. More whistles, fainter this time. Could it have been a relay system?

When we moved on, two men from the rear of the column sent the word up that they had spotted what looked like flashlights on the skyline, blinking for a second. (I never mentioned it, but we saw lights in No Man's Land a few times when we were on New Bunker. Sometimes they were matches that were lighting cigarettes in the distance, or sometimes they were cigarette coals not so far away. Sometimes they were green, and sometimes they resembled pocket flashlights. These lights were not seen often; I don't mean to give the impression that the Chinese held candle parades out there.) In spite of the relay system that announced our arrival, we kept moving forward.

From the ——— squad, ——— platoon sector of the MLR, Old Bunker looks like this.

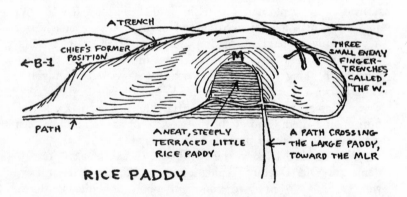

RICE PADDY

The mission of last week's Diesel was to enter the W-shaped group of trenches, but they never made it. This is the hill on which an old college friend, Leslie Baker, who used to play fine bop trumpet at the Hotel Harrington in Canton, this is the hill (I say) where Les got wounded several months ago. I wonder if he knows that the Chinese have the hill now. He probably wouldn't care. The old marine command post, a cave which is no longer visible, was located in the following place "M" in the above drawing.

For clarity I'll refer to that little terraced rice paddy as the "terrace." As we approached the terrace, the lieutenant halted us and we were deployed in an L shape, facing the slope of the "W." In this position we were able to deliver fire on any part of the immediate skyline. When the base of fire was in position, the scouting party went forward; Cahill, myself, Lt. Sandler and Cpl. Medve. With each step, I made note of the nearest crater and was ready to leap into it as soon as we were fired upon. Most of our attention was directed on the "W" trench area. There was no doubt in anyone's mind that a group of Chinese soldiers were watching us as we crept along the lower part of the terrace.

Reaching the other side, we lay down. It was a windy night. The moon appeared briefly every minute or so, until a bank of clouds obscured it. My BAR was trained on the "W." If a single Chinese had fired one round, I would have emptied an entire magazine at the skyline, and so would have the other twelve men.

Our mission was to see if Waldron's body was lying in the terrace; and also to look for a flame thrower that had been left out there during the raid. We saw neither.

The distance between we four and the "W" was somewhere between twenty and thirty yards. Evidently the Chinese were waiting for us to ascend the slope, as they had waited for McGinnis to ascend the slope, before opening fire. But none of us took a step up that slope. We were easily within grenade range.

In a whisper that was much too loud, Lt. Sandler said, "About face—move out." When we reached the other side of the terrace, we came across a clump of what resembled yellow poppy. I had noticed it from the MLR that morning. The base of fire fell in column behind us, we rounded the knoll, out of sight of the "W" and returned to the MLR.

Cahill said later that he had heard a movement in the dirt above him as we did the about-face. Jesus, we were lucky. The captain was highly relieved when we entered the CP. He debriefed the four men of the scouting party. We told him that Waldron was not out there.

Old Bunker has a definite personality. From down in the

rice paddy, it looks like two huge, well-formed breasts. So much for the outline. The hill mass itself is almost facial. No eyes, or features; but the general look of it is a giant's head, scowling.

March 29th, Hill 229

A little package today from home. I should mention that letters and packages come often. Today's package contained four Penguin books: Plays by Sophocles, *Candida* by Shaw, *Imitation of Christ* by Thomas a Kempis, and a little stiff-backed volume called *Some British Beetles*. I'm afraid none of them will be read until we go into reserve once more.

Every afternoon I carry a blanket up to an old deserted bunker just behind the MLR and write in this thing. I write until it becomes late afternoon. I loathe late afternoon, and this is so distracting that I stop scribbling as soon as I notice that the shadows are beginning to lengthen. It always makes me think of New York, when the street lights go on and crowds of people leave the office buildings. Late afternoon means that it will soon be time for the patrols to get ready to depart. Only when it becomes totally dark does this uneasy feeling go away, or diminish. Late afternoon is the time of day when the men are at their lowest.

Last night I went along on a ———— squad reconnaissance patrol. Sgt. Van Horn was the point man, I was behind him, Lt. Buell was behind me, then Pfc. Haals with the sound-power, Pfc. Ankers with the pro-6, Cpl. Lo Castro, and last of all Pfc. Bartlett. The patrol was scheduled to leave at 1:30 A.M. During the early part of the night, Barefield and I stood watch on one of the two listening posts in the squad sector; Big Dick and Little Peter.

When the column moved out, at 1:30, I was immediately impressed by Van Horn's stealth as we descended the MLR slope below Bunker gate. He has a reputation for this, and for being a good man to have around in a fire fight. He made no sound whatever as he moved. This takes talent.

The first check point was the little wooden bridge. Then we

216

crossed the narrow paddy and ascended the Hedy-Bunker ridgeline, passing the spots where our four-man ambush had been set up the other night. We turned right and moved in the direction of New Bunker. Check point two was the highest point of this ridge, a small knoll which overlooks Sniper Ridge. There is vegetation on this ridge, it is difficult to move silently through it. We remained at check point two for an hour. Twice we heard a faint whistle behind us.

We moved out again, and soon came upon the left flank bunker of the New Bunker outpost—Lorretta. We had left the vegetated area and were moving across light sand-shale. We lay down within fifteen yards of Lorretta, on the other side of the concertina, and Haals whispered, "Check point three," into the phone. We turned left and moved north, into the gradual slope that leads eventually into the vast rice paddy down there in goonyland, with its network of trenches. During the briefing we were told that the first Chinese trench begins within two hundred yards from New Bunker. It runs east-west and is believed to be occupied. It is probably from this trench that we have seen wisps of smoke rising during the day, which we presume to be smoke from stoves. Van Horn knew exactly how far to go and we halted halfway between New Bunker and the Chinese trench, which none of us have seen but which we know is there. At this point we turned right and moved parallel to it. We crossed a wide draw. This draw begins below the B-2 bunker and continues as far as the lowlands. The ruins of the tiny village are contained within it, but we didn't go down that far. This was one of those "see what there is to see" patrols. Lt. Buell knew better than to go snooping around those ruins. It was here that we had seen the green lantern the other night. We halted on the other side of the draw—check point four. Looking up at the skyline, we found that B-2 is not visible. Hogg and Pugnacci had believed it to be when they occupied it. It was very strange walking around the outside of New Bunker, over ground that we were so nervous about before.

The Meander lay behind us; that is, between B-2 and our column. I reminded Van Horn of this. We went on, moving east, parallel to and in front of New Bunker. Within a few yards we came across the Meander and found that it was almost filled with dirt, rocks and some flattened out rolls of U. S. concertina wire. It is only two or two and a half feet deep. We stepped across, and turned south in order to skirt the flank of B-1. The old hacienda looks entirely different from out there. The B-1 bunker is on the skyline. I'll never know why we weren't blasted off the map. The men on B-1 were watching us, of course, but could neither be seen nor heard. The sky was overcast last night; no moon.

Check point five was established in front of B-1. We lay there for a while, then descended the southern slope, passing the graveyard. Van Horn suddenly tumbled to the ground and motioned vigorously for us to do the same. Down in the paddy, we could barely make out movement, not far away. Haals reported this to the captain in the CP and was informed that what we saw was a friendly Cadillac—another recon patrol. When we got back, Lt. Buell raised a stink about this. We might have decided to open fire on them, believing them to be Chinese. In other words, we should have been informed that we were working near another marine patrol.

We returned to the lines at 4:30 and were de-briefed by the captain. There was a tremendous can of coffee waiting and a large box of doughnuts, just the kind I like—no holes, plain, various shapes, sometimes called crullers I think. When no one was looking I filled my sweaty helmet with them and got away with about fifteen.

April 3rd, 1953. Hill 229

Last night: another Diesel, led by Lt. Buell. Two squads, plus two machine-gun crews. Our point of departure was (that is to say, we left the MLR) at Hedy gate, which does not look like a gate.

Hedy gate is where the seven-foot-deep trench begins which ends on outpost Hedy, thus connecting the outpost with the lines. The tank slot, on the other hand, is the beginning of a road which was leveled several months ago, that is, the road was put down several months ago. No tanks use the road any more. The last one that did—a flame-thrower tank—was knocked out by a 76-mm. barrage and is still in position in front of Hedy. This is the tank that was burned the other night.

About halfway between Hedy gate and the outpost, we climbed out of the trench and crawled across the tank road. A small, steep slope on the other side of the road, leading down into a series of dunes. This terrain is new to me, and I would have lost any sense of direction were it not for the Panmunjom searchlight directly west, and the quad-50s that fire occasionally from the lofty ridge behind the MLR.

We entered a draw which has apparently been used by hundreds of other patrols. A nightmare of communication wire. Tremendous bunches of black strands through which we constantly tripped.

Tumbleweed, who is probably ashamed of the slight squeamishness he displayed on New Bunker, showed up at the briefing that afternoon and announced that he wished to volunteer for the patrol. He was loaded down with bandoleers of ammunition and grenades, and, with his deadpan, he was very comical. He looked as though he had been on Guadalcanal for a year. He had not been to the showers yet, a lapse of three weeks. The lieutenant replied, "Sorry, lad. You spend the night standing watch. And I want you to be thinking about ways to make yourself more presentable." Presentable to whom? Has Buell been reading about Sparta, too?

As I mentioned, I don't actually know where we were last night—somewhere northwest of Hedy, a considerable distance out. During the briefing the lieutenant had said that he hoped we'd make contact with the enemy. We hoped so, too, and were decked out like a bunch of movie marines; soot from the stoves all over our faces and hands, little twigs of pine in our helmets, and armed to the teeth. There were thirty of us and, although we moved silently, we had the confidence of a damned regiment.

The moon was not out but the shallow puddles of water in the paddies reflected the stars. We halted near a ridgetop. The base of fire, including the two machine guns, were deployed. We waited an hour. Then the lieutenant sent Sgt. Henion's squad down the slope—a hundred yards down. From the ridgetop we commanded a view of goonyland proper. The network of enemy trenches stretched out below us. Of course we couldn't see anything—except three distinct fires in the distance, possibly from an earlier white phosphorous barrage. Henion and his men returned in twenty minutes. They had seen or heard nothing.

On the way back we were spotted or heard by a forward observer. Five 60mm. projectiles landed nearby, but we kept moving and nobody was hurt.

A tremendous hill mass was visible, west of Hedy, a larger hill than any of the others in this sector. This was outpost Ingrid, the million-dollar outpost; so called because of the collection of mine fields that cover its forward slopes. There are also a number of big oil drums, filled with napalm, which have been placed within the mine fields. These can be detonated by means of an electric charge emanating from the outpost itself.

No contact was made last night.

April 4th, 1953. Hill 229

A description of procedure: When an NCO is told that he is scheduled to take out a patrol, and told the number of men he will need, he goes around to each bunker in his squad or platoon sector and asks for volunteers. Most of the places in the patrol will be filled by volunteers; the others he must choose. The point is that there is no rotation system in marine patrolling. No one has to volunteer for anything. A man could conceivably spend all his nights on line standing trench watch which, though safer, is a drag.

To say that sleeping on watch is frowned upon would be a howling understatement. The punishment for those caught is extremely severe—not death, as in the old days, but a good fat court martial, with a sure bust to private, and a long stretch in the brig, or rather naval prison. One might think that it would be impossible to nod off under such circumstances: being in a combat situation, and knowing the punishment if caught. But it is not impossible. I shouldn't underrate the hardships of the latter stage of the Korean war—let us hope this is the latter stage—but it is true that our schedule is such that we can get all the sleep we want on line, unless things become a shambles as they do from time to time. Even so, most of us have spent our lives sleeping at night and one never seems to get accustomed to staying up all night, just standing or sitting in a trench. In general, the men are extremely alert during the early hours of the night. After two or three o'clock one has to fight off drowsiness, if all is quiet. This happened many times on B-1. Although no one actually went to sleep, we were constantly nudging each other when a head would begin to drop slowly onto the man's chest. The hour from 3 to 4 is the worst. After that, one looks forward to dawn and the sleeping bag. The early hours are the daydream hours; it is then that the fantasies are in full swing.

Sgt. Barefield came around yesterday afternoon and asked if I would care to go along on his four-man reconnaissance patrol. Knowing Barefield's military aptitude, I asked for particulars. He explained the mission. The more he talked the more I realized that this could well be the end of four innocent men; a suicide mission. Actually, this patrol was routine; the same route was covered by a different patrol each night. But, Barefield—oh, never mind. [The drawing on page 222 shows our check points.]

Barefield is a nice guy. He is a gentle soul, and more considerate than any other NCO around here. But he is dangerously simple and should not be asked to lead men on a patrol. For some strange reason I agreed to go along with him. I don't mean to imply that it was because of loyalty or anxiety for Barefield's safety; I just found myself accepting.

There's no sense describing that patrol except by way of a

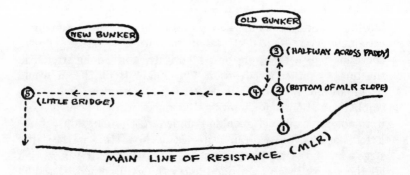

MAIN LINE OF RESISTANCE (MLR)

few comments. The idea of approaching Old Bunker, that scowling face, accompanied by only three other men, was slightly unnerving. The fact that Barefield has a very bad sense of direction, as well as an overdeveloped imagination, made it worse. I was frankly afraid that he would get lost in the paddy and lead us ALL the way across instead of halting halfway. I conned him into letting me take the point, but he was reluctant as hell. It would be so much better for him if he weren't gung ho. The fact that the sky was overcast lent some cheer to the venture; at least the Chinese would be less likely to spot us. The patrol was an UTTER *shambles.*

No action—thank God. But we made more noise than a herd of dinosaur. We lost use of the radio—a tube blew, we think, and since we carried no sound-power, we were unable to maintain contact with the CP beyond check point three. The result was that, as we approached New Bunker, we were spotted and/or heard. They had not been alerted because the captain was waiting for us to call in from check point four. We were mistaken for Chinese. The men on New Bunker called for a flare. Two were sent out. We were exposed, in the middle of the paddy. A machine gun opened up—we think it was Lorretta —and the rice paddy was sprayed. We hurtled for cover among the craters. Kostis, always in command of himself, reacted first; he shouted, at the top of his lungs: "A Cadillac! A friendly Cadillac!" No more bursts from the machine gun. From New

222

Bunker, someone shouted, "What's your name?" "Andrew J. Kostis." A pause, then the voice from New Bunker: a mumbled, "Sorry." Kostis shouted back, in a very loud voice, "Oh, that's O.K., ace. Anytime." The entire conversation was surely audible for some distance, so we trotted home quickly.

When I got to sleep this morning, I had lousy dreams, thanks to Barefield and his patrol. I seemed to sleep with my eyes partially open. Whenever I moved around inside the bag, and some light would show through the opening, I dreamt that the light was a white phosphorous explosion, and I reported this to the CP. I also dreamt that Higgins woke me up to stand trench watch. I woke up because of this and started to get dressed. Never again with Sgt. Barefield. Ever.

In describing the raid on Old Bunker the other day I mentioned that a machine-gun crew had fired tracers into the objective at dusk. The men that did this were Bamburger and Reshevsky, who are not machine gunners. The story is that they stole a gun from an army supply depot while we were at Camp Myers, and sneaked it up to the MLR. Bamburger and Reshevsky were among the thirteen men wounded by the amazing 60-mm. shot the other evening. Dan Keppard said that Bamburger's legs were shattered and that he might lose one of them. The machine gun is still here in our squad sector and it is somewhat of a comfort.

April 7th, Hill 229

Standing next to Mother Connant's supply tent, which is at the bottom of the slope behind the MLR, this is what one sees—looking up toward the MLR.

It's a long way up there, a stiff climb. I left out all the details; the bunkers, ammo dumps, gullies, little plateaus. Our squad sector is out of sight to the right, around a wide bend. We have two patrol gates: Ginger Gate and Tunnel Gun. (There is a marine outpost to the right of our right flank called Ginger.

223

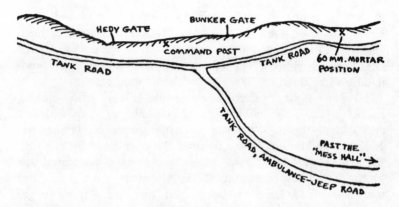

Here are the names of some of the other marine outposts: Kate, Ingrid, Marilyn, Hedy, Dagmar, Ava, Corrine, Berlin, East Berlin, Reno, Carson, Vegas, Elko, New Bunker.) The ——— squad, ——— platoon, occupies the company right flank. Tunnel Gun is a machine-gun bunker in our sector. There is an opening in the trench beside it. To give some idea of the distance shown in the drawing—the distance between Hedy gate and Bunker gate is about 250 yards. It is a long walk from the ——— squad sector to the company CP.

I have already described the terrain to the north. Looking south from the MLR trench, the terrain is even more extensive. The group of tremendous craggy mountains that surround the city of Seoul can actually be seen from where we are. They are at least twenty miles away. The outcrop—and it certainly is an outcrop—looks like this.

It is referred to as Castle Rock.

224

April 8th, 1953

Another Diesel last night. Some business. I mean, we got some business. When the volunteers and chosen ones were gathered, we were all taken down to the CP. Lt. Buell took us in, one by wide-eyed one. There is a cleverly camouflaged aperture in the north wall of the CP bunker. The lieutenant pointed out our route through the aperture, a very practical way to conduct a briefing. We were allowed to study the terrain through field glasses. When I came in he smiled and said, "I wondered if you were going to come along." (Watch that stuff, sir. Throw away that Symposium before it's too late, man.) Later we were briefed more thoroughly outside. There were sixteen of us. Our mission was to go out to a strange fortification known as the Pentagon. It is a circular trench with several angles in it. It is located startlingly near outpost Hedy; 150 yards north of it. We were told that it is used as a listening post by the Chinese.

At quarter to ten we lined up beside Bunker gate and smoked, awaiting the word to move out. The column was already formed. A small, apelike figure walked past me and went up to the point man, who was Pugnacci. He asked Pugnacci who was "the NCO in charge of the point." There wasn't such a thing, but since I was third man back in the column, Pugnacci replied, "Corporal Russ. Two men back." The figure came up to me and said, "How would you like another point?" I said, "Huh?" He said: "Another point man. I'll be way out there, see? Way out in front of Pugnacci. Like a ghost. You won't even see me." It was still dark out, the moon hadn't risen, and I couldn't recognize the man. I asked him who he was. He said: "Never mind. Listen. When we move out, I'll be right behind you. When we get past the little bridge, I'll move on up ahead. You won't see me after that, but I'll be out there." I said, "It's O.K. with me." By then I had recognized the voice. It was Top Sergeant Schiff, who is as gung ho as they come. He has been volunteering for damn near everything, which is something a master sergeant is not expected to do. Captain Krupp has pointedly suggested that he calm down and stay where he belongs, in the company CP. Lt. Buell told us this. It is for this reason that Schiff was being so secretive. He is something of a ham actor and has an affected though unoffensive tough-guy style of talking. Dan Keppard tells me that Schiff has two Purple Hearts and a Navy Cross, and the rumor is that he wants a Congressional Medal of Honor. As a matter of fact he was acting positively suicidal the night of the Old Bunker raid, racing around the rice paddy under that barrage, leading stray troops back to safety. He fell into line behind me, armed with a carbine and several grenades. The carbine had a bayonet attached.

Lt. Buell made his usual last-minute check on the column. Our faces were blacked, and we hoped that Schiff would not be recognized. But the lieutenant peered at him for a moment and said, "I appreciate this, Schiff, but—negative." The lieutenant, instead of saying, "No," always says "negative." He took the phone and said, "Tom? (Lt. Casimetti) This is Buell. The first sergeant's up here, saying goodbye to us, but looking pretty eager. I'm sending him back to the CP. Keep an eye on him." Schiff is due to return to the states in two or three days.

We moved out. I carried the sound-power and was surprised at its weight. The spool of wire is called a "speed reel." They must have weighed close to forty lbs. There were two of them, one under the other.

We descended the slope, crossed the bridge and the paddy and climbed the Hedy-Bunker ridge at a northeast angle. Soon we approached the Lorretta gun bunker. New Bunker has received a probe since we left and those boys must have taken it badly. When the gunner spotted us, he slammed the bolt of his weapon home—twice. Lock and load! meaning that he was preparing the gun for immediate use. There is no safety mechanism on the Browning machine gun; gunners normally keep the breech clear unless they expect trouble, in which case they manipulate the bolt twice, thus loading the weapon. We all hit the deck. The lieutenant yelled, "Friend! Friend! This is Buell. Hold your fire. We're friend." The men on New Bunker had been alerted this time. Buell called the captain and asked him to give the Lorretta gunners hell.

226

Hedy-Bunker ridge is extremely wide. It is composed of a series of little valleys, gullies, draws and ridges. We crossed over to the northern slopes of the ridge and crept west. After moving for three or four hundred yards—not as the crow flies, but making numerous detours in order to explore as many gullies as possible—the first speed reel played out to its end, that is, the bottom sound-power spool of wire ran out. Cpl. Stark was the man in front of me, and he kept moving ahead. I was unable to move an inch further until the bottom reel was cut and the wire attached to the other. We were in unpredictable territory and I hesitated to call out to Stark. He disappeared into the darkness. This is an easy way to lose two men. Pugnacci and Stark just kept going unaware that I was holding up the remainder of the column. Tumbleweed was behind me. When he caught up, I whispered frantically, "I can't move! Get the lieutenant!" I told the next man, Barnet, to run up ahead and stop the point. The lieutenant arrived, concerned and fatherly. "Tumbleweed tells me you're sick. What's the trouble, lad?" I was frothing at the mouth, mad at everybody. "Bull shit!" says I. "That idiot Stark never bothers to look behind him, so when the speed reel ended he kept going." Stark appeared and I told him I'd wrap my BAR around his neck if he did that again. Why did I blow out the back? They were the ones who might have gotten lost. The new reel was attached, the old reel detached and we were on our merry way.

Soon thereafter we came within sight of the Hedy finger. (Outpost Hedy is at the end of a terrain finger that juts out from the MLR.) It was still dark but we could see the outline of the demolished tank on the skyline.

As prearranged, the lieutenant instructed me to set up the base of fire. Five of us left the column. We found a good spot, northeast of the Pentagon. We deployed on the low summit of a knoll and prepared to support the assault element if necessary. I've got to stick in all these military terms somewhere. Assault element, deploy, attack phase, etc. The Pentagon is said to be hidden from view until one is right on it. This is because all of the terrain in that area, with the exception of the Hedy finger, is composed of a seemingly endless expanse of knolls and gullies. The Pentagon then does not command high ground, as most outposts do. It is merely one of the knolls. The lieutenant alone knew exactly which knoll and pointed it out to us, the base of fire, before we departed.

We were not squeamish—the Pentagon being a listening post rather than an outpost—and we set up within thirty yards of the knoll. Frankly I didn't really know where it was, the terrain is so peculiar out there. But I knew about where it was, so that we could have provided covering fire.

Two hundred yards to the south, Lt. Casimetti was standing by with a rescue squad in the Hedy trench. As a further precaution, the company mortars—three 60-mm. tubes—were registered on the Pentagon.

The main assault element was the flame-thrower team, two men. The other nine men served as their protection. To be a member of a flame-thrower unit is probably the most dangerous position a man can have. Two of them were killed during the Old Bunker raid. This is how the assault was conducted. We watched it from the nearby knoll.

The eleven men were in an echelon formation.

When the line of men reached the skyline—they crawled up to it—the flame-thrower team was brought up. Then three grenades exploded on the other side of the slope. This is what had happened. The Chinese had heard the marines as they crawled up to the skyline, and had thrown grenades. The eastern edge of the Pentagon is located approx. forty yards down the slope—according to the men in the assault element that we talked to later. The grenades had exploded short of their mark, that is, on the other side (the Pentagon side) of the slope. From this information we might suppose that three Chinese man the Pentagon listening post—since three grenades exploded in close succession.

Lt. Buell marked time. No more grenades. The flame-thrower men were given the word and they crossed the skyline. The other nine men were poised to fire their weapons; we could see that much. The flame-thrower man got up on one knee and lit the "match" by squeezing one of the handles on the gun of his weapon. The muzzle spluttered with sparks. When he squeezed the other handle the air pressure was released and the napalm flowed past the sparks. Whoosh! I've forgotten the name of it, but this is the kind of fuel that is used for shorter ranges. It billowed into a cloud of smoke and flame and rolled down the slope. Everyone was caught within the light of the swelling flames. The burst of fuel lasted for only four or five seconds. When the flame-thrower operator closed the pressure valve, he and his mate immediately backed down the slope. The blast of flame was certainly visible for miles, so we withdrew rapidly, expecting a mortar barrage. I forgot to mention one important thing. Before the flame-thrower went to work, the lieutenant ordered all nine men to heave a couple of grenades down the slope, in the direction of the Pentagon. As soon as they detonated, the flame-thrower team came up.

The base of fire guarded the rear of the column during the withdrawal. For some reason the Chinese did not send out a barrage, but we got out of there fast anyway, almost running. We climbed a few knolls, went past the demolished tank, and entered the trench of Hedy. This trench—connecting the outpost with the MLR—is partly covered with boards. Eventually the entire trench will be. What purpose do they serve? I'll find out. When we reached Hedy gate, we stood around while the lieutenant counted noses, the usual procedure. I saw one man slip away furtively and disappear down the tank road. The lieutenant counted sixteen of us, the original number. The man that slipped away had been M/Sgt. Schiff. This means that Schiff must have been wandering around out there virtually alone. This takes unspeakable guts, and is also extremely dangerous. The obvious danger is that the man could be more easily captured than if he were among a column. The other danger lies in the fact that he would probably have been fired upon if anyone in our column had seen him. Pugnacci is a remarkably alert point man. Had he seen a lone figure ahead of him, or anywhere around him, I'm fairly certain that he would have fired. Or, he would at least have halted the column and investigated. How Schiff finally included himself within the column—on the way back—is a great mystery. Ghost indeed.

April 9th, Hill 229

These notes are being written at TOP speed. All of them, except one I did at 1st Ord. Bn. I looked over some of the previous entries and should have been appalled at the clumsiness and stilted writing; but there is no time to worry about continuity and correct English; when I get home, there'll be no hurry; I'll be able to sit down at a desk in a warm room in a comfortable chair and insert some grace into this jumble of words. (Oh, don't be falsely modest, my boy. You are aware that there is a possibility of your getting killed, and you're writing this the best you know how. Isn't that so?—There is not the slightest possibility of my getting killed. However, I am writing this the best I know how.—Well, we'll have to do a little better than this, won't we?)

There were some happenings on Big Dick last night. This is one of the listening posts in front of our sector. The one in front of the ——— squad sector is called Little Peter. I like to call our listening post Gigantic Phallus. The other is a bit too crude. Cpl. Lauroesch and Pfc. Bartlett stood watch on Big Dick last night, with a sound-power. During the night they heard noises in the brush below them. They threw grenades. A few minutes later they heard a voice, way down in the rice paddy. According to both men the voice said, "Come on down, marine."

Another similar tale: The ——— platoon sent out a recon the other night, over the same route that we used during Barefield's patrol. On the way back from the Old Bunker area, they thought that they were being followed—noises behind them. A voice called out to them. The man who told me about this (Pfc. Mead Wilkes, who was a member of that patrol) reported that the voice said, "This is Lieutenant Casimetti."

We are told that there are no mine fields in this area, with the exception of the slopes of outpost Ingrid. For this reason there are no definite avenues of approach either for us or for the

230

enemy. Therefore that wild two-man ambush that Dan Keppard and I worked out at Camp Myers can't be done in this sector. There are a number of paths out there but also so many intersections that it would be a waste of time to gamble on a particular spot for the ambush. Besides that, who the hell wants to blow up a column of Chinese? Not me. I've got nothing against them. Nobody ever bothered to tell us why we should be angry. Something or other about the U.N. or something like that there. And aggressors and stuff. I don't know. And I'm willing to bet that none of the other men up here know either. It might be nice if somebody told us pretty soon.

Idea: Most of the casualties in a raid are inflicted during the withdrawal, or so it seems. Since the purpose of a raid is to climb the enemy slope, fire into the trenches, and withdraw as quickly as possible—why not use cavalry? A stable of say, forty horses could be set up in some rear area. The horses could be trained to climb hills while mounted, moving toward men firing blanks from the practice objective. If those thirteen men had been mounted during the Old Bunker assault and armed with light automatic weapons—carbines or Thompsons—the result would have been vastly different. They could have gotten out there fast, made the assault, and could have withdrawn long before the rain of mortars fell. If this idea were put into practice—which, as we all know, it will never be—a scheduled assault unit could be withdrawn to the stable area in order to practice the mounted maneuver.

Thank you very much.

About armored vests: They weigh eight pounds and are each man's most valuable piece of equipment. We are required to wear it whenever we leave our bunkers. It must be zipped. It is made of several spun-glass or nylon plates, each about 6″ by 6″. The plates (I remember now) are made of nylon and the shoulder portions are made of pliable spun glass. At first they seemed heavy, but we got used to them quickly and they are a comfort. They will not stop a rifle or machine-gun bullet (same size bullet), but they are supposed to stop burp-gun slugs. They will stop almost all kinds of shrapnel. No bayonet thrust could possibly penetrate the plates. They look like this.

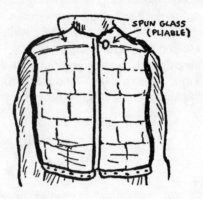

The man's arm and waist movement are not hindered in any way.

Armored shorts are not too common. They are loaned out to point men and assault squads. Lt. McGinnis was not wearing a pair during the raid. Ironical that he was hit in the area that would have been semiprotected. The shorts are made entirely of spun glass. They look like this.

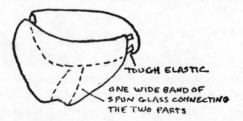

Both the vest and the shorts are covered with a strong material, a dark, green cloth.

Cpl. Cal Tibbels took out a small recon the other night and I went along for the ride. Our route included the Hedy-Bunker ridge. Cal didn't know the terrain—he just got back from NCO school—so I magnanimously took the point. No contact. Saw nothing, heard nothing. Quiet night.

Although it may sound as though these patrols are becoming routine—emotionally—each one has been a hair-raiser so far, whether we see anything or not. When I have the energy I'll describe what a point man does. That's the most challenging job of all, and strictly volunteer.

When I announced that I was joining the marines—this was at a time when I was something of an idler, dissatisfied with the way things were, and hard to get along with—Mother remarked, "Oh? Flirting with death?" She is one of the few people who know that my life is one big acting problem, a Stanislavski improvisation. At any rate, the invisible movie cameras have been collecting some fine material. The director only orders takes when I tell him; I have my unattractive moments. As a matter of cold fact, the only time I'm not reluctant to allow the cameras to shoot is when I'm talking to Garbo. That's awful hokey I know, but it's true. But I'm not going to worry my dolicocephalic head about the motive for her being here; I'll let the cats in the cutting room take care of that. And I'm also not going to think too hard about why I volunteer for everything. And I'm not going to think too. I'm not going to think. I'm not going to. I'm not going. I'm not. I'm. I.

April 11th, Hill 229

Hogg is back. He looks like he was clawed by a leopard, but he is all right. He had the humor to remark that the scar will possibly make him more attractive to his wife. Hogg, Pugnacci, Kostis and myself are living in a fairly comfortable bunker. Kostis, as I've mentioned before, is a member of the cool school. His favorite band is a fairly unknown outfit from Mexico led by Perez Prado. Andy would do the mambo well. It is a great dance for

233

cool ones. Kostis is half Greek and dark. Something of a pretty-boy, but he has fine features and large black passionless eyes—a concentrated study in boredom. He is quite vain, won't get a haircut; spends a great deal of time combing his hair. I have an imaginary picture of we two meeting, say, five years from now in some dance hall in New York. We are like brothers right now—in fact all four of us in the bunker are like brothers. I would walk up to Andy, in the dance hall—he would be doing a cool mambo with a cool chick. I would burst forth, "Andrew, my son! Hello! Hello!" Andy, I am certain, would give me the heavy-lidded stare and say, "What do you say, ace?" Back at Camp Rose I mentioned that someone had stolen a unit of morphine from Dan Keppard's medical kit. It was the Cool One. He has since admitted this to Dan, who told me. Kostis is from the Bronx.

Lester Higgins has left. We will miss that large violent man. He lives in Chicago and his ambition is to become the gigolo of a wealthy, elderly woman. Except for Dan and Higgins, I've never known any colored guys. I like to think that Higgins' humor is typically colored. It is based largely on the way he enunciates and emphasizes certain words. He always called me "Russie-May." Referred to himself as "Higgie-May." Never used the word "I." M/Sgt. Schiff is gone, minus Congressional Medal of Honor but miraculously still alive. Pfc. Dunbar Bloomfeld—O, Sasebo carniferous anti-tank mine double hanghead—is also gone. Bloomfeld can go back to Calumet City and brag that he never killed anything over here except several rats.

I took a vacation from No Man's Land last night and went exploring, behing the MLR. Hogg was working a group of yo-bos in the Hedy-MLR trench. They were putting down more boards over the trench. I paid him a visit. Later, we went out to Hedy for a look. The trench runs into the rear of the outpost. We did not actually enter the outpost because of several rolls of concertina. We talked to Pfc. Williams, who was standing watch on the other side. We exchanged sea-stories across the wire. Despite our mendacity (learned that word today), I was able to pick up

234

some information concerning the layout of Hedy. Just call me Herodotus Russ.

Hedy is a small, compact outpost, composed of a number of covered fighting-holes. Living conditions there are worse than they are on New Bunker. They are also harassed by watchful snipers. It may be a sea-story, but Williams said that he sees figures crossing the skyline between Hedy and the MLR almost every night. It is for this reason that the trench is being covered with boards. When Hogg and I heard this, we returned at once to the yo-bos, who were working alone and unarmed. The forwardmost position on Hedy is called Charlie-hole. According to Williams, the occupants of Charlie-hole have reported twice that they heard the sound of digging *beneath* them. That would certainly be an interesting way to capture Hedy. If the Chinese are digging a tunnel into Hedy, they probably began it at the Pentagon, 150 yards to the north. The work would not be too difficult since the ground is sand-shale. But this is highly doubtful.

Hedy is manned by one squad, and two machine-gun crews. New Bunker is manned by a platoon—about forty men—and four machine-gun crews. Lt. Knight is back on Hedy again after a short break. There are larger outposts in the marine sector; company-sized, for instance; but I don't know which ones.

Williams mentioned that Riley was killed because he was a souvenir-hound! "He was a fool," said Williams. "I don't feel a bit sorry for him; only for his folks."

April 12th, Hill 229

Ammunition rusts easily. The cartridge cases become discolored, a greenish mold on the brass. The rounds are used, rusty or not.

Today each squad ammo dump was filled up with a supply of the newly developed grenade. They resemble little teapots. They are olive-drab color and not corrugated like the old-type fragmentation grenades. They are smaller but a bit heavier. Not being corrugated, they explode into a hundred or more sharp splinters of steel. I believe that the old type explodes into even

235

sections; twenty-four squares. We threw some in front of the MLR to see what they were like. Compact, easy to throw, anarchist bombs.

Sgt. Suender, who is from Asheville, N. C., and who has never heard of Thomas Wolfe, took out a recon last night. They found an old cadaver, left of Hedy, near the western slope of the Pentagon knoll. The body was naked, and they were unable to determine whether it was a Chinese or an American. While they were examining it, they were spotted from the Pentagon and fired upon. One man, De John, was hit, not seriously so we are told. The body is possibly that of a marine who went berserk three months ago, and who—so the story goes—grabbed a BAR one night, leapt out of the Hedy trench and headed for goonyland before anyone could stop him.

It is not mentioned out loud, but I am acting (ham acting) squad leader of the ———— squad now. The lieutenant finally acknowledged Sgt. Barefield's ineptitude. Barefield will not take part in any more patrols. The lieutenant has made him his assistant, in such a way that Barefield's feelings are not hurt.

Hedy was probed this morning, severely. Four men were wounded, including Lt. Knight. Also corpsman Woods. The raid occurred immediately before dawn, and the Chinese unit is said to have been clobbered by our mortars during the withdrawal. Kostis and I—to the rescue— ran up to the Hedy gate and waited there, hoping, literally hoping that some Chinese would enter the Hedy-MLR trenchline so that we could play Horatio at the bridge. We were at the gate when the four wounded men were brought out. Knight and another man were unconscious and on stretchers. Woods and the other man were walking. A jeep ambulance was waiting, out on the tank road. Lt. Buell climbed down to the aid station to see Lt. Knight before the men were loaded onto the helicopter.

236

April 13th, Hill 229

Reconnaissance patrol procedure:

Recon patrol last night, myself in charge. Pugnacci, Tibbels and Kostis. We talked Kostis and Tibbels into exchanging their carbines for BARs. With a total of four BARs, we were a formidable quartet.

Briefing in the afternoon. The captain reminded us that only under the most dire circumstances does a recon patrol return fire if attacked. In the operations room of the CP bunker, he showed me the regulation map of the company sector—the company front as it is called. The map is covered each day with a fresh layer of transparent acetate or onion skin. The captain marked the route and check points of our patrol with an oil crayon. He also tested me to see if I knew the code names of the mortar concentrations. The password for the night was "Green pastures." At dusk I picked up the prc-6 and later went up to Tunnel-Gun—our exit point—to see that the new sound-power wire had been laid in from the CP. The wiremen had brought up a new speed reel and it lay nearby. I walked along the MLR and studied our actual route. This is always advisable, especially for the point man. In most cases, the check points are easily recognized since they are (usually) prominent terrain features, *i.e.*, a large clump of bushes, a junction of two paths, a bridge of planks across a stream, etc. Often the area between two check points is indeterminable, unless there happens to be a path leading from one to the other. If this is so, it is possible to pick out what might be called personal check points—a minor terrain feature of some kind.

On a map, the terrain compartments, terrain features, patrol routes, etc., are obvious to the eye. Everything appears neat and well defined. This is also the case when one looks down at the terrain from a high vantage point. But when a man is actually out there, the entire setup is different to the eye. The angles are different.

Another task which a patrol leader must carry out is to brief his men. This is pure delight, especially if one is power-mad, as one is. The men listen attentively and ask many questions. The patrol leader's word is law. When the patrol is under way, there is never any talking, never a discussion or a criticism of procedure. Even during Barefield's last patrol, no one said a word. If there is any criticism, it will be made during the patrol leader's briefing, for it is then that the patrol leader explains, among other things, how he intends to conduct the mission. The captain's briefing is a general one; the patrol leader is usually allowed to fill in his own details—the personnel, the weapons, etc.

This is the second patrol I have taken out; the other having been an ambush patrol. Something I forgot to mention: Jane Owens sent me a box of art equipment which arrived when the battalion was in reserve at Camp Rose. Pastels, crayons, stiff paper. I lacked interest—and nerve—to use the stuff, except once. I had in my belongings an elaborate Christmas card on which was printed a map of the world. "Merry Christmas" was printed within the boundaries of the larger countries in the particular language. Using a black crayon and a small pad of stiff, coarse paper, I copied the Chinese equivalent of Merry Christmas on four separate sheets.

I saved them. During the briefing for the ambush patrol, I produced them and gave one to each of the men, who knew better than to laugh out loud. My juvenile idea is that, if one of us is captured, he could impishly pull out the card and hope that the Chinaman's sense of humor is basic enough to respond to the blatant, and thus might evade immediate sessions with the thumbscrews. After the ambush, the men returned the cards. I passed them out again yesterday during the briefing.

Incidentally, each man carries a Geneva Convention card explaining that, if captured, he expects to be treated under the rules set down at the Convention, etc. Signed by MacArthur.

We blackened our faces and hands and departed at 1 A.M. Earlier that evening, Cpl. Hanna, in charge of an ambush set up on the Hedy-Bunker ridge, had spotted what he believed to be a Chinese patrol. They in turn spotted Hanna's unit and appeared to lay down about forty yards in front of them. Hanna was evidently vague as hell when reporting all this to the CP. The captain told him to wait until the Chinese began moving again. If they moved toward Hanna, he was to open fire. According to Hanna, the figures appeared to crawl backwards and disappear on the other side of the skyline. No shooting.

We reached the paddy at the bottom of the MLR slope within an hour. I was determined not to make any noise; this is why it took so long. Check point two was at the edge of the paddy. We crossed the paddy by following a large dike—not on it but beside it—which could have provided excellent cover. We were halfway between check point two and the base of Old Bunker when a loudspeaker began blaring. It was located far to the east, probably on the hill known as Siberia in front of the Charlie company sector. As usual, we only heard parts of the program but it was so interesting that we halted and lay down close beside the dike and listened. One isolated phrase sticks in my mind as one of the typical comic-book phrases: "Ike is one of the leaders who could bring about peace in Korea; but, like the rest of the big-money boys, he is not interested in peace."

A woman sang a song, a very sentimental one but quite moving. "The Last Rose of Summer." I looked back at the other three men and could see the outline of their brush-covered helmets. They were listening, too, not aware of each other, and maybe for a moment unaware of the surroundings. When the song ended, a woman said, "Did you enjoy my song, marine? If so, then fire your rifle twice and I will sing another." A wag on the MLR fired an extremely long burst from a machine gun. It echoed for several seconds. A few miles to the east, in the Army sector, five or six parachute flares hovered above the mountains. Artillery rumbled in the distance, a kind of muffled thunder. The woman sang another song. It was unfamiliar, a semi-art song. This was followed by a haunting, 1920-type number played by an American dance band of that period. I listened hard for the sound of Bix Beiderbecke or at least Henry Busse. It may have been Whiteman.

I had an imaginary picture of the Chinese nearby, listening

to the record, thinking how well it must typify the atmosphere of money-mad, capitalist, warmonger infested, modern America. Poor bastards really do need a new propaganda system. Never the twain will meet.

We made no contact last night, so I won't bother with our route. I'll describe some of the duties of a point man.

On a dark night, the normal interval between men is as follows, using a six-man patrol as an example:

←O TEN TO FIFTEEN   ←O   ←O   ←O   ←O ←O
(POINT)   YARDS AHEAD

The interval between the other men is five to seven yards, with the exception of the last man who stays close to the man in front of him and whose attention is given to the rear. The point man then is way out in front of the others. It is his responsibility to detect any signs of an enemy ambush. Unless he is completely alert, he is the one who will lead the others into an ambush, and he will be the one who steps on a land mine or tripwire. There are two hand signals most commonly used by point men. If he holds one hand in the air above him, it means that he has spotted something that he wishes to investigate. At this signal the men behind him will lie down and cover him with their weapons as he scouts. The other hand signal is a sweeping sideways movement of the arm, indicating to the others that he is about to move forward and for them to follow at the usual interval. There are other hand signals which are used occasionally; one for instance meaning, "Come here—I want to talk to you." Another: "You're getting too close to me. Maintain the proper interval." When a point man sees something that really worries him, he will merely drop down flat on the ground, and everyone behind him will do the same.

The strain on a point man is constant and he is usually exhausted by the end of the patrol. Always volunteers. There are some men, like Van Horn, who are great at it and who feel obligated to offer their services often. There are good point men and bad ones. Barefield is the worst, but as we have seen, he won't have to go out again. Pugnacci is fairly good but he is apt to drop

240

his concentration from time to time. Kostis has stated flatly that he will never ask for the point. I am about average but learning fast. The important thing, of course, is to be interested in it, and Sgt. Van Horn is the best instructor around. It may sound a bit phony, but—to me—being a good point man requires talent. It is a beautiful thing to watch a good one at work.

One more comment. This applies not only to point men but to the movement of all men while in No Man's Land. The usual method of locomotion is not merely to walk or step. The idea is obviously to move as quietly as possible. In an ideal sense, a man will support himself on one leg and with the other free foot he will poke gently at the ground in front of him. When he finds a spot that is free of twigs or leaves, he will put his weight on that foot and so continue the process throughout the entire patrol. I have never seen Van Horn move any other way. The pace is dreamlike; the first time I went on a patrol I was amazed. Kostis and I talked about it today, about the actual rate of movement. We went outside and performed a little experiment. I moved across a piece of terrain near our bunker, as though I were leading a patrol at night. Kostis timed it. In three minutes I had taken twenty-six steps—not quite nine steps a minute. When a patrol is near an enemy position, the rate of movement is infinitely slower.

One of the reasons why I'm not a very good point man is because I have a bad sense of balance. Very little of the terrain in this sector is even, only the long narrow paddy between the MLR and the Hedy-New Bunker-Old Bunker mass. The Hedy-Bunker ridge and the dunes around outpost Hedy are somewhat precipitous. It is difficult to maintain balance on one foot while the other is gingerly testing the ground ahead.

Last night, when we returned to the CP to be debriefed, the captain's face brightened. "Welcome home," he said. "Negative report, sir," said I. We returned the armored shorts that we had borrowed.

Lieutenant Buell is gone. Not home, to a rear area. He is now a "rear-echelon pogue," as we call them. Second lieutenants —cannon fodder—do not spend all of their overseas time with a line company, as enlisted infantrymen do. So Virgil Buell gets his rest with a headquarters unit and will return home alive and unscarred. I didn't get a chance to see him before he left. I would like to have gotten his home address, in Rye, N. Y. We are both due for discharge next November. Nothing would please me more than to meet him in some grey-flannel-suit bar in New York, call him Virgil, and get stoned with him.

April 15th, 1953

By candlelight; 4:30. No one else in the bunker. It is very windy outside. I'm going to take my time on this one. The climax of the events I'm going to describe occurred less than two hours ago.

Yesterday afternoon the word was passed around that there would be a raid tonight or tomorrow night. The objective would be the Fan, a Chinese outpost northwest of the Pentagon. We went down to the CP to volunteer for it and learned that a recon patrol, led by Lt. Guyol of the ——— platoon would go out that night in order to reconnoiter the target area in preparation for the raid. Kostis wasn't interested in this, but the lieutenant said he'd be glad to have an extra man along.

Lt. Guyol was in charge of the unit that relieved us on New Bunker. When he and his unit were relieved, he went down to the showers and shaved his beard—all but the chin section; leaving a natty goatee which is refreshingly out of place around here. We were first introduced to him at Camp Myers, where he delivered a lecture on military courtesy while smoking a pipe. We were impressed; he was relaxed, witty, and he made a dull subject quite interesting. Andy referred to him as a cool stud. A personable man; well-formed and obviously intelligent. Immediately popular with the men because of his knowledge of how to be friendly without being familiar.

After the briefing I asked Cpl. Hanna what kind of an officer Guyol was. "Number fucking one," he replied.

Faces and hands blackened, we left Hedy gate at 11:15, crossed the tank road one at a time, and picked our way through the tremendous tangle of barbed and communication wire; moving northwest—toward the Yolk. The terrain out there, as I have mentioned, is a series of sandy gullies and a couple of low, broad hill masses which are themselves a group of gullies. There were seven of us on that patrol; I only know the names of three: Guyol, Cpl. Hanna, and Pvt. José Rivera.

A mention of the weather is essential. It was, and still is, one of those windy nights when large banks of compact clouds are swept along, sometimes obscuring the moon. One other important fact; Lt. Guyol was the point man. This was a brave but unnecessary move on his part. The captain would have raised hell had he known. An officer is expected to take the most protected position in the column, namely the middle. Infantry second lieutenants used to be called "platoon leaders." During the Second World War they usually led their men in a literal sense, but so many were killed this way that they changed the routine a bit, calling them "platoon commanders," and tactics were modified so that lieutenants are the most protected men in their units. This makes better sense. But Guyol took the point.

Somewhere out there we made a 90-degree turn to the right and headed toward the Pentagon area. The Fan was off to our left, far down the slope. We had just executed the turn when the lieutenant halted the column and we lay down. There was a corpse up ahead. The lieutenant called the CP; we heard him say, "Let's have some instructions." We lay there for quite a while, the lieutenant alternately examining the body and talking to the captain over the wire. Presently we moved on, filing past the corpse. Hanna turned to me and whispered, "Is it a marine?" I looked down at it. Face up, no armored vest, no shoes. There were leaves and bits of debris lying about. The body was well camouflaged, as though it had lain there for some time. I decided that it was an American; why I can't say. I avoided looking at the face. We moved on.

The body lay at the entrance to a long gully, at the beginning of a gradual incline. We reached the end of the gully, on higher ground, and the lieutenant began to cross the skyline. A Maxim machine gun opened up, firing in our direction. The lieutenant, unharmed, bumbled back into the gully and we set up a hasty defense. The enemy gun seemed very close, as though it were on the other side of the ridgeline. I was undergoing a fit of the shakes, the old fear fever.

Guyol spoke with the captain again. One of the things we heard him say was, "No, that would necessitate our crossing about twenty yards of open terrain, exposed to the Fan." Guyol had two choices. We could either retrace our steps and leave the gully near the body, or we could try to cross the skyline at another point. Guyol chose the wrong one. We reformed the column; he began leading us up the side of the gully. The forward slopes of outpost Hedy were just on the other side.

In the meantime the captain had given two orders—this is a logical deduction. First, he called for an immediate mortar barrage on the Fan. Second, he contacted outpost Hedy to alert them of our approach.

When Lt. Guyol reached the skyline he was perfectly silhouetted. In spite of the fact that he was moving low to the ground, the moon made him conspicuous against the light sandshale. Two automatic weapons opened fire: a Maxim from the Fan, and a BAR from Hedy. As we learned an hour later, not all of the men on Hedy had gotten word of our approach. A marine known as Red Joe saw the figure crossing the skyline 150 yards to the right front of his position, and, believing it to be a Chinese, he opened fire. The lieutenant was hit; probably by a BAR, possibly by the Maxim also. He tumbled out of sight, down the opposite slope. There is only one way to describe the way he screamed, he sounded like a pig being castrated.

Having heard two automatic weapons on either side of us, we considered ourselves surrounded. Cpl. Hanna, second in command, took the phone and reported what was happening, emphasizing the fact that we were surrounded. We weren't, of course, but no one knew it at the time, not having recognized the sound of the BAR. Hanna urgently requested that a corpsman be sent out with a rescue squad.

The screaming was maddening. I couldn't bear it. Jo Rivera committed the bravest act I've yet seen by leaping suddenly across the skyline to retrieve the lieutenant. Rivera is a small man, but he brought the officer back in a matter of seconds. He was not fired upon.

The lieutenant was hit in the midsection. We laid him down and formed a perimeter defense around him. Rivera administered the only first aid possible; he collected our compress bandages and used them to try to stop the flow of blood. But what we needed was a corpsman, and morphine. Every breath the lieutenant took was a loud, agonized groan. "Ohh—I can't stand it!" he said. "Somebody DO something!"

We all knew that he was dying. I was guarding the lower entrance to the gully, weeping bitterly. The Chinese on the Pentagon and the Fan must have heard Guyol's outcries. We had laid him among a scattered pile of debris; some C-ration cans and pieces of tin sheeting. He often jerked his legs convulsively, kicking about the debris. The sound was terrible. In order to relieve the pain, or distract himself from it, he uttered a couple of words with each breath, with the same inflection of agony each time. He asked Rivera to hold his hand, and then to squeeze it hard. "Harder!" Between gasps he told Rivera that he would write him up for a medal, for having retrieved him. Rivera replied, "Never mind about that, sir. That was just something had to be done." Guyol told Rivera to ask him questions, to get his mind off the pain.

"How old are you, sir?"

"Twenty-two."

"What's your first name, sir?"

"Ned."

"Where do you live, sir?"

"Laramie, Wyoming."

Then a flash of pain—he cried out, "Oh, God—let me pass out! I'm scared!"

Rivera told him to lie still. "It's only a flesh wound, sir. Everything is O.K."

"More questions." He raised up and yelled to the rest of us, half delirious: "Don't bunch up!" Then, "More questions!" Rivera was tremendously shaken.

245

"How old are you, sir?"

"Twenty-two."

"Are you married, sir?"

These were Guyol's last coherent words.

"No . . . Don't even have a girl . . . mother."

By the time the rescue squad arrived he was having severe convulsions, kicking wildly among the cans and the tin sheeting. Corpsman Truro administered morphine and he was placed gingerly upon a stretcher. Before we reached the MLR the groaning ceased. It was somehow important to us that we get him back to the lines before he died, but Truro said we didn't make it.

A jeep ambulance was waiting at Hedy gate. I walked to the CP and was the first to arrive. It was crowded with people who had heard the news. Everyone quieted down. The captain said, "Let's have it," and I began to relate all that I had observed. Up to that time I thought I was pretty calm and that I was stating the facts in a composed manner. But before I had gotten two sentences out, the captain pushed me gently down on a pile of sandbags and said, "Somebody better give this man a cigarette." When the other five men arrived the captain cleared the CP and questioned each of us in turn. Three of us believed that Guyol had been killed by the Chinese Maxim, at least, three of us made that assertion. The other three believed that he had been killed by a burst of fire from outpost Hedy. But no one knew for certain. When we had finished, the captain said, "I wanted to hear your versions before telling you that Red Joe called in from Hedy and confessed to Lt. Casimetti that he was the one." "Confessed" was the word the captain used. "And now I want you all to be very quiet. I have a terrible task to perform." Then he called battalion headquarters.

April 16th, Hill 229

Bruno said that Guyol was hit in the kidney and the liver.

The combat patrol that was directed against the Fan was postponed. Instead we went for a stroll through a shadowy ter-

246

ritory known as Three Fingers. This is the relative location of that area.

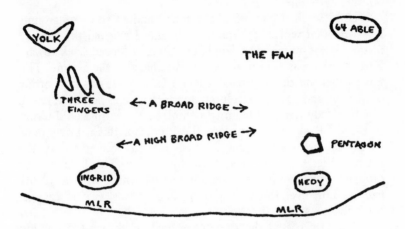

This is the story we got at Lt. Sandler's briefing. Three Fingers is to the Chinese what the Hedy-Bunker ridge is to us. Both are considered No Man's Land. However, Three Fingers is so close to the Chinese main line of resistance that it is a sort of goony stomping ground, in the same way that we are fairly at home on the Hedy-Bunker ridge, it being so close to our lines. We were told that we would be the first patrol to enter this area since the battalion occupied this sector.

Only two men volunteered for the point, Van Horn and myself. Lt. Sandler isn't acquainted with the "work" of either of us, so he told us to guess a number between 1 and 10. I won, or rather I lost.

The objective is not visible from the MLR. The captain allowed me to study his operations map. I had been out in that area twice before—not that far out though. Once with another Diesel, on April 3rd, and the other night when Lt. Guyol was killed. On the map, the only personal check points I could find were two broad flat ridges.

There were thirty of us. At 9:00 we filed through the tank

revetment left of Hedy gate. The ground is soft and completely devoid of vegetation, and we were able to move silently, in a northwesterly direction.

Until we had covered about four hundred yards of ground, I was familiar with the terrain. Each time I reached the summit of one of the numberless knolls out there, I looked back toward Hedy until I was able to recognize the shape of the skyline. This was so that, on the way back, I could fix my eyes on this portion of skyline and lead the column towards it; our point of return was the Hedy trench. One might think that a patrol could return to the MLR at any point along the front, but this is rarely done —only in case of emergency. When a patrol becomes lost, the patrol leader will call in and ask for a flare. The flare will be dropped over a prominent terrain feature which will be identified for him over the sound-power, and in this way he can get back his sense of direction.

After we passed the second personal check point, I got lost because the MLR was no longer in view, and we were forced to move circuitously because of the uneven terrain. So I was leading twenty-nine men into enemy territory by radar. The slope suddenly dropped off into a steep descent and a terrain finger came into view. Which one of the Three Fingers it was I don't know. It was a short fat one, about thirty yards long. I halted the column—for the hundredth time—and went back to the lieutenant, asking permission to take three men out to the end of the finger, a scouting party. He said O.K. Four of us crawled out to the end, where we found a large flat rock but no people. I sent one man back to tell the lieutenant that it was safe to bring the rest of the column along. When they arrived, the lieutenant set them up in a perimeter defense, a very tight one. It looked like one of those aquacade shows where all the girls form a circle and touch toes. We were almost as tight as that. And there we remained for two hours, pugnacious as hell. Except for harassing and interdictory machine-gun fire from our lines, and stray mortar projectiles that whistled overhead, we heard no strange sounds and saw no figures. The sky was not light enough for us to see into goonyland proper, although the looming Yolk was clearly visible in front of us. God, the terrain is strange out there. Someday I would like to see it in daylight.

When we withdrew at 2 A.M., three mortar rounds exploded nearby. We had probably been heard by a forward observer, and one of their mortar crews were doing a "search and traverse" mission. After an interval of about one minute, we heard a POP! in the air above us and we dived for cover. A pale yellow flare ignited and began the slow descent. We could hear it burning. We still don't know whether it was a Chinese or an American flare. As soon as it went out, I led the column—at a very rapid rate —across the skyline of the first broad hill mass, into the relative cover of the reverse slope. Another series of mortars exploded behind us. We reached Hedy gate at 3:45.

A snatch party, led by Sgt. Mackay of the ———— platoon, went out to look for the body that Lt. Guyol had found. Shortly after Mackay left the MLR—this was after our Diesel had returned— the moon came out, very bright, and the captain called Mackay and told him to come back.

Red Joe has been relieved of duty. He was sent to a rear area yesterday.

April 17th, 1953

Drew Pearson predicted that the war would end today—or so the word is being passed around the campus. Several truckloads of prisoners were exchanged last night—again, this is the word. The narrow neutral corridor is located a mile or two to the west. It runs between Munsan-ni (behind our lines) to Kaesong (behind Chinese lines). It is a strip of land running generally north-south, with a road in the middle. Panmunjom, the site of the farcical truce talks, lies somewhere in the middle. Panmunjom is not a village, it is merely the name of one of the tiny provinces, a rice paddy. Last night, we all saw moving lights from that area, probably truck headlights, involved in the prisoner exchange. I haven't mentioned it before, but we have often seen moving lights way, way back in the Black Hills—probably supply trucks.

A man named Barney Lipschutz was shot in the leg today by a sniper. He was standing in the tank slot next to Hedy gate.

I walked down to chow yesterday at noon and met a jeep that was grinding laboriously up the slope. Lt. Buell was in back. I was very glad to see him and made no bones about it. The fact is, I didn't have time to react in a military manner, so I blurted out, "Well, hi-ya, man!" Buell grinned, self-consciously. Lts. Guyol and Knight having been put out of commission, Buell was recalled from his rear-echelon job.

Yesterday afternoon I talked over an idea with Kostis, Pugnacci and Hogg. We made a decision and went down to the CP to talk to Captain Krupp. We were somewhat indignant. We wanted to know why the dead marine hadn't been brought back, the one that Lt. Guyol had found. The captain was surprised; he said that Guyol had told him over the wire that it was the body of a Chinese. I was then the first person that had suggested that it was a marine. He asked me why I thought so. I replied, "I don't know, sir. I just got the impression that it was a marine." We four would like to go out, we said, and get the body, whatever he was. The captain said that he was grateful. He would have been forced to pick out another Rolls-Royce (snatch party), an ugly job for him and for the men he picked.

Jo Rivera, Hanna, and the rest of the men that were on that patrol with Guyol, had gone out to New Bunker. Therefore, I was the only man available who knew exactly where the body was. We learned through the captain that Sgt. Suender had been sent out for the *other* body; the naked one, believed to be the man from Fox company who went berserk.

The captain left the details to me—there wasn't much he could do in the way of briefing. I pointed out on the map where the body was, but the map is not detailed enough to make it clear. He said that we must do the job before the moon rises.

We left Hedy gate at 9 P.M., faces and hands blackened. Andy carried the stretcher. Pugnacci carried a coil of thin rope, fifty feet long. Hogg carried the sound-power. We had no prc-6.

The next two hours were pretty awful. Guyol's death was

tragic enough, but the events of last night were traumatic. I *thought* I knew where the body was. But the moon was not out, as it had been that night. It seemed as though all the gullies looked alike. I remembered that the body lay in what looked like an old stream bed, right in the middle. So all I could do was lead the men up one gully and down another. What made it so ghastly was this, and I doubt if I can express the effect it had on us:

It was very dark. What the eye saw was a series of gradations in color; from black to dark grey to grey, small patches of each. An occasional rock. Each rock and each small patch of grey became the head of the dead man. Each one of them. But that wasn't all. I didn't mention it during the account of Guyol's last patrol, but the body stunk, the air around it was saturated with three months' decay. Last night we caught faint whiffs of it, many times. From this, we knew that the corpse was somewhere nearby. Each and every time my eye caught sight of one of those light patches, my heart almost stopped beating. I would creep up to each one and stand over it until I was sure. But I was never really sure, so I would extend the muzzle of the BAR toward it, until the metal clinked against the rock. Each time I heard the metallic sound I was tremendously relieved. By this time I didn't care whose body it was; I wanted to get the hell out of there. The feeling I had about Guyol's death got to me, too, and I didn't want to enter that gully again. I regretted bitterly having instigated this Rolls-Royce.

Sometimes the smell would get stronger, and whenever I saw the image of the rotted head I would consult Pugnacci, who was behind me, in low whispers, asking him if he thought that was it. But I was only stalling. Each time I had to go up and touch it.

When we did come upon the body, there was no doubt. I didn't have to poke at it with the muzzle. For the first time since we left Hedy gate, I stood erect, and rubbed my face with my hands. I was conscious of the fact that I might get sick, and I was taking a moment to find out. Pugnacci thought I was about to pass out, and he came up and grabbed me from the rear. I knew that it would take quite an effort even to look at the body and I didn't want the other men to watch the process. Andy was told to cover the bottom entrance to the gully. Hogg and Pugnacci watched the shallow ridges on either flank.

I wasted a minute or two crouched, getting nerve. Pugnacci had given me the coil of rope; I finally moved over, and fixed my eyes on a spot two or three feet away from the dark form. Out of the corner of my eye, I made out a pair of feet. This meant that I might not have to look at the face. I examined them. The man was lying on his back; his feet and ankles protruded out from a little dam of rocks, probably built by a Korean farmer long ago. He was wearing tennis shoes. This identified him as a Chinese. The shoes were of canvas, light grey or faded yellow in color. There was a round, flat rubber patch covering the area of the ankle bone of each shoe. Later, examining one of the shoes by candlelight in the CP, we saw that this patch was the trademark, a profile of an American Indian—of all things. When I had looked at the body during Guyol's patrol, it appeared shoeless, because of the light color.

Taking infinite pains not to move the body—for fear of booby-traps—I removed the laces of one shoe and then removed the shoe. There was no need to be so gingerly, the legs and ankles were like stone. Kostis appeared at my elbow and said, "I think someone's coming this way." He pointed to the west, indicating that he had seen movement in that direction. I kidded him about this later; no one else but he would have been so casual. I said to him, "This is a goony. So the captain won't want him. I got one of his shoes to prove it isn't a marine. Tell Hogg and Pugnacci to get ready to move out." I had an idea that the captain would think we had chickened-out, if we returned saying that it was a Chinese. But seeing the shoe, he wouldn't doubt our story.

We ascended one of the flank slopes, crossed the skyline and passed over two gullies. When we were about one hundred yards away from the body, and well hidden in another gully, I called the captain over the sound power, telling him what we had found and that Kostis had seen figures. The captain sounded cold as ice. From the tone of his voice I gathered that he thought we had turned yellow and just wanted to get home. He said, "I don't care who it is. We want the body. Stay where you are for a few minutes. If you don't see or hear anything, go back and get it." The anger I felt helped overcome the fear. We went back, the others resumed their former positions, more watchful than before. As quickly as possible, I tied one end of the rope around one of the ankles, and then walked down the gully, playing out the entire length of the coil. Kostis moved down with me, still watching the shadows to the west. I yanked the rope. No give. I yanked harder. No give. Kostis put down his carbine and we yanked together as hard as we could. Something gave. I went back and took a look. The man's legs were spread wide apart, but that was the only difference. Apparently the torso was so rotted that it had sunk into the harder sand-shale of the old stream bed, and there it clung tenaciously.

I want to mention one thing before going on. I did not volunteer to be the one to examine and handle the body. I volunteered only to take the point. We discussed the matter before leaving the MLR. Hogg and Pugnacci flatly refused to handle the body, "unless absolutely necessary." Kostis said that he would if I lost my nerve. Here we dropped the matter. The word is going around today that we flipped a coin out there, sitting around the body, and that I was the one who lost. A colorful tale but not true.

Examining the body more carefully this time, I found that, except for the feet and ankles, it was half buried in the shale. Lopping the rope several times around the other ankle, I walked down the gully again. We pulled once more but failed to dislodge the body. There was only one thing to do, and it is something we laughed about later, but not at the time. All four of us lay down our weapons—no laughing matter—and did a One-two-three-Pu-u-ll." Something gave and we fell over backwards. The others returned to their positions and I went up the gully for a look. We had pulled it apart. The pelvic carriage and the legs were separated from the upper torso. The man had probably been hit by a mortar, a direct hit in the stomach. Either that or the rats had feasted on rice and fish-heads. I knew that we would never be able to collect the parts without a shovel. Not looking, I ran my hands across his chest. The material was padded quilt, in little sections—the winter uniform. I found no pockets or papers or equipment of any kind. We withdrew immediately, crossing two or three gullies as before. The captain was more obliging this time, that is, he was slightly sympathetic. He made a very unhappy suggestion though. He asked me to try to slip the rope under the man's neck, with the possibility of working loose the upper torso that way. We returned to the gully for the third time. It was too dark to discern the facial features. The face was half buried. There was no sense in trying to scrape away the hard earth underneath. Hogg crept over and whispered this in my ear, "We're crazy to hang around here. Why don't you set off a grenade under the body and we can tell the captain it was booby-trapped?" I admit considering it.

I was searching for pockets again, Hogg had just gone back, when a heavy object landed on the sand twenty or twenty-five feet up the gully. It exploded after I had sprawled flat on the ground. From which direction had the grenade been thrown? We had no idea. I joined the others and we raced down the gully. Another grenade exploded behind us. We halted near the place where we had halted twice before. I requested a mortar barrage but the captain replied that he didn't know exactly where we were, that he couldn't take the chance. He said, "You're on your way in, aren't you?" I said no, and began to describe our position to him, so that he could call in mortars. The captain became very excited. He said for us to get the hell out of there, "before you're followed." He also said, "Come on home!" I wanted to say, "Gee, thanks."

When we returned, minus the stretcher and the coil of rope, and without the body—only his tennis shoe—we felt badly. But Krupp greeted us like long lost sons, and apologized in his reticent manner for asking us to stay out there so long. As long as we could find no equipment or papers, there was no need for the body itself. He told us to sit down and have some coffee and doughnuts. It may seem unlikely, but we were all very hungry.

We sat around for a while, enjoying the bright light of the Coleman lanterns and the smell of the coffee. Something to do with the communal father-image also. We watched the captain at work. He sat before the operations map, wearing a pair of earphones. He talked successively with New Bunker, Hedy, and two recon patrols—one led by Cal Tibbels. The other three ghouls left and I remained, drinking coffee and talking occasionally with the captain. He asked some personal questions. I realized that he is a deeply sentimental man who does a great job of covering it up. This is an old hackneyed story—the sensitive officer who weeps because he must order men to go into No Man's Land. But Krupp is not a character of fiction. He didn't exactly tell me his life story last night, but through the deceptive coating of Old Corps toughness, I got his number.

Later, I went outside and made the long hike along the tank road to our bunker, and I was very much afraid of the dark.

April 18th, Hill 229

Lt. Buell called the three squad leaders together (Sgt. Van Horn, Sgt. Henion, and myself) and said that two squads would have to make the relief on New Bunker that night. Van Horn and Henion wanted to go; I was willing to stay. I figure we can raise more hell on patrols than defending the outpost. There are only seven of us left, and three of us have Purple Hearts. I don't mean to imply that we are slowly being massacred; it is simply that our platoon is under strength. A replacement draft is due shortly. Cpl. Lauroesch, Pfcs. McMaster (Tumbleweed), Pugnacci, Kostis, Hogg, and Cpl. Tibbels. Lauroesch has been given charge of the yo-bos and will not be available for patrols. The function of our squad is a curious one. Not counting Lauroesch, there are six of us left. Tumbleweed is not dependable on patrols, so there are five really. A squad from the ——— platoon has taken over our sector of the line, and we have moved our gear into a bunker near the CP. We are not responsible for any section of the trench. We fill in where needed. Our primary function is patrolling.

Last night a Rolls-Royce attempted to retrieve another body believed to be that of a marine. Again they were fired upon from the Pentagon. No one was hurt but they were forced to withdraw. I'll be god-damned if we're going to volunteer to get *that* body.

There's no reason to mention this except that I don't want to forget it. Andy sings two songs, regularly, and no others. "Autumn Leaves" and "When I Look into Your Eyes."

Andy, in strict confidence, told me that he uses opium. At first I didn't believe him, but he showed me a little wad of it. It looks like dark gum or pitch; raw opium according to him. He buys it from one of the yo-bos. Twenty-five bucks a gram. Andy prepares it by placing a tiny bit of it in a metal spoon, mixing it with a drop or two of water, and melting it over a candle. He owns a hypodermic needle which he stole from another corpsman. He also places chunks of it on the end of a cigarette. He said that it dries up the moisture of the skin and makes him itch. He is continually sloe-eyed, but that is natural to him.

He wanted to introduce me to the stuff, but I turned him down. I'll give it a whirl later maybe.

Andy has a nickname for Captain Krupp, whose first name is Ray. It is based on the fact that the captain was so insistent that we get that body. Ray O'Ghoul.

He refers to Sgt. Barefield as the Joe Bfsxtd, after the Li'l Abner character who always has a black cloud hanging over his head.

Ray O'Ghoul allowed us to study the sector map today. There used to be several villages in what is now No Man's Land of our sector. There is a vast network of octopuslike trenches out there, a complex system, especially behind Old Bunker. Tae doksan is not on the map, but the captain said that there is a tremendous trench behind it: "Twenty feet deep, and wide enough to drive a truck through." Intelligence (G-2) tells us—we have heard this many times during lectures—that the Chinese occupy fortified hills as far as twenty miles behind their forwardmost po-

sitions. Their lines are called a fortified zone. We occupy a fortified belt. There is actually no Chinese MLR, that is, one
continuous trenchline running east-west. They occupy hills and
other strong localities, a much better method of defense. They
defend in depth, unlike us, with only one strong line. Once our
line is breached we would be in bad shape.

Another bit of information: A marine outpost, known as
O. P. 8, spotted a Joseph Stalin-type heavy tank the other day,
just as it was being pulled into a cave in the enemy sector. Lt.
Buell said that he was unaware that they were using them.

Hedy is called the weakest spot on the MLR.

We have learned to stay inside at dusk. There is almost always an enemy bombardment at this time. One of the communications men was sitting on the crapper yesterday during the
late afternoon. An 82, streaked in, and landed ten yards behind
him. It was a dud, and it is still sitting there, three quarters buried.

Even though the tank was burned out, there is still believed
to be a sniper inhabiting it during the day.

April 20th, Cunaxa

I was sitting under a tree the night before last, thinking. I
fell asleep and had a dream. I saw my house in the dream, and a
gigantic thunderbolt hit it, and the house caught fire. The skilled
soothsayer from Lacedaemon, Kostis of Sparta, has made clear
the meaning of these portents. Zeus Almighty Cloudgatherer
Thundershaker has made a choice. We slaughtered a bull and
made the usual libations, and then sought out our companions, the
noble Hoggus and Pugnacious, worthy hoplites both. We decided
to become a "provisional fire team." We talked to the captain
about it, with the following results. Since we four have no definite sector of trench to cover, we are a semi-independent unit.
We will be on call for special missions. This relieves the captain
of having to order men to go out on extra-curricular missions. Instead, we will be called upon. We will be expected to retrieve

257

bodies, lost equipment, reconnoitre new territory in preparation for a raid or a combat patrol—or any other job that would require volunteers. Also, we told the captain that we would be willing to be farmed out to other units, for use as point men. Hogg, who is married, is excepted from this last function. The captain, in his dour way, was delighted. We call ourselves The Captain O'Ghoul Suicide Squad. May Zeus have mercy on The Sacred Band of Thebes, whom we shall turn to dust before our campaign is ended. And may Hephaeston never forget that he forged our armored vests, or rather our helmets. I, Xenophon, am the leader.

Ray O'Ghoul put us right to work. Our mission was to cover a certain piece of terrain and take note of any equipment that we might find, bringing back as much as we could. We were also to return to the Chinese body and look again for equipment. It had been overcast all day and it looked as though the night would be a dark one. With this in mind, I checked out a Thompson to use at the point. The weapon is designed so that a man can carry it with one hand. It is a handy piece to carry when one crawls over barbed wire or climbs steep slopes—using the three-point crawl. There is an extra handle behind the trigger guard of the Thompson. It is a relatively light piece (10.5 lbs.) and is short. It can be fired with one hand if necessary. The disadvantage of the weapon is its limited range, about 100 yards, as compared with the five- or six-hundred-yard range of the BAR. But the latter weapon is twice as heavy and almost twice as long. Since it promised to be a dark night, I figured that any firing would be at close range.

Kostis was second in line, carrying my BAR. Hogg carried a carbine. Pugnacci, bringing up the rear, carried a BAR. We each carried four grenades, the new fragmentation type. Pugnacci carried one smoke grenade also. He was instructed to set off this grenade if we were hit from close quarters. Our forward point of advance was to be the second broad ridge in the vicinity of the Yolk.

We waited beside Hedy gate for several minutes, as our eyes became accustomed to the dark. We moved out at 10 p.m. We found the body without much trouble, although it took more than an hour to get out there. We picked up a helmet nearby, with the letters LT. F. P. DUDLEY stenciled in white on the outside. From this point (check point three) we proceeded northwest. We ran across several duds, one U. S. 105mm. shell.

And possibly a Chinese heavy mortar projectile. We found an old rusty carbine. The stock was broken and the front hand guard lay nearby. We picked this up.

At about this time, the moon came up—or rather, the sky became clear. I realized that it was a mistake to have brought the Tommy gun. I felt naked without the BAR. At our furthest point of advance (according to the set check points), we set in for an hour, watching and listening. The only unusual noise we heard was a loud metallic CLINK some distance away, in goonyland. It sounded as though a mortar tube had been dropped accidentally upon a base plate—instead of being lowered gently.

Before we withdrew, I crawled over the skyline with the binoculars for a long look at goonyland. The top of the ridge was irregular enough so that I could cross it without being silhouetted against the sky. The other three moved up to the skyline then and gave cover to their daring master. There was a small defilade area on the other side, a natural foxhole, and I sat in it. Yolk loomed ahead, really loomed, a tremendous hill mass. Several yards below the foxhole, there was a shiny metal object of some kind. I left the hole and crawled down to it; a flashlight. I know exactly where that spot is. Someday I would like to find out how close I came to an enemy trench when picking up the flashlight, armed with that weak-sister Tommy gun.

We returned to the lines, by another route, at 3:40 A.M. The captain was highly pleased. He said, "That's the kind of patrols I want." The flashlight is a medium-sized one, made of aluminum. There are Chinese characters on the cap and along the small switch. The two batteries inside bear a Chinese trademark, with a picture of a golden bell. The flashlight is in working condition. The captain called Major Heintoff at battalion headquarters, reporting the discovery of the helmet bearing the name. He had this to say concerning the flashlight: "This verifies those reports of lights that the men are always seeing out there. Not *all* of them are the reflection of stars in the rice paddy." While being debriefed I went into another acting bit. I sat on the ground, Oriental-fashion, and spoke as tersely as possible, no facial expression. Only the facts. It came off well.

April 21st, Hill 229

The 31st replacement draft arrived last night, and the —— squad has three new men. Pfcs. Louis Bengis—Brooklyn, Vernon Pymm—Gary, Indiana, and Jack Hampden—Indianapolis. All city fellers. They won't join our patrols, or even go out on listening post, for three or four days. They stand trench watch. Last night I took each of them up to the MLR and "set them in" —that is the expression used around here. There was nothing to worry about, I said. The Chinese never come near us up here, only on New Bunker, I said. It was dark when I took them up and they couldn't see much of the terrain. This worried each one of them. Remembering how scared I was the first time I stood trench watch, I told them how far away Old Bunker was, and that nothing ever happens on the MLR itself. Last night's password was "Texas Aggies"; I taught them how to challenge someone coming along the trench. Cpl. Lauroesch, at my request, made periodic visits on them during the night.

When we (others) returned at dawn, I went up immediately to see how the new men were doing. Pymm and Hampden challenged me and seemed to be in good shape. Bengis however had had a bad night. After answering the challenge, we talked awhile. I noticed that he was clutching a grenade in his hand. When the sky began to lighten, he relaxed and confessed his fears of the night. He said that he had intended to throw the grenade at anyone who came along the trench and failed to answer his challenge properly.

In regard to stealth and alertness, our patrol last night was the most perfect I've ever seen. Our mission, boiled down to one sentence, was to locate any listening posts that might be covering the Fan. The Fan is a mighty strange position. It is the only outpost I know of that is located specifically on low ground. It lies three or four hundred yards northwest of the Pentagon, at the bottom of a smooth, gradual slope. We were not expected to go roaming around the Fan; we were to find a vantage point from which the slope leading down to the Fan could be studied, through field glasses.

A raid is being planned for the near future, on the Fan. The last time anyone bothered the unit on the Fan they—a company of marines—were clobbered. It was during this action that the tank in front of Hedy was knocked out.

We were to approach the Fan from the southwest. We did this, found a fairly good observation point, and set up a perimeter defense. Our vantage point, roughly speaking, was within that area where the gullies and the ridges begin to smooth out along the edge of that vast, smooth slope. Here we lay for three hours, taking turns with the glasses. Nothing was seen, nothing extraordinary was heard. We knew that the Fan trenches were located at the bottom of the slope—approx. 150 yards from our position, but it was not visible. On the aerial photographs that we studied, the Fan looks something like this:

We established the following information—unverified: There are no listening posts in connection with the Fan. We studied every foot of that slope, and could find no defilade areas in which a man might conceal himself. Lt. Guyol was fired upon by a Maxim from the Fan. It is probable that there is an automatic weapon at the end of each of the four fingers of the Fan. Just a guess. And because our tank was hit by fire from the Fan, it is also probable that an anti-tank weapon is included in the fortification.

The slope is an even one, and the angle is not steep. The forward slopes of Hedy are the beginning of the incline; the Fan is at the bottom.

Obviously anyone caught moving across the skyline—along that slope—would be cut to pieces by machine guns from the Fan. This type of fire is called "grazing fire." It is probably because of this that the raiding party of a few weeks back were hit so badly. And it is because of this that we did not go near that slope last night, although we were near the top of it, on one flank.

When we got back to the CP and were debriefed, the captain said to me, "Good boy." Boy hell. Old curmudgeon.

April 22nd, Hill 229

A Mercury (ambush) last night, on the Hedy-Bunker ridge. Near 1 A.M., Hogg, on the right flank, spotted two figures as they were about to descend the slope on the other side of the skyline; that is—according to his description later—he saw them just as they were crossing the skyline and moving out of sight down the other side. He fired a long burst in their direction, thereby throwing the rest of us into a panic. The figures, he said, were about fifty yards away. When he explained, in whispers, what had happened, we moved out quickly in that direction, roughly north-east, and tried to follow. We crossed the skyline and lay down, and found ourselves in a unique position. There, out in front of us, lay a number of old, deserted bunkers, which I may have mentioned having seen when on New Bunker. Van Horn's sniper worked from one of these bunkers. We could see no one. The low, broad hill mass of New Bunker was visible to our right. The two Chinese might have been hiding in one of the demolished bunkers, but I had no intention of going down there to hunt, Suicide Squad be damned. In order to cross the space between ourselves and the line of bunkers, it would have been necessary to expose ourselves, with no available cover, for a distance of about forty yards. No, thank you.

We reported all this to Ray O'Ghoul, suggesting that these dilapidated bunkers are probably where one or two snipers hide during the day—the jokers that continually harass the left flank of New Bunker. He said, as we hoped he would, that he would send a combat patrol out there in the near future.

This is written later the same day. A Diesel is going out tonight, to the area mentioned above. Our fire team is included.

April 23rd

A strange Diesel last night. The communication man carried two speed reels, and both of them ran out before we returned home. This means that we covered a hell of a lot of terrain. Included within the sixteen-man unit were four men, each carrying a ten-pound satchel charge. Lt. Sandler, the Southern gentleman (my guess was correct; he is from Virginia, graduated from U. of V.) was in command.

We entered No Man's Land at Ginger gate, descended the wooded slope, crossed the paddy—angling toward New Bunker —passed New Bunker, and climbed the Hedy-Bunker ridge. It took us an hour and a half to get that far, which was good. The slower a patrol moves, the less sound it makes. Up to then, I had been the point of a column. On the ridge, we changed the formation.

FIRE TEAM

263

Each member of our fire team was in a "key" position. This was arranged by Lt. Sandler at the briefing, and was very complimentary to us individually and as a unit, ifIdosaysomeself. Har!

The interval between men was six or seven yards. In this spread-out formation, we traversed the entire length of the Hedy-Bunker ridge, that is the leeward side of it, that is, the side facing the MLR. We combed the area, as the process is called. We were looking specifically for spider-holes in which snipers are said to live. It sounds like right out of a comic book, but there are men who have seen them—Cpls. Mackay and Colia.

Theoretically, we covered a strip of land seventy-seven yards wide, and mighty long, but we found no holes. The movement was extremely difficult. Many times two or three of the flank men were out of sight to the rest of us because we were crossing gullies and ridges. Most of the terrain is wooded on this ridge and we made a hell of a racket. A column would also have made much noise; but far less than we made last night. In a column, the men behind the point follow the path he has taken, and that path will be the least vegetated passes. But we were all spread out, and nervous about maintaining the formation so that we wouldn't lose anyone. Lots of noise. Since we were combing the ridge, we couldn't move in column.

At one point there was an accidental discharge among the ranks and we scattered for cover, believing ourselves to be ambushed. The word was quickly passed that someone had caught his weapon in a bush and we reformed and went on. Soon we came into the clear and were able to see the skyline of the Hedy finger, with the disabled tank at the end. We could also see the Pentagon knoll. We made a flanking movement, circling around not far from the tank. Fifty or sixty yards away. A 180-degree turn. Cpl. Lo Castro crawled up to the lieutenant—no, before he crawled up, the word was passed along for everyone to stop and lie down. Then Lo Castro came up and told the lieutenant that he had seen "heads bobbing up and down on the skyline, right next to the tank." The lieutenant called Captain Krupp and requested mortar fire. The tank is located only a few yards in front of one of the flank holes of Hedy; so the barrage had to be carefully executed, and it was. The first round landed more than one hundred yards north of the outpost—somewhere along that slope I was describing a couple of days ago. Each successive round exploded closer to the tank; they were being "walked-in." Lt. Sandler finally said, "On target" into the phone and the searching and traversing ceased. It was a waste of time, not enough rounds were sent out. Four I think. Only one of them landed near the tank.

When we had completed the turn, we changed formation again.

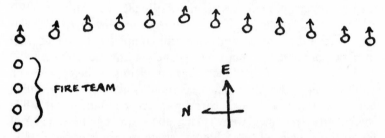

Lo Castro's unit covered the flank because that end of the skirmish line was nearest to goonyland. The point is that we were now on the opposite side of the Hedy-Bunker ridge, which is the windward side and almost devoid of vegetation. It is also somewhat rocky; both sides are. In this formation we covered the other half of the sprawling ridge. We found a great deal once we arrived at the group of demolished bunkers. Here is another diagram, to show our general movement:

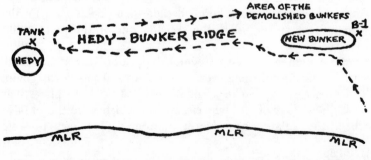

265

These bunkers, we learned, were built and once occupied by marines. U. S. sandbags. (Chinese sandbags are larger, the mesh of the burlap is not so fine.) We found several small caves, prone shelters, boxes of U. S. machine-gun ammo, grenades, entrenching tools and cartridge belts. We also found an old trenchline that had been hastily dug. About twenty yards long. Once among the bunkers, we split up into several groups. Each bunker and cave had to be searched. The routine was to throw an armed grenade into the bunker, then enter it. Nothing was found except several 7.9mm. cartridge cases in two of the bunkers. These two bunkers then were possibly the ones used by Chinese snipers during the day. No one was around last night; we made too much noise as we approached. There were eight or nine or ten bunkers out there. I'd say most of them were completely caved in, that only two or three of them could possibly accommodate a man.

There is no doubt concerning my claims to being a ghoul. After last night I am a full-fledged ghoul. There is safety in numbers, and I felt it enough to go wandering around a bit while the other fifteen men were poking about among the bunkers. I found the remains of two Chinese, within ten yards of each other. The first notice of them was a shocker. The nearest one was almost completely buried in the sand-shale. His fleshless skull was above ground, also one foot with tennis shoe. The other delightful gentleman was lying face down. Most of him was above ground. The padded clothing was mostly shredded, the white cotton exposed in some places. There was a burp-gun cartridge belt around his waist. It was unbuckled. I put down the BAR and tugged at the straps of the belt. Pfc. Haals was nearby; he stopped to watch with a horrified expression on his face. Finally with a giant tug I pulled the skeleton out of the ground and took the belt.

The men were being assembled; I slung this soggy, fetid, putrid, rancid, foul thing over my shoulder and joined the group. The men carrying satchel charges were instructed to place their packages in four of the bunkers, two of which were the ones in which the 7.9mm. cartridges were found. The charges were

266

planted, the forty-second fuses were pulled and we raced down the skyline for cover. The explosions were impressive, throwing up tremendous geysers of sand, mingled with small rocks. Each lofty geyser cast a shadow over us for two or three seconds, then the bright moon would appear again. No symbolism intended.

We withdrew, crossing the rice paddy. All the way back I was thinking about one thing: Orientals and their patience, as compared with Americans and their lack of it. The thought wasn't as profound as it sounds; I was merely appalled at the goddamned noise we made going back. Right in the middle of the rice paddy, IN FULL VIEW OF OLD BUNKER, the lieutenant twice had to stop the column and tell the men to stop talking. *Talking.* We were all sweating heavily, and were pretty tired; we wanted to hit the sack, and because of this we became careless. I expected a rain of mortars but none came. We returned through Ginger gate.

April 24th, Hill 229

We all have a craving for fruit but we don't get enough, one small can a day. Complicated deals to supplement this: trading of, say, two cans of pork&beans, a pack of butts, plus a promise to clean the other man's weapon—all for a can of crushed pineapple. A slight exaggeration, but only slight. My thoroughly practical solution: The company C-rations are brought up to a supply point every evening before midnight. I have stolen two boxes—gigantic boxes—of rations. Cherry, grape, mixed fruit, pears, pineapple, apple sauce and prunes. They are hidden in a deep ravine near the bunker. A fruit fit. Prunes are the least popular.

C-rations come in the following varieties: Pork&beans, meat-&beans, frank&beans, chicken&noodles, beef stew, hamburgers. I must have forgotten one. There are also cans of dry rations: hard tack, jam, powdered coffee, powdered milk, sugar, cigarettes (Philip Morris, Camels, Lucky Strike, Chesterfield) candy bar, cookie. A minute can opener in each individual ration. This chow is not bad, we don't mind it. Heat tablets are used to warm the food.

A simple story. I was thirsty yesterday so I tipped a five-gallon can and filled a canteen cup with the cool, clear liquid. I wolfed down three or four large gulps. Kerosene. An hour or so later, I was lying in the bottom of the trench, belching the foulest kind of oily breath. Soon thereafter, a glorious, gushing bowel movement and all was well again. I mention it as one of the rare times when I have suffered.

While we are in the crude department: Pugnacci was farmed out last week to lead a ———— platoon recon patrol, while suffering from dysentery, sometimes referred to as the green-apple quickstep. Halfway between the Yolk and the Pentagon, he called the column to a halt, rushed them into a perimeter defense around him—throwing the men into a panic—and went potie-potie. Just a little barracks humor is all.

April 25th, Hill 229

A routine recon last night: THE fire team. Northwest of Hedy. It certainly wouldn't have been a routine recon if we had run into anything. We made an experiment. Hogg and Pallas exchanged their carbines for BARs and we filled our magazines with tracer bullets, that is, every fourth round. It was necessary to steal a box of machine-gun ammunition to obtain the tracers, removing each one from the metal clips. On the patrol, we each carried six magazines, less than half of the standard unit of fire. This is the usual procedure for men during recon patrols; the idea is to avoid contact with the enemy, and if contact is made, the idea is to get out as quickly as possible. With Leonidas as point man, we don't anticipate walking into any ambushes, and the difference in weight is important. Here is our theory: In the fire fights I have seen, it was a matter of our firing blindly at muzzle blasts, or shadows. We had no way of knowing whether

268

our fire was effective or not. By using tracers, the shooter can direct his fire accurately. Since it is night, it is still impossible to aim by means of the gun sights; however, with tracers the trajectory is visible and the impact area can be adjusted. What I'm trying to say is roughly comparable to a man watering his lawn with a garden hose—no, better yet: a fireman directing a stream of water into the window of a burning building. The fireman aims the hose in the general direction of the window. He then watches the path of the water and adjusts it accordingly. The shooter, watching the trajectory of the red tracers, adjusts his fire accordingly. The obvious disadvantage lies in the fact that the shooter's position is given away as soon as he fires. But it no more reveals his position than when he fires armor-piercing or ordinary ball slugs. The muzzle blast of all automatic weapons is perfectly visible for a considerable distance. There is never the slightest doubt where the shooter is located. Even when he is using that ridiculous attachment known as the flash-hider.

For example: That night that the yo-bos and I were laying down a concertina roll in front of B-1 on New Bunker, we fired back at a line of muzzle blasts along the earth shelf, not knowing whether our aim was good or bad. Had every fourth round of our fire been tracers, we could have sent out an accurate cordon of fire, spraying the shelf.

April 27th, Hill 229

The rumor is that we are about to be pulled back into Corps reserve. If it is true, this means that the entire 1st Marine Division will be taken off the line. It will be the first time this has happened since the Inchon landing. The feeling is: "It's about time." It would be great to get off this god-awful hill.

It rained heavily last night. Lt. Buell and Sgt. Van Horn went out with the O'Ghoul fire team last night and pulled off a tricky reconnaissance patrol. It was the longest patrol I have ever made, not in distance covered but in the time it took to get out and back. We left at 8:30 and returned shortly before dawn, completely drenched. Nothing happened, absolutely nothing, so I'll just make a few comments.

If it had not been raining so hard we would never have been able to go where we did. On March 20th we made a similar patrol, led by Van Horn on point. The difference was that, instead of merely skirting the flanks of New Bunker—Lorretta, B-3, B-2 and B-1—as we did on the former patrol, last night we ventured far down the slope before turning and moving parallel with the forward line of the outpost. We'll never know how close we came to the enemy trenches, but I'm certain that we came very close. It was a pitch-dark night; no light whatsoever. The sound of our snail-like movement was covered by the sound of the hard rain. The interval between men was nonexistent because we hung on to each other, or rather, we touched the back of the man in front—except Van Horn who was the point. When we were on New Bunker, Van Horn divided his time between B-2 and B-3 and was much better acquainted with the terrain in front of those positions than I. So I asked him to take the point. He was glad to, of course. The remarkable thing is that Van Horn was leading us purely by intuition. He couldn't see a thing. When he led us as far down the slope as he dared, we turned to the right and got down on our stomachs and crawled. Once our clothing got completely soaked it wasn't so bad, although we weren't exactly comfortable. The nice thing was that we were just uncomfortable enough to forget the danger, but not alertness. The lieutenant kept passing the word up to ask Van Horn if he was lost. Van Horn replied each time that he was not, meaning only—as he admitted later—that he had not lost his sense of direction. I certainly had. At one time it seemed to me that we were heading north, that is, after we had made the turn and were supposedly moving east. I was so sure of this that I had something like the following thoughts: "We'll just keep going until we fall into a goony trench, or until we're shot at. In either case, we'll know that we must go the *other* way then. And it is so dark that nobody could hit us anyway; they'd only be firing at noises." I said this kind of thing over and over to myself. Then I heard a voice, off to the right, call out, "Life!" And I figured: Oh, well

—what the hell. It was bound to happen sooner or later. Van Horn yelled, "Belt." The password, Oh. "Van Horn, where the hell are we?" "Right in front of B-1," he said.

I made a measurement while we were out there. Before we began that blind descent into goonyland, we lay near the Lorretta bunker for quite a while. I'm sure I know exactly where we were then—a tiny gully about twenty yards NW of Lorretta. When we began to move down the slope, I counted the steps that we (I) took until we made the turn to the right, and began to crawl upon our bellies like reptiles. Eighty-four steps. If I ever return to Korea I'd like to walk out there and see just how close we did come to falling in an enemy trench. The remains of all the trenches, even though they be filled in, should be visible for many years to come.

Van Horn is tremendous. It is a wonderful accomplishment when a point man can convince the men behind him that he knows what is going on. What was the purpose of that strange patrol? None of us care now; we were just exploring. During the briefing we were given the same instructions as during the briefing for the March 29th patrol; so we were doing some extracurricular snooping.

April 28th, Hill 229

It's still raining but not as hard. Kostis has taken the point of a ——— platoon recon, and Pugnacci went along for the ride. They're out somewhere left of Hedy now. The date is actually April 27th, but I'll be scribbling off and on past midnight, Lauroesch and I are alternating with two other men standing watch on Little Peter. Two hours on, two hours off.

Morale of Able Company is soaring; we are definitely being pulled into reserve. A group of Army officers were wandering around this afternoon, inspecting the area and asking inane questions. According to Lt. Buell, the entire division is being withdrawn in a few days. Our division is not being replaced by an Army division, it is being replaced by two Army divisions, plus a

271

unit of Turks. One might call this a favorable comment upon the First Marine Division. Mightn't one?

April 28th, Hill 229

I was sitting there drinking coffee, about to do some more notes, when the captain sent for me. He was angry; Cpl. Lo Castro had taken a recon out to the area north of outpost Ingrid, and had been fired upon by a long-range Maxim. Lo Castro had withdrawn without asking the captain's permission, leaving the sound-power phone in his haste. The captain obviously wanted Lo Castro and his men to return fire, even though this kind of thing is not encouraged by battalion headquarters. Ray O'Ghoul was disappointed that Kostis and Pugnacci were already out on jobs. He told me to pick out whoever I wanted and bring them to the CP for a quick briefing. We were to carry out the mission that Lo Castro had made a stab at. Lauroesch, Nate Bell—just back from the hospital in Japan; he was hit in the butt during the Old Bunker bombardment—and the three new men: Bengis, Pymm and Hampden. The captain asked me if I wanted to take Lo Castro's men along—undoubtedly as a punishment—but I said no, six men would be enough. Twelve men would make too much noise, especially if six of them were pissed off, as Lo Castro's group would have been had they been forced to go out again.

We left through the tank slot left of Hedy gate, at 2:30 A.M. The rain had stopped and there was a slight wind, and an unmistakable odor of spring. The moon was barely visible, a dim ball of light. We moved west, parallel with the MLR, until we cleared the loose strands of barbed wire and the areas of brush. We came upon a running stream and a half-hidden path that was new to me. Following the path, which followed the stream, we bore northwest. The stream flowed into a large rice paddy, the path became the path on top of a large dike. We crossed the paddy and arrived at a sharp corner of one of the first series of broad ridges out there. This corner sits directly in front of Ingrid.

272

The drawing is made as though we are looking west. The knoll shown in the foreground is the end of the hill mass that, further east, becomes the series of dunes. The path curves around

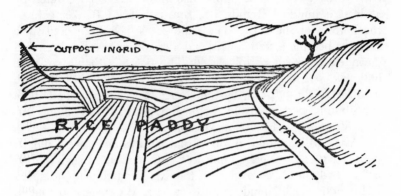

the edge of this knoll, presumably heading north. This curve, to further clarify the location, is approx. six hundred yards west of outpost Hedy and approx. four hundred yards north of the MLR. This is the border area between Able Company and Easy Company of the Second Battalion.

We were not anxious to round that curve; it was here that Lo Castro received fire. So we "set in" for a while, waiting and watching through the binoculars.

Despite the starkness of the drawing, this is the only area in this sector of the front that could be called beautiful. The clouds were dispersing and we could see the complex arrangement of the lines in the rice paddy. There are large patches of yellow poppy at various points beside the path. They were still wet from the rain, and they may have been part of the pleasant odor in the air. It was a real balmy night. The frogs in the paddy were croaking frantically, until we came along. As soon as we approached that corner of the paddy they stopped croaking. This made us very uneasy, this natural signal system. This may have been why Lo Castro was spotted. As soon as the frogs got wind of us there was a deathly silence. Come on, you little green idiots! Brekekekekex Ko-ax Ko-ax! We noticed something else out there that was quite interesting. Most patrol paths are covered with literally hundreds of strands of black communication wire. No, I take that back. But there are always many, many strands, and we have seen some paths that must have been covered by at least a hundred strands, *i.e.*, the path from Bunker gate to the bottom of the MLR. The same paths have been used since this war became a static affair, and a strand or two has been laid down each time a patrol passed. The point is that there were only two strands of communication wire on the path that we used last night—that is, by the corner of that ridge—and those two strands were probably dropped by Lo Castro's phone carrier. We thought this was remarkable.

We had been told to follow that path as far as we could, or until our speed reel played out. We only had one. Bengis carried it. We had already covered more than six hundred yards—a speed reel contains eight hundred yards of wire. We were also told to retrieve the sound-power phone that Lo Castro had left.

After waiting for an hour or so, we moved out. The interval between the point and the second man, Lauroesch, was wide—fifteen to twenty yards. I moved on my stomach for short distances, would stop, study the terrain ahead through the glasses, then crawl a little further. The logical spot for an ambush was the end of the ridge, where a unit could command a view of both angles of the path. Since we were skirting the end of the ridge, we were a bit nervous. The knoll was covered with small pine trees, that smelled GREAT, but they were sparse enough for us to study every foot of ground up there. Not a soul. (Famous last words.) Lo Castro said that he had received fire from a long distance away. We found the phone and did an about-face, returning to the spot where we had previously "set in." I intended to cross the end of the knoll, rather than follow the path around it as Lo Castro had. Before we made the ascent, the captain called and asked where we were. Between check points four and five, was the answer, check point five being that indeterminate spot at which the speed reel would end. I told him that we didn't consider it advisable to follow the path around the end of the knoll, that we might draw fire, that we were about to climb to the end of the low knoll to take a look. The captain said, "It's four o'clock. Come on home. We'll try again some other time."

The three new men handled themselves well; it was their first time out. In general, they will have to learn to move more quietly. Fortunately the ground was soft from the rains. I'm glad nothing happened; no telling how they would have reacted. At least they got a taste of No Man's Land. Discovering new terrain is a somewhat fearsome thing. I shouldn't have said, "There's no telling how they would have reacted." It may sound corny, but they are marines; they have been taught how to react immediately to orders and, almost as important, they know how to use their weapons. They wouldn't be here otherwise. And who would have given these "immediate" orders? Why, old Doctor Scitzo.

The speed reel gave out as soon as we turned around. When this happens the wire is cut and contact with the CP is established by means of the prc-6. And when the patrol re-enters the MLR trench, the wire is cut at that end. This insures against wire-tapping by the Chinese.

April 29th, Hill 229

A little sturm & mishmash last night. Lt. Buell has hemorrhagic fever and has been evacuated. This can be serious. We don't know how sick he is. Van Horn has been made platoon leader. He took out a fourteen-man Diesel last night, utilizing the O'Ghoul fire team. Corpsman Truro was included.

Left at 8:30. No moon. Five new men came along, including Bengis from our squad. G-2 has informed the captain that the Pentagon has been fortified. This was discovered by means of aerial photographs. The men on Hedy have been hearing the sound of digging from that area ever since we pulled that last Diesel in that area. (The flame-thrower assault—when the Pentagon was believed to be a listening post.) The aerial photographs show that a new trench has been dug, apparently a communica-

275

tion trench which—as it was described to us—looks something like this.

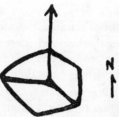

Our mission was to draw fire from the Pentagon, and thus determine the approximate strength of the unit occupying its trenches. Another diagram.

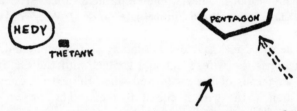

HEDY · THE TANK · PENTAGON

Broken arrow shows the direction of our approach during the flame-thrower assault of April 8th—when M/Sgt. Schiff was playing phantom.

Black arrow shows the direction of our approach last night.

We left through Bunker gate, descended the slope, crossed the bridge, crossed the paddy and climbed the Hedy-Bunker ridge. In column, we moved west along the ridge until we came within sight of the burned-out tank. Then, as pre-arranged during the briefing—we actually rehearsed the movement behind the MLR yesterday afternoon—we shifted from the column into an unusual formation.

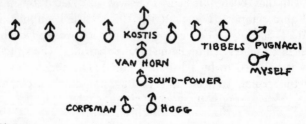

KOSTIS · TIBBELS PUGNACCI · VAN HORN · MYSELF · SOUND-POWER · CORPSMAN · HOGG

Kostis was the point man, although he was less than five yards in front of the skirmish line. Pugnacci and I covered the right flank, which was exposed to goonyland. Although we could not see them, the vast network of trenches were spread out far down the slope. The area down there, directly north, was obscured in shadow, and one's imagination played weird tricks. As Pugnacci said later, "You can tell that's a place where you're just not supposed to go."

When we executed the shift, we were 200 or 250 yards east of the Pentagon. We lay there, waiting for the moon to rise above the Hedy hill mass. Once the moon came out, we could be seen —and fired upon—from the Pentagon. Something about guinea pigs. But we were not completely lacking in cover; there are hundreds of small shallow gullies, made by the erosion of water, in which we lay. The sky began to lighten in the west and soon the bright moon appeared, barely peeping over the skyline. This was our signal. We rose and began moving forward, *very* slowly. We veered gradually to the right, so that Pugnacci and I were forced to descend the slope even further. I caught sight of a path, eight or ten yards below. It ran east-west. There were no strands of communication wire visible. Going east, it disappears in the direction of New Bunker. This might be the path used by snipers that occupy the Hedy-Bunker ridge. I was afraid right then. I mention this only because, when the boom fell in, a minute later, I wasn't particularly afraid. The presence of that vast shadow covering the paddy—the light of the moon hadn't reached it yet—was ominous and spooky.

After creeping twenty or thirty yards toward the Pentagon, we halted, lay down, and waited. At this point the fun and games began. An enemy mortar tube—startlingly close—began pooping off a rapid series of rounds. The tube was located behind the Pentagon, but further down that slope. We could see sparks and a tongue of orange flame from each muzzle blast. Pugnacci and I had time to look at each other, and the look we exchanged meant: "Well, that's the way she goes."

The incoming rounds landed behind us, and we received

small arms fire from the Pentagon at the same time. I can't say how many Chinese fired at us, but it seemed as though the entire skyline of that knoll was covered with the little sharp white fingers of light that were the muzzle blasts. It was a good-sized force. At least one squad, probably more. Some of the men estimated that it was a platoon. This seems plausible, since the Pentagon is so near to our outpost, Hedy.

Pugnacci and I returned fire immediately. I have always admitted it when I got scared, but, as I mentioned, I wasn't scared then. It's nice to be able to mention that once in a while. Sgt. Van Horn began pulling out the unit, two or three men at a time. Pugnacci and I, being the flankers, were the last to be withdrawn. We had both fired several magazines. Our ears were cracking. We were within ten yards of each other and enjoyed a certain amount of cover in one of the rivulet beds. When the last group of men disappeared, we rose and sprinted up the slope and tumbled across the skyline. The Chinese were firing at us from a distance of about 150 yards, which is damn' close on a moonlit night. That's when I got scared; when we made that sprint. The only casualty was Pvt. Ankers, who was shot through the foot. The mortar barrage was fortunately inaccurate, except for one dud which landed according to Van Horn, who doesn't often bull shit, five yards from him.

Van Horn had asked Louis Bengis to carry a twelve-pound satchel charge, in case we ran across another sniper cave or a spider-hole. As we lay on the reverse slope of the Hedy-Bunker ridge, waiting for the barrage to lift, Bengis noticed that the pin of the fuse-lighter had become dislodged. It occurred to him, naturally, that perhaps the fuse was burning. He picked up the satchel and heaved it as far as he could; it went over the skyline but did not explode.

Cal Tibbels had found a Chinese bangalore torpedo before the shooting started, which he dropped during the withdrawal. And Sgt. Van Horn had found a potato-masher grenade, which he brought back to the CP. To arm this grenade, you have only to unscrew the wooden cap, which is attached to a string inside the wooden handle. When the string is pulled, the fuse is lit.

As soon as we were debriefed, the captain dismissed everyone except our fire team. Within twenty minutes were were back in No Man's Land. From the halls of Mon-te-zu-u-*u*-ma, to the shores of Trip-oli (da *dum* dee dum) Ray O'Ghoul wanted the satchel charge and the bangalore torpedo. The captain is sustaining a reputation at battalion headquarters for bringing in assorted gear. So, quaking in our boondockers, we went back to the same area. Since Bengis knew where the charge lay, we took him along. It took us less than an hour to get out; we used a different route. The moon was high and we were thinking about the sniper that is said to occupy the burned-out tank. If one was there, we were under close observation. I found Hogg a defilade area, put him in it, and told him to keep his carbine trained on the tank. We approached the skyline near the area of our previous withdrawal, and we went after the satchel charge first. Bengis pointed to a portion of the low skyline and indicated that it was about here that he had thrown the satchel. He and Pugnacci provided cover; Kostis and I crawled out. At first we could not find it, and were forced to wander aimlessly on our stomachs. We hadn't the slightest doubt that we were being watched, incredulously, from the Pentagon. We wish to thank them for not opening up; they would have had us cold. When Kostis found the charge, we returned quickly to the reverse slope. The fuse-lighter had been pulled, but it must have been defective.

We searched for the bangalore torpedo. We could not find it. I called the captain and asked him to ask Tibbels to describe where he had dropped it. Strangely enough Tibbels had also been sent back into No Man's Land as the leader of a routine reconnaissance patrol, northwest of Hedy. In less than a minute I was talking to Tibbels himself, which was something of a surprise. Evidently the captain had hooked up our wire with his, making a three-way party line out of it. Tibbels described as best he could the location of the bangalore. We still couldn't find it, and called again. The captain was irritated by the fact that Tibbels had dropped the thing. We soon found it, and got the hell out of that area.

The torpedo is an ordinary piece of lead or steel pipe, with thick metal caps on each end. The pipe is filled with a hard yellow substance, like C-3. It is detonated by a fuse inserted in a small hole near one end of the pipe. The torpedo is about three feet long and is used to blow apart barbed-wire entanglements, thus creating a path for an assault force. The torpedo is simply slipped underneath the wire and set off. The name might imply that it is launched, but it is not.

Some disconnected facts concerning last night's action: Out of the fourteen-man unit, only six men returned the enemy's fire: Van Horn, Lo Castro, Rollins (a new man), Hogg, Pugnacci and myself. Kostis was busy pushing men over the skyline. Pugnacci checked later and found that he had fired seven full magazines—140 rounds. I fired about the same, not quite 120 rounds. Hogg was one of the first men that Van Horn pulled back, but he fired a full magazine—30 rounds—with his carbine. Lo Castro fired three and a half carbine magazines—about 100 rounds. Van Horn, who was busy pulling the men back, managed to fire several bursts. I don't know how much Rollins fired. The captain was highly displeased by the fact that not everyone fired his weapon, and said so. He asked each man whether or not he had fired. Fourteen men, all firing automatic weapons at the same target might have caused a great deal of damage. As it was, we doubt that any of our fire was accurate, although it was definitely effective in providing cover during the withdrawal. Van Horn has a cheerful note to add. He said that, as Pugnacci and I made that sprint, we were followed by a spray of slugs that kicked up the sand behind us. This probably means that one or two slugs landed nearby.

The most colorful tale of the evening concerns Frank Rollins, one of the new men—the only new man that fired. When the Chinese opened up, Rollins tried to wrench the satchel charge from Bengis's grasp. He wanted to run up to the Pentagon with it and drop it in the Chinese trench—a one-man Kamikaze. Lo Castro told us about it later and Bengis backed him up. Lo Castro said that he thought that Rollins had gone off his rocker and that he had pointed his carbine in Rollins's face, telling him to stay put or he would cut him down. This was Rollins's first patrol. We hope he is not another Schiff, bucking for a Congressional Medal of Honor. I guess that's the way that medal is won; a guy loses his mind and also his instinct of self-preservation. If he stays alive long enough he will undoubtedly cause some damage. But Rollins would have been killed crossing that wide area of open terrain which was illuminated by moonlight. He is a weird-looking cat, very tall—at least six feet two—and very skinny —he couldn't weigh more than 130 pounds. He is still in his teens, and has a girlish face. (This face has caused some alarm around here already. If he put on a wig he would not only look like a girl, but quite an attractive girl. Watch it, Russ. Forget about those Spartans before it's too late.) Van Horn is strange-looking also. He is tall and slender, has very bad teeth, and dark hair and complexion. His face is covered with smallpox scars. He is from Lawton, Oklahoma. Career marine.

May 1st, Hill 229
Writing by candlelight in the bunker again. There is an angry bombardment going on outside. We are safe inside, and hope that everyone else is inside, too.

Much carryings-on. Ray O'Ghoul sent us looking for trouble again. May 1st is the big Communist holiday—May Day—and he wanted to have a strong force in front of the MLR in case the celebration became too boisterous. As a matter of fact, they got pretty god-damned audacious.

Lt. Buell is still at Able Medical Company. It was Sgt. Henion's turn to take out the Diesel. I will be next. Henion asked me to take the point. It was (is) a fairly dark night and I took along the binoculars. They are large and cumbersome but well worth the trouble. The second point—or the second man in the column—was Pfc. Haals, who has been around. He never volunteers for point but always likes to be near the front of a column. But he was too close. He hugged my tail from the time we left

281

Bunker gate until we reached the Hedy-Bunker ridge. He would often stop me and point out likely places of ambush. This was enterprising of him but distracting, also unnecessary. We both saw a light further along the ridge, caught a glimpse before it went out. Possibly a signal system, announcing our approach to the Pentagon. There were sixteen of us and we made some noise.

It was fortunate that I carried the binoculars. The Hedy finger was barely visible; I was afraid that we might cross too close to the Pentagon. Through the glasses, I searched for the tank and found it. We were within fifty yards of it, that is, right at the base of the slope leading up to it. Our mission was two-fold. First, we were to scout the tank for snipers; second, we were to attempt to draw fire from the Pentagon, and then engage in a fire fight.

Haals was still too close. Before beginning the climb, I told him to broaden the interval considerably. We started to climb. The time was close to 11:30. The dark form of the tank looked ominous as hell, lying on its side. It looked as though it would fall over on us, and there was the possibility that a sniper was within it. The tracks had been blown off and all of the armament removed. A huge shapeless monster. I stopped ten yards below it, waiting. The word was passed back for the four-man scouting party to go to work. They snooped around the bulk for two or three minutes, found no sign of life, and resumed their positions within the column. Now came the difficult part.

We were to cross the skyline near the end of the tank road. We were exposed to view from the Pentagon on both sides of the skyline. On the opposite side, we would also be exposed to the Fan, located northwest of the Pentagon. When I was within a very few feet of the top, I noticed that Haals was creeping along *beside* me. I leaned over and whispered hell in his ear, making a rather melodramatic speech. "If we walked into an ambush," I said, "it would be *I* who would get clobbered first. Why should there be two of us?" adding that I have good eyes plus a pair of binoculars. "Get back down the slope with the rest of the column," said I, semiapoplectic. There are some outfits that use two-man, even three-man, points, but I don't dig it.

In this immediate area we could smell death. The mutilated body of the marine lies somewhere near here. A snatch party examined it the other night and found only a pair of legs.

I poked my head above the skyline and found that there is a strange little razor-backed ridge, running parallel to the tank road. In cross-section, the skyline there would look something like this:

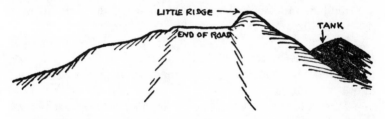

This is what the view would be from Hedy. The razor-back hump is two feet high.

For several minutes, I looked over the sloping terrain in the direction of the Fan and the Pentagon. No sign of life. The moon was not out, but it was fairly light. I crawled over the hump and across the end of the tank road. When I had reached the other side, Hanna made the cross. I moved down the slope to make room for him. We were not more than seventy-five yards from the Pentagon. The Fan was two or three hundred yards away, but we were in a perfect position to receive grazing fire. Next across came Pfc. Bartlett, who like an idiot, did not bother to come across the skyline on his stomach; rather he walked in a crouch. The Chinese on the Pentagon must have caught sight of this for, as Sgt. Henion began to crawl over the hump, the shit hit the fan.

One light automatic weapon opened fire on us—it wasn't a burp gun. Then a heavy automatic weapon opened up and green tracers streamed over our heads. Then lots of weapons, including all of our own. Bartlett fell to the ground unconscious, but came out of it within a matter of seconds. He believed that he had been hit by a stone, dislodged by a slug. Henion, Hanna, Bartlett and myself returned fire at once; two BARs, a carbine, a Thompson. The situation became tremendously confused. We four believed that the other twelve marines had been cut off, and that they were directly under enemy fire. And they believed us to be cut off. Actually, it was they who produced the most fire power and therefore they who received the most fire in return. Our main worry was that the Maxims on the Fan might fire. Fortunately they did not. We were at a disadvantage, not having any method of communication; the sound-power and the prc-6 were with the other twelve men.

Our concentrated exchange of fire power lasted from three to five minutes—a comparatively long encounter. These next bits of information, concerning the other twelve men, were made known to us later.

Mayfield was killed immediately. Pugnacci lay across his legs and fired an almost continuous barrage of slugs, emptying all of the magazines he carried, nine of them, and then began firing Mayfield's carbine. According to the account, not one of those twelve men retreated to the tank for cover, although it was only ten or fifteen yards behind them. Possibly they were too frightened to move; nevertheless, not frightened enough to prevent them from returning fire. With the exception of Mayfield, Brackett, Etherton and Collins—the last two named were wounded—the entire unit returned fire. The story is that Kostis saw to it that some of the men overcame their stupors by shouting at them to start firing in order to cover *us*.

Sgt. Henion alternated between firing his Thompson and shouting at the top of his lungs, trying to make contact with the other twelve, whom we could not see. As I mentioned, the Chinese on the Pentagon did their share of boisterous celebrating. The fact that there was so much shouting going on between the separated groups—I found myself shouting gibberish—may have led them to believe that they had inflicted heavy casualties. A Chinese snatch party was sent out from the trenches of the Pentagon.

The enemy fire slackened. We like to think that our concentrated fire power actually neutralized theirs. It is true that the green tracers stopped streaking overhead as soon as our fire became centralized.

We four began to withdraw, sidling back toward the left flank of outpost Hedy. There were intermittent bursts of fire from both sides. Grenades began to explode near us. Henion shouted at us to heave all the grenades we had. The Chinese snatch party was close by. Not one of us saw a sign of them. We knew only that they were close enough to throw grenades. They were out of our line of sight, in a gully. Pugnacci, who was among the other group, said that there were five or six of them and that they were moving around fast, probably looking for bodies. These Chinese were seen—by Pugnacci and some of the other men—shortly after our barrage commenced. The captain, anticipating trouble, had already seen to it that the company mortar tubes were registered on the Pentagon. For some reason the barrage was inaccurate at first, the rounds landing so close to the fourteen men, in their tight group, that they were forced to withdraw and seek cover, dragging their wounded. I offer this as the excuse for the fact that the snatch party was not fired upon by that group. It was a matter of bad timing.

We four threw all available grenades and then found our way back to Hedy, a matter of twenty or thirty yards, and immediately became tangled among the barbed wire. The marine mortar barrage increased in intensity. Some of the men on Hedy saw us and made our position known to the captain, who then contacted the other group and told them to pull back, that we were safe. Within a few minutes we were together, waiting in the Hedy-MLR trenchline as the heads were counted. Fourteen, including poor Mayfield. All in. We moved back to the MLR through Hedy gate and rushed down to the CP, the safest place on the MLR—thirteen layers of sandbags overhead.

Captain Krupp had pressed the panic button, as they say. Within fifteen minutes every tank slot in the sector was occupied by a gun tank. Block Six—the huge ridgeline four hundred yards behind the MLR—was occupied by troops who had been pulled out of their sleeping bags in reserve areas. Block Six is a segment of the secondary MLR.

The Chinese counterbarrage commenced shortly after we reached the Hedy trench. It was going full blast when I began writing—it sounded as heavy as the barrage after the Old Bunker raid—but died out at least an hour ago.

During our withdrawal, a machine gunner on Hedy reported to the captain that he spotted a small group of figures out there ahead of us. This must have been the snatch party. After we got out of the way, he fired at them.

Stan Bartlett had an incredible experience, an incredible piece of luck. The blow that knocked him momentarily unconscious, which he believed to be a rock, was in fact a slug which grazed his skull. It passed through his helmet above the left eye, grazed his temple, and made an exit out the left side. He discovered this of course when he saw the holes in his helmet. He says that he will take the helmet home, which should be of great interest to his folks.

Mayfield was shot through the chest. I didn't know him. He was a colored guy from Philadelphia. Nice-looking gent, unmarried, wanted to play baseball. Etherton was shot in the thigh; Collins's wrist was grazed. These were the only real casualties. Pugnacci picked up some splinters from one of the grenades thrown at us, and so did I—tiny splinters, tiny cuts. I have a larger cut above the knee, which I strongly suspect was gashed when we got hung up on the wire. Nevertheless my pants leg was good and bloody and Ray O'Ghoul made an examination and sent me down to Corpsman Truro, who promptly marked me down for a Texas League Purple Heart. If my parents get one of those god-damned ghoul telegrams ("Cpl. Martin F. Russ has received wounds, on May 1st, 1953, in action against the enemy"), they'll surely think I've been maimed for life, so I'll get off a quick letter.

May 2nd, Hill 229

I saw Danny at chow today. He is in good shape, working at the forward aid station next to the chow bunker. Some idiot put my name on the casualty list and Dan was a bit worried. Here's the way I feel about it. It would be nice to return to the States with a Heart—a real one—but since I'll be discharged as soon as we hit Treasure Island I wouldn't be able to parade around with the ribbons even if I wanted to. And I'll never brag about having a Heart. As far as I'm concerned, the medal will represent all those times I've been scared, and for just having been over here.

A recon last night. THE fire team, plus Frank Rollins who had the honor of being asked to join us. Our forward point of advance was the middle finger of Three Fingers. Unknown to the captain, we made an agreement to go out to that point, and keep going until our speed reel gave out. We sat on the end of the finger for more than an hour, surveying the terrain below through the glasses. There was a graveyard halfway down the first broad shelf of earth; we decided to head for that.

On the way out, even though we had moved like shadows, those damn frogs stopped croaking and the peepers quieted down. This is always very disturbing. The frogs and the peepers produce the same kind of sound that you might hear in the countryside on a spring evening at home. We hear it all the time at night here and, therefore, become accustomed to it; that is, we are not aware of the sound. On patrol, our ears monitor this sound and are sensitive to any other sound. But when the frogs and the peepers hear us and stop honking and cheeping, it is as though the earth has stopped revolving. And it is easy to imagine that the Chinese nearby have noticed this, too, and that they know we are coming. So last night we left the paths and took to the hills. The movement was much slower, but we avoided the paddies and the frogs and the peepers honked and cheeped as usual. Approaching what we will call the final skyline, we had one bad moment. There was a movement up there, and we stopped and looked through the glasses. It looked like a helmet;

287

as though the man were sitting on the reverse slope, less than fifteen yards away, with only his head visible to us. And it moved every so often. Using hand signals, I sent Kostis and Hogg on a flanking movement to take a look. They moved off to the right and then crawled up to the skyline. It turned out to be a little bush, moving in the soft wind.

While we were waiting on the edge of the middle finger of Three Fingers, a marine machine gunner, located halfway between Hedy gate and outpost Ingrid, fired a routine harassing&interdictory mission. These are fired many times throughout the night, along all sectors of the front. They are not usually directed at specific targets, but at possible areas of approach: large gullies for example. The gunner can't see what he's shooting at, but he doesn't have to; he will have zero-ed-in the weapon during the day. At night all he has to do is squeeze the trigger, move the traverse and elevation mechanism back and forth in a tiny arc, and his bursts will spray a particular area of terrain. The possibility is that his beaten zone—or impact area—will coincide with the location of an enemy patrol. Marine patrol leaders are always informed where the beaten zone is. However, last night we entered the Easy Company sector as we played our little game of moving forward until the speed reel played out. In order to approach Three Fingers from a new angle, I led the patrol quite far to the west. We made the turn, crossed a wide gully and reached the beginning of our objective. As I mentioned, a machine gunner fired a harassing&interdictory mission as we were studying the terrain below. The gunner's beaten zone was the wide gully we had just crossed. We watched the red tracers streak toward us from the rear—a beautiful sight in a way—watched them burn out in the sand, and thought how lucky we were to have left the gully as quickly as we did.

We descended the gradual slope.

The speed reel came to its end shortly after we had started back, which was perhaps fortunate. We found cover in a thin, narrow indentation in the ground and surveyed the terrain once more, and cut the wire. There seems to be a path below the graveyard, running NW-SE. We mentioned this to the captain later, hoping that he would set up a combat patrol or an ambush down there. He replied—something like this: "I'm not going to send anybody out where they don't *have* to go. The 25th (Army Division) is relieving us in a couple of days. So—we're going to sit tight and play it cool."

GROUP NINE

███

Camp Guyol

██

May 5th, 1953

We seem to be in Corps reserve, at least the 1st Battalion is. The ride down here was the END. Spring is here for real, but we didn't know for certain until the sun came up during the truck convoy south. We saddled up some time past midnight, said good luck to the soldiers that replaced us, and climbed off the hill, 229, joining the rest of Able Company at the bottom. The mess people brought vats of hot coffee to us and we spread out among the ravines, along the dikes, or along the supply road, drank coffee and talked or slept. But hardly anyone slept, too excited and happy to be off the top of 229. The trucks arrived at 4:30 and we climbed aboard. We moved out. It grew light and the sun came up. A clear, dewy morning, promising a hot day. Unlike the terrain on the MLR and in No Man's Land, the hills and mountains to the south are covered with greenery, including many-colored patches of wild flowers. One of the most startling sights of all were the rice paddies. It had never occurred to me that these fields *worked*. Near the front, of course, they don't work; they are ruined. But south of the Imjim they are going concerns. The farmers wade around, sometimes knee-deep, in the water, wielding their crude hoes. The weather is balmy. Kids come around from the neighboring villages to shine our shoes for inspections or to take our laundry to be done by their folks.

The first night back we went whoring, Kostis, Pugnacci, Hogg and myself. It was strange to find ourselves creeping along dikes, skirting small paddies, halting abruptly whenever we heard a noise—there were numerous sentries posted in a wide perimeter around the camp, to watch for people like us. It was as though we were on another O'Ghoul patrol, except that there were no Chinese, and we carried no weapons. I felt naked without the BAR, even though it wasn't needed. I had the point again and enjoyed it in a thoroughly different way. And I vowed that I'd clobber the first sentry that tried to stop us. None did, we evaded them all. The officer of the day was also out there, we heard him challenge and catch some other night-crawlers.

The rice shoots, in neat little bunches, are just appearing above the water. In some places the water is quite deep. We knew the direction of the nearest town in relation to our camp, but not its name or exact location. We passed a tiny hamlet, occupying the end of a narrow wooded ravine. All we could see were the candles that burned inside three or four thatched huts. We felt as though we were passing a Chinese outpost. But it was all for the invisible movie cameras, and we were outplaying John Wayne again.

We saw a fire burning in the distance and we went toward it, climbing along a series of gentle slopes. As we came closer we heard singing and soon made out the figures of Korean men and women, young and old, seated around the fire. Some of them were drinking from tin cups, and some were singing a happy kind of Oriental blues. They smiled and nodded vigorously to us as we passed. A young boy rose, left the group and caught up with us. We asked him to lead us to the town and he understood. We walked for a long time, maybe three miles, but we enjoyed the walk. There was no hurry. No one said a word. We came to a main supply route, and the boy told us to lie down on the ground because a truck was approaching. When it passed by we rose and sprinted across the road, finding the edge of the town a hundred yards in on the other side, nestling along the bottom of a series of very steep ridges which towered above. The town, as we approached it, was nearly obscured among the leaves of many trees, but we could see the light of candles and lanterns.

We had never seen a town like it. Obviously my powers of description are limited when it comes to Korean towns. I was totally unable to translate my garbled impressions into writing after I had seen Inchon and Seoul; and this town—to hell with my impressions. It was like an anonymous town that one wanders through in a dream. Dreaming of a town like this, I usually meet or at least, see a faceless but beautiful dark-haired girl. Several Faceless Dark-haired Girls appeared unto us but they were not exactly beautiful. But it made no difference; we leered in the lewdest possible manner at each and every one of them, from the ancient mama-sans to the little ones with bangs.

The town was small; it might measure roughly three hundred yards by three hundred yards. We wandered around the streets, fascinated. Open-air stores, tended usually by one man seated near a dim kerosene lantern. Sometimes a woman would be seated nearby. Everybody inscrutable as hell, of course, except us. Their faces looked so strange, yet they weren't hostile. They *observed* us. The smell of the kerosene-soaked wicks was fine. Andy found the entire business extremely amusing, it was too unreal. His running comment, which he seemed to be addressing to himself, was in the form of half-audible bad imitations of an Oriental accent, muttered under his breath as we moved along. "Goood eve-a-neeng, mos' honoraberr Korearn genterrman . . . Mos' admiraberr, mos' in*curti*berr Orienterr papa-san andt hees a-missee, mama-san." He was sometimes acknowledged by a stone-faced nod.

We met no other Americans in the town, which was fine. The houses were low, one-story jobs, with sometimes a single room projecting from the side of one of the fragile walls. Lattice doors, papier-mâché walls. The young boy, preceding us, entered several houses and was yelled at by the inhabitants of each. Finally we were led into one of the shelters and told to sit down on the dirt floor of a tiny room. Six candles protruded from the walls, burning at a 45-degree angle. After considerable haggling with a Korean Bloody Mary, the price that was agreed upon was three dollars apiece or a piece. Without studying her too carefully, I chose one of the women, and she led me outside and into her stall, further down the street. The walls were papered with Japanese and Korean newspapers and candles were protruding from the wall. There was a wind-up phonograph on a small bureau and several Chinese records. Also pictures of Korean soldiers, herself, her parents, and a picture of some mountains. There was a dusty blanket on the floor. She smelled as though she hadn't bathed for several days, but I liked that. I wasn't quite well-kempt myself.

Later I walked around the town, looking at the weird merchandise sold in the open-air stalls. Strange, dry vegetables and weeds and seeds, all shapes and colors. I bought some very extraordinary pastry, which I want more of.

May 8th, Camp Guyol

Memorial services were held yesterday at the regimental parade ground. There were thirteen companies of marines present. A four-mile walk. General Ballard made a speech, a typical droning, platitudinous, meaningless speech. I doubt that anyone listened. A chaplain and a rabbi spoke. Isolated phrases that I remember. ". . . in glory . . . that they will not have died in vain . . . not forgotten," etc. None of those men died gloriously. And most of them died in vain. Only the ones that died while saving the lives of others did not die in vain. The most disturbing thing of all is that not one of them knew why they were dying. I still have a book called *The Greek Way* by Edith Hamilton. I have underlined a sentence or two. "Why is the death of an ordinary man a wretched, chilling thing, which we turn from, while the death of a hero, always tragic, warms us with the sense of quickened life?" I don't know, Miss Hamilton. You tell me. You're the one who felt that sense of quickened life. I never felt it.

The roll of the dead was read off. Many, many names, some familiar. Edward Guyol. John Riley. Willy Mayfield. Waldron, Carlough. All ordinary men, no heroes.

As usual during mass formations on a hot day, several men passed out.

May 9th, 1953. Camp Guyol

Sgt. Zarcone has started a boxing team. Why not give it a whirl, sez I? He tumbled us out of the sack at 4:30 this morning and ran us ragged. Then calisthenics before chow. Tomorrow morning is going to be murder.

The Seoul liberty rotation began as soon as we came into reserve. Andy brought back another lump of stuff that he claims is heroin. His reaction to it is startling. He will sit perfectly still on the edge of his rack for literally hours at a time. At infrequent intervals he will rub his face hard with the palms of his hands and then return to catatonia. The stuff makes him irritable, and his face becomes blotched with little light patches. I let him turn me on, as the phrase is, the other day. He led me up to a ridge behind camp and we sat down. He sifted a small amount on a bent piece of paper, like a tiny trough, and held it under my nose.

He said if I blew any of it away, he would shoot me. (Twenty-five dollars a gram.) I drew up hard, the powder went in like snuff. In a few minutes I was partially high but didn't feel good or bad, merely nowhere. Booze is better.

There is an English tank outfit within three miles of us. Hogg has made friends with one of the tankers. His Dickensian name is Tom Morley. He brings an offering of rum from the Commonwealth each time he comes. His personal weapon is a Sten gun. The weapon costs less than three dollars. BAR costs more than 350 dollars. The effective range of the Sten gun is about seven inches, judging from the look of it, which is like a toy sparkler gun. Tom Morley says that he will soon be sent home and then he will be sent to Inja.

May 10th, Camp Guyol

A workout with gloves today to loosen up rigid muscles. I'm not certain that this is really fun—to have a man stand in front of you and snap his gloved fists at your face. "Why?" I said to myself. "Do I have to? What is it that we are proving to ourselves now? Haven't we been through all that in No Man's Land, having found that it didn't prove a god-damned thing?" Zarcone says I have a good left, fair right, terrible footwork, good defense, terrible stamina. He suggested that I should try to get used to being hit in the face. He is possibly intimating that I am yellow. That is correct. I turned in my jock strap this afternoon, and will sleep peacefully tomorrow morning until six o'clock while those other fanatics go thundering down the main supply route at 4:30.

May 11th, Camp Guyol

At 4:30 this morning I felt someone shaking my rack. Sgt. Zarcone. "Come on, big boy," he said. "We got no other light-heavyweights, and we're going to have a match with the 2nd Battalion next month. Get up! Roadwork!" This was a cue I've anticipated for several years. "On your way rejoicing," says I, going back to sleep. The next thing I knew was that I was lying on the ground, with the rack on top of me. "Zarcone," I hissed, aspeyed, "I'm going to kill you." We squared off, I in my nakedness. I took one wild swing at him, missed, and fell down, still half asleep. "I'll take care of you later, ace," said the sergeant, and he left.

June 21st, 1953. Camp Guyol

A great deal has happened during the last four weeks. In short, I was finally forced to go to N.C.O. school, or should we say *Sturm-Soldaten Schule*. Boot camp was nothing. The only comfort was that master sergeants, tech sergeants, and staff sergeants underwent the same training as the buck sergeants and the corporals. I didn't even attempt to take notes. This was our usual schedule:

5 A.M. reveille
5:05 outside, dressed. Physical exercise under arms.
5:45 chow
6:30 police call (working outside; removing grass, butts, paper, raking, etc.)
7:00 inspection of tents, weapons and personnel; followed by close order drill on the parade field of sand.
8:00 to 11:30 classes, very formal
12 noon—chow
1 P.M. to 2 a class
2 P.M. to 6 P.M. field problems
6:30 chow

Four nights a week there was a field problem. Every third day we marched to the Imjim during the noon hour, bathed and washed our clothes. We were issued large notebooks, covering the following subjects—·matching the lectures given in class:

military courtesy and discipline, 2 hours.
interior guard (guard duty), 3 hours.
leadership, 2 hrs.
drills and ceremonies, 7 hrs., in the field.
technique of fire, 1 hr., in the field.
map reading and compass, 7 hrs., in the field.
signals and basic formations of squad and fire team movement, 2 hrs., in the field.
terrain appreciation—a euphemism if there ever was one; learning how to estimate the distance of various targets—1 hr., in the field.
introduction to offensive combat, 1 hr., in the field.
demolitions, 2 hrs., in the field.
scouting and patrolling, 4 hours, in the field.
offensive combat, leadership in, 1 hr., for each man, in the field.
organization, function and equipment of Marine Corps, 1 hr.
raids, 1 hr., in the field.
ambushes, 1 hr., in the field.
tank and infantry co-ordination 1 hr., with tanks, in the field.
attack on a fortified position, 1 hr., in the field—a dummy outpost
attack on a river line, 1 hr., in the field—Imjim river.

patrols, combat and reconnaissance, 2 hrs., in the field.
field fortifications and individual protection, 1 hr.
guerrilla warfare, 2 hrs.
operation of an infantry unit in wooded terrain, 1 hr.
retrograde movements, 1 hr.
rifle platoon tactics in defense and offensive, 2 hrs., in the field.
security missions, 1 hr.
military information, 4 hrs.
co-ordination of supporting arms, 2 hrs.
The UN in Korea, 2 hrs.
communications, 2 hrs.
amphibious operations, 2 hrs.
supply economy, 2 hrs.
administration, 1 hr.
mines and booby traps, 2 hrs.
first aid, 4 hrs.

We marched in formation everywhere we went. Each man had to assume each of the following posts for a day: company commander, first sergeant, platoon leader, platoon sergeant, platoon guide, squad leader. We were given grades for almost everything we did. We were given two written examinations before graduation. We were each required to give a ten-minute lecture on a military subject of our own choosing. On the final day, we were marched out to a series of ridgelines, given sheets of cardboard and a pencil, and told to draw a map. "You are a company commander. Your company will occupy that ridgeline. You will probably be attacked tonight. Draw a map, showing exactly how you will deploy your units. Show the location of the command post, mortars, anti-tank weapons and machine guns."

Those four weeks were undoubtedly the most valuable training, excepting actual combat, that I've received. And in a way it was fun.

Last month the Army and the Turks lost outposts Vegas, Reno and Elko to the Chinese. The Commonwealth division lost their positions along that sector known as the Hook.

Some ideas: in night fighting, the sights of small arms weapons are useless; one can only aim roughly along the barrel. Why not stamp a luminous dot on the rear of the front sight?

A patrol usually carries a prc-6 and a sound-power for communication. Why not use two prc-6 radios with hand-set attachments—earphones, small microphone—and dispense with the bulky sound-power, its heavy speed reels, and the expense and trouble of all the wire?

Some kind of portable shelter should be perfected, for use during withdrawals from a raid, or for use during the digging-in phase after a unit occupies a newly taken position. As we have seen, most of the casualties are inflicted during withdrawals.

Camp Guyol. (Undated)
Kostis, Pugnacci and I had a narrow escape last night. We decided to let Andy turn us on—skin pop style, heroin through the needle. This happened after evening chow. We waited until it was dark and then eluded the sentries on the north side of camp. By the time we reached the Commonwealth post exchange&beer joint an hour later we were stoned. We walked in, ordered some Asahi, and began throwing darts at a target board. I got sick and went outside. It was raining. I sat down on the ground and leaned against the wheel of a truck, and fell asleep. When I awoke there was someone standing over me. It was very dark, but I could see that he was drunk as hell. I was being pissed upon, so I scrambled to my feet and stumbled into him, trying to swing but all tied up. It was Pugnacci. He hadn't seen me and was mortified at what he had done, but we laughed. When we returned to the large tent, it was fairly crowded. We played darts again. Not one of us had said a word to any of the English. They were making much noise, singing, yelling. There were three large colored photographs on the wall near the top of the tent. Queen Elizabeth, the prince consort, Bonnie Prince Charlie. A toast was made to the queen. We continued throwing darts, silently. One of the English yelled at us, "Hey, Yank. Why don't you toast our beautiful queen?" Andy threw another dart. Then I threw one. "Hey, Yank!" Pugnacci threw a dart. We were quickly surrounded by a number of angry faces. "Yank. I suggest you pay

tribute to our beautiful queen, you know." We stared at them. "Now!" the man said. What could we do? We were marines. We would never live it down if we backed out. But we would die anyway. Frankly, I don't know what the hell I intended doing. Nothing. Pugnacci started to throw another dart at the target, but someone was standing in front of it. Pugnacci, bless his little butt, picked up a bottle of Asahi, raised it over his head, and shouted, "All hail to the bee-OO-tiful queen!" All was well and we were bought many Asahis. And Cadbury chocolate bars.

(AUTHOR'S NOTE: The following three entries, concerning events which took place immediately before the truce, were actually written after the truce. They seemed anticlimactic in their original position, so I've switched them to here.)

Shortly before the truce, a new marine outpost was established, called Boulder City. The circumstances leading up to its fortification as an outpost were as follows: The Chinese made a series of attacks, mass attacks, on East Berlin. The casualties were extremely heavy; unit after unit was replaced. Finally the higher echelon decided to evacuate East Berlin. The segment of the MLR behind East Berlin then became the outpost, Boulder City. So the tactical situation was something like this. (The Chinese, of course, occupied East Berlin as soon as we departed.)

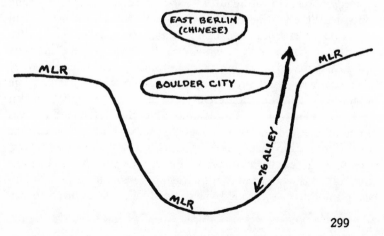

The Chinese then launched heavy assaults on Boulder City, for several successive nights, but failed to overrun it. The marine casualties were appalling. Had the enemy taken Boulder City, they would have commanded a view of several of our important supply routes. Incidentally, Boulder City covered the area that we, the ———— platoon of Able company, occupied last January and February. The day after the cease-fire, detachments of marines and Chinese gathered on Boulder City to collect the dead. Many of the Chinese wore white cloths over their lower faces to cut the odor. Others, so it is said, placed garlic in their nostrils. I would have given anything to have seen Chinese at such close range. . . .

Our little group, occupying the Wyoming line outpost, was relieved by a detachment from the 1st Marines—Item company. The machine-gun section leader told us the following tale, which took place the day before the truce was signed.

The forwardmost position on Hedy was Charlie-hole. A marine standing watch in it that day spotted a sniper, firing at the MLR from a foxhole. The sniper was one hundred yards or so northeast of the marine's position. He took aim and fired at the sniper, who fell backwards out of sight. The marine decided to get himself a prisoner. He found a roll of communication wire and tied one end of it around his ankle. Another marine—his companion in Charlie-hole—played out the wire as the first marine crawled through the parapet. The terrain to the right front of Hedy is such that a man can move forward and be fairly well concealed by following the line of the crisscrossing gullies.

After several minutes of crawling, he appeared along the slope on the other side of which was the sniper. The other marine in Charlie-hole saw him. He continued to feed out the wire. The other man suddenly tumbled across the skyline, his weapon at the ready. A concussion grenade exploded in that area and the marine in Charlie-hole quickly pulled up the slack on the wire. He continued pulling; there was no weight at the other end. The story is that this man—the one who was lost—recently signed over for a six-year reenlistment. But he is probably not dead. The theory is that he was seen leaving Charlie-hole, and that a small ambush was prepared. The first thing that occurred to me as the story was being told was that I would probably have done the same thing—although I would have taken someone else along for cover.

The man from Item company also said that it had been discovered—he didn't say how—that the Chinese had been digging a tunnel into New Bunker, that—had the tunnel been completed —it would have breached the outpost somewhere on the right flank.

The last two patrols, shortly before the truce.

I was having one of those fine, hot-afternoon dreams when Van Horn shook me awake, said that the forward party was moving up to the MLR and were expected to be ready in thirty minutes.

The fighting here in the spring was comparatively static. The Chinese lines remained generally intact, as did ours. Neither side made any major offensive moves, content to send out occasional raiding parties and ambushes. However, when the signing of the truce at Panmunjom seemed imminent, the enemy—during the final few days of fighting—launched several massive thrusts at some of our outposts and strong points. During those last nights, that is, before the final enemy offensive, patrols and ambushes of both sides were scheduled as usual. Van Horn and I took part in two of these patrols.

In this stationary type of war it was possible for a unit in reserve to study the "standing" situation of a particular position on line before that unit actually relieved the unit then defending the position. This was accomplished by a skeletal forward party whose job it was to memorize patrol paths, sectors of automatic fire, mortar concentrations, boundaries of mine fields and barbed wire; and whose job it was to learn as much of the activities to be expected of the enemy as possible, by questioning the members of the unit about to be relieved. A forward party usually consisted of platoon commanders (lieutenants), platoon sergeants, and infantry and machine-gun-squad leaders.

Within half an hour, the forward party of Able company had

boarded two trucks and were plummeting along a dusty road, heading north. We carried a minimum of gear, having stored most of it with Mother Connant, who would bring it along later—when the rest of the company moved up on line. My equipment and personal gear were as follows: Weapon, magazine belt, helmet, armored vest, blanket, toothbrush and powder. I didn't bring this notebook. Nor shaving gear.

Here is a map drawn from memory of that sector of the MLR which Able Company was to occupy within a week:

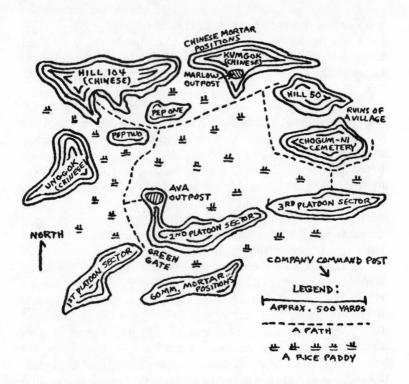

Our three hills were rather low. The crest of the hill occupied by the ——— platoon was no more than one hundred feet above the rice paddy. The fields of fire were excellent. A larger hill mass is likely to contain saddles and draws—defilade areas, ambiguously referred to as "dead spaces," due to the fact that although these areas are inaccessible to the fire of our machine guns, they are within areas of mortar concentration. There's a muddled definition if I ever heard one.

Another decidedly defensive advantage was the size and flatness of the vast rice paddy separating our hills from those of the enemy. This area, in the event of a mass attack, could have provided no cover at all against our artillery and mortar bombardment.

Each squad sector, defended normally by ten to fifteen men, was supported by two light (30 cal.) machine guns. The over-all platoon sector was supported additionally by two of the regimental .50 cal. guns. With such an efficient defensive arrangement, the company was able to utilize a comparatively large number of troops for reconnaissance and combat patrols.

The particular unit then occupying this sector was Fox Company, 1st Marines. Sgt. Van Horn accompanied one of Fox Company's patrols the first night we got up there. For some obscure reason there had been room for only one member of the forward party, and I was unable to wangle a spot. So I passed the night standing watch in the MLR trench. The following morning I hunted for Van Horn to ask him a few questions—the route of the patrol paths, etc.—but was unable to find him.

A thirty-man combat patrol was scheduled to go out that night, and I asked to go along. A small recon patrol, preceding us by three hours, reported having sighted a long enemy column approaching the small, brush-covered knoll called Pep One. The recon returned at 11:30. The word spread around rapidly and the usual pre-patrol excitement was increased—by the prospect of engaging the enemy. Pep One, we knew, would be one of our check points.

To most of us, patrolling was part privilege. I seem to have a more normal outlook, now that the truce is signed. I've been thinking about it lately and am astounded, really astounded at the naïveté I displayed. It's written all over these notes. I was grateful to be able to take part in the adventure. Asinine as it may be, it is true, and there's no other way to put it.

The area known as No Man's Land is, no matter how one considers it, morbidly fascinating. For several months this strip of land separating North Korea from South—in some places less than a hundred yards wide, in others more than a thousand—has been the most treacherous piece of ground in the world. Terrible battles have been fought here, but the armies did not move on; they entrenched themselves in caves, bunkers and trenches which were deepened and strengthened as the months passed. On this same corridor of land, men of many nations have been killed, wounded or captured. Ragged infantry companies were replaced by fresh troops, who were then subjected to the same gruesome adventures until they in turn were replaced. Both sides became so strongly fortified that few men ever ventured out there in daylight and returned.

Gazing out there at night, it is easy for one's imagination to run rampant. Not only does one often see objects which are not there, but also one hears nonexistent noises. One night, on Hill 229, I stared out there for so long that the very aspect of the shadows, the clouds and the sky, were transformed into a massive hall, the walls, ceiling and floor of which were so far apart that one loud noise—an artillery shell, a mortar round, a grenade—re-echoed in my mind for several minutes. Someday, ten or twenty years from now, I will pay a more casual visit to Korea and perhaps then find myself incongruously nostalgic thinking about the days when I was a marine. . . .

The men of the combat patrol were assembled by midnight, immediately behind the opening in the MLR trench called Green gate—same kind of setup as Bunker gate on Hill 229. Our mission was roughly as follows: Proceed to the foot of Hill 104, at which point ten men will be detached. Under the cover of overhead fire provided by the remaining twenty men, the detachment will assault the hill, etc.

The patrol leader was Lt. deGourdier. I never saw more of him than his silhouette, for I missed the afternoon briefing. S/Sgt. Rau was second in command. Three Navy corpsmen accompanied the patrol and were stationed at even intervals along the column. Also included were two light machine-gun crews. To maintain communication with the CP, two men carried prc-6s and one man a sound-power. In the thirty-man file, I was number sixteen, located immediately behind one of the gun crews. Back at Camp Guyol, shortly after we arrived, I was issued a brand-new BAR, which I made into something of a hot rod by removing the following parts: flash-hider, front-sight cover, bipod assembly, front and rear sling swivel and base, rear-sight assembly, and shoulder support plate. For once all the magazines were full, that is, I carried 360 rounds on this patrol. When the word was passed around that the recon had spotted a Chinese column, many of the men went to the ammo dump and collected a complete issue of rounds.

We passed through Green gate soon after midnight. A private known as Wang was the point man. He was closely followed by two men: the second and third points. This separate group of three moved in advance of the main body of troops. As soon as we descended the small slope in front of Green gate, it became apparent that the trail itself was ripe for ambush. It was bordered on both sides by waist-high rice stalks capable of concealing a large number of men. There were no land mines in this paddy, nevertheless it would have been too much of a production to wade through the mire and the brittle rice stalks; the noise of our movement would easily pinpoint our position to any nearby enemy.

The trail runs along for a hundred yards or so to where it meets another path coming from outpost Ava. Beyond this junction the path curves slightly to the right and heads north. Across the level paddy, a distance of approx. three hundred yards, the path intersects at right angles with another path which crosses directly in front of Pep One. Three languid ming trees are growing at this junction.

The column neared the other side of the paddy after an hour of creeping, punctuated by long delays as Wang searched behind bushes and listened for sounds, etc. Nearly across, the column halted once more and the men lay down as usual. Wang had found a taut trip-wire stretched across the path. Following the wire over to the left side of the path, he found a POM-Z stake

305

mine—of Russian design—planted in the ditch. This mine resembles a crudely corrugated potato-masher, the end of which is stuck into the ground. It can be deactivated. Wang, with this in mind, passed the word back for the lieutenant to come up.

While Wang waited for the lieutenant, a Chinese soldier watched him from behind a bush, less than fifteen yards away. Nearby, other Chinese infantrymen awaited the signal to attack. During the delay, the men in the column had bunched together somewhat, particularly near the front. Some of the men were almost beside one another. It is so easy to get careless on a large patrol. I know that I felt quite safe at this time. The dim outline of Pep One was visible up ahead. It is a small but clearly defined knoll. I was gazing calmly at it, lying flat on my stomach, when the total silence of the humid night was shattered by the voice of one burp gun, close by. This is what had happened.

When the officer arrived, accompanied by S/Sgt. Rau, Wang pointed out the trip-wire and the stake mine to him. Lt. deGourdier, barely armed with a .45, crawled over to the right side of the path, following the wire. Meanwhile Rau lay down in the ditch and covered him with his carbine. The wire disappeared into a clump of bushes, behind which the Chinese was lying. The lieutenant fumbled into the growth, probably curious to know where the wire was secured. He had time to say "Oh!" before he was shot. He fell among the foliage and was captured. This patrol incidentally was his first and last (I read recently that Lt. deGourdier was one of the prisoners of war returned to UN custody at Freedom Village, Munsan-ni during the month of August. He was a litter case, wearing a torso cast, but was recovering reasonably well from a *number* of bullet wounds).

Following that initial burst, which was the signal, the shit *really* hit the fan. A tremendous volume of fire, coming from our right front, at a distance varying from twenty to fifty yards. These were the first muzzle blasts that I noticed. (This is a bad time to interrupt, but before I forget to mention it: Van Horn wasn't a member of this patrol.) Fire of equal intensity came from our left front but at a greater distance. The ambush had been deployed in an inverted V formation, and the fire from its apex was obviously the most deadly.

Of the first ten marines in the column, nine were hit by slugs. Wang alone escaped. He wisely refrained from returning fire—he was practically in their laps—and lay perfectly still in the ditch a few feet to the rear of the POM-Z. S/Sgt. Rau was not so wise. He fired his carbine at the first muzzle blast and then catapulted into the brush in an attempt to retrieve the lieutenant. He was apparently killed in hand-to-hand combat. Wang later said that he thought he heard Rau yell, and not from pain. He was found a half an hour later by a rescue party; skull caved in, his body punctured in several places, his own weapon and bayonet—found nearby—covered with blood.

The dark valley was filled with a variety of noises; the raucous chattering of automatic weapons producing sharp fingers of orange light and in the case of the two or three enemy machine guns producing a series of brilliant greenish white tracer trajectories. Slugs were striking the deck close by. Some grenades were probably thrown, but I was transfixed, aware only that I was pinned down under enemy fire, but nothing like a scene in a war picture.

In a fire fight, or any type of severe combat, time is indistinguishable. I may have remained immobile for minutes or only seconds. It was an enormous effort to move anything but my eyes; limbs were leaden as in a nightmare, and the old fear fever took hold. It is difficult to describe this state, terror. Physical terror I mean. It is a rare emotion in this age. Every soldier that has been in combat must have felt it. The immediate problem is to overcome it as quickly as possible. If he cannot, he ceases to function as a soldier. I sweated profusely from the summer heat, and yet I was very cold and shivering convulsively. After an interminable period I overcame the thing and rolled over into the ditch along the left side of the path, gaining a fair amount of cover.

I wondered why our two machine guns were not firing. Four of the gunners had been hit, and the others were unable to set up the weapons as rapidly as they might have wished. The BAR was already cocked, and I began squeezing off short bursts at the uniform (and fairly distant) line of muzzle blasts on the right. I recall that following each burst I tried to bury myself in the ground, anticipating disaster in the form of grenades or accurate return fire. Most of the other men had overcome their inertia and were firing their weapons.

The intensity of the enemy fire power diminished perceptively as our individual fire took effect, but the damage had been done. Most of our casualties were inflicted during the first ten or fifteen seconds of the encounter, the Chinese having gained the advantage of surprise.

Six marines were killed. Fourteen were wounded, and one —Lt. deGourdier—was captured. By the end of the action the Chinese probably suffered as many casualties, considering the late mortar barrage. According to a man named Welch, we had a prisoner for a few seconds later in the action but, rather than be hindered by escorting him back to the MLR, Welch and another man killed him.

In a short time the remaining machine gunners had assembled one of their weapons and were laying down long bursts. The gun was close by, and I could see the gunner lying in the ditch behind the weapon, which had been set up on the edge of the path. The familiar PHUM-PHUM-PHUM racket must have made every live marine out there feel less than irretrievably lost. So the situation had seemed up to that point. Several of our wounded began to return fire also. In spite of the utter chaos of those first few moments, the matter really boiled down to a question of which side was the better trained; which side could establish fire superiority.

It is said that the Chinese will not attack an enemy force unless that force is greatly outnumbered. I estimated there to have been thirty to fifty Chinese engaged in this ambush; most of the others made broader estimates.

Three main factors saved the patrol from annihilation: the ability to return rapid and accurate fire, the aggressiveness of the men during the withdrawal, and the borders of high growth which shielded most of our movement. The main battle lasted for less than five minutes, I would guess. During this time no one changed position other than to roll into the ditch. When the enemy fire had been generally neutralized, the laborious withdrawal phase commenced. Ghastly figures appeared along the path, recalling a certain description by Ambrose Bierce. One man, coughing and spitting blood, crawled over my legs. Other small groups passed by bearing dead and wounded.

The shooting at this time was intermittent; bursts aimed at noises or shadows. I began to crawl forward. Grenades exploded occasionally, not many; only two men were treated for shrapnel wounds. Each time someone fired from a relatively short distance on either side of the path, I would fire back a short burst, and in this manner I emptied several magazines—trigger happy. Moving forward, sometimes crawling over the legs of men who were firing, I came upon a casualty sprawled across the trail, moving rhythmically from side to side. He uttered no sound and made no response when I whispered, "Where are you hit?" in his ear. I dragged him into the ditch. The front of his flak jacket was covered with blood; he was wounded in the side of his neck. I couldn't find his first-aid packet, so I broke open mine and applied it to the wound, wrapping it twice around the neck and tying it firmly. The man was losing a great deal of blood. Such a wound as this, where an artery is severed (as it probably was in this case) requires a tourniquet although a tourniquet can hardly be applied to a man's neck. He died later from loss of blood, but not in No Man's Land, if that is any consolation. I dragged him toward the rear and was relieved shortly by two men. During the exchange we heard a movement in the brush and lay on the ground instinctively. A grenade exploded nearby. The wounded man's grenade pouch was within reach so I removed one, pulled the pin, and lobbed it in the direction from which the noise had come. One of the other men did the same. When they went off, we separated, and I moved forward again, encountering two more groups of stretcher-bearers who were moving in the opposite direction.

Enemy fire was now negligible. People could be heard crashing through the rice stalks in the paddy. The enemy force had probably been split up into separate groups, the most integrated of which was working in the vicinity of our right front.

Still moving forward, I came to a curve in the path. No one was visible up ahead. I decided that I had gone too far. The goddamned chill again. I saw that two figures were lying in the ditch a few yards ahead; whether Chinese or American, dead or alive, I couldn't tell. I fumbled for a grenade and two men abruptly emerged from the low jungle twenty or twenty-five yards up the path. They moved stealthily but rapidly toward the two prone figures. Their style of movement looked idiotic; they minced or tiptoed rather than crept. The one in the lead was slight of build and short; he wore a visored cap and a modified Sam Browne belt. He may have carried a pistol in one hand; it was too dark to be certain. He knelt down beside one of the prone figures—which I figured then were marines—and the other one moved past him, lay down in the very middle of the path, and pointed his weapon—a short shoulder weapon, probably a pp-S—in my general direction. I was mesmerized; the distance between us could not have exceeded fifteen yards. Traumaville, end of the line. It's taken me a month to even think about writing a description.

The first Chinese hovered nervously about the wounded marines; he was up on his knees. I couldn't see what he was doing. A moment later he began dragging one of them into the ditch, by the wrists. The other Chinese rose up on one knee, swung his stubby weapon in the other direction, and stood erect. He looked like a terrible puppet. The BAR was not in firing position; it was necessary to bring it up from my side. I did this quickly, planting both elbows on the ground with an audible thud. I squeezed off an unnecessarily long burst before the Chinese could react. The muzzle blast was blinding. For the first time I realized what a flash-hider is for; to shield the shooter from the brilliance of the muzzle blast. When my eyes became again accustomed to the dark, I saw that one of the Chinese lay crumpled up near the edge of the paddy. The other was nowhere in sight. The marine had been dragged only a few feet; his feet and ankles protruded from the first level or step of the paddy. At this moment—as I took notice of these things—I was fired upon from that area in which the two Chinese had appeared. This was evidently the tardy covering fire of two or three men assigned to support the small snatch-party. I heaved grenades in that direction. After the explosions I could still hear people moving around in the paddy. Someone fell noisily into a puddle off to the left.

The nearest marine began to crawl toward the other, and I crawled up to both. The conscious one was a Navy corpsman, who later told me what had happened. (He had been giving the other man first aid, he said, when he heard movement nearby. He had of course lain perfectly still when the two enemy soldiers appeared. One of them stepped on his wrist and removed the .45 that he was holding lightly, before dragging off the other marine.) I whispered something like this to him: "Let's get the hell out of here. There's no one else up here, and we're liable to get left behind," etc. He replied that there were several other marines up ahead, and then examined the other man to find out whether he was alive. We went over to him. He was alive, and fortunate to have been unconscious. Being dragged away into No Man's Land by a Chinese is not likely to cheer a man's soul. The corpsman administered first aid—another neck wound—and we lifted him and carried him to the rear. After covering more than a hundred yards, we met a group of four who were searching for casualties. They relieved us, and one of them informed us, confidentially, that "the paddy's *crawling* with goonies!" We followed the group to the emergency forward aid station, a distance of another hundred yards. The area was crowded with loaded stretchers, corpsmen and "angels" as members of the rescue party were called. The latter group, hastily assembled behind the MLR, had been rushed out as reinforcements but were being used instead as stretcher-bearers. Things were too much of a mess, people were too urgent for anyone to stop and ask questions of another, and some of us believed that Lt. deGourdier,

311

S/Sgt. Rau and private Wang were still lying out there in the paddy somewhere. In fact, the latter two were among the first evacuated.

All activity at the forward aid station was momentarily suspended—a fire fight up ahead; a chorus of burp guns followed by the sound of BARs and carbines. This is what had happened. Seven marines, under the command of a Corporal Smith, had remained in place out there in order to cover the withdrawal. They became aware of the fact that they were being quietly surrounded. They drew their group close together and deployed in a tight perimeter defense, having decided that their salvation lay in defending a stationary position until help arrived. Unfortunately they had no radio. This detachment, two of whom were already wounded, was attacked by a squad of Chinese as they were debating whether or not to send a man back to get help. The estimates of the number of Chinese that attacked were between ten and twenty—it was probably a squad. The attack was almost immediately squelched by the accurate and concentrated fire power of the seven men. The fire fight lasted for less than twenty seconds. The detachment withdrew as quickly as they could, which was not very quickly at all, four of them now being wounded.

An emergency squad of six men was assembled at the forward aid station. Within ten minutes we approached the isolated outpost. We were vigorously challenged. No one could recall the password at first, so one of our group whispered hoarsely, "Angels, god-damn it, ANGELS!" As we pulled them back, one of them asked if we had seen any Chinese on the way out. Noises only.

The enemy mortar crews, located behind the hill mass called Kumgok, went to work as we withdrew. No counterbarrage was allowed because we weren't entirely accounted for; the people in the CP didn't know exactly where everyone was at that moment. The bombardment of 60mm. variety, was ineffective; the strike zone was some distance away to our left. Before long, however, projectiles of heavier calibre landed nearer to us and we were forced to hide in the ditch for cover. Movement was considerably slowed up, but we managed to reach the forward aid station. None of the men picked up any shrapnel. The enemy infantry, in all probability, had started for home.

As soon as heads were counted—a poor choice of words— as soon as each man was accounted for, the radioman gleefully called the command post, requesting the counterbarrage. Our mortar crews, certainly suffering from extreme frustration by this time, finally went to work. Within a minute after the radioman had given the all-clear, we heard the sound of mortars being dropped into the tubes behind our lines: THUNK-THUNK-THUNK. 60mm., 81mm., and 4.2-inch projectiles arched into the low clouds above us and roared downward into the northern end of the paddy, chewing up the jagged slopes of Hill 104 and Kumgok. The din was tremendous, and in a way gratifying.

Stretcher teams continued to relay the dead and wounded to the MLR. I lay down in the ditch, oblivious of occasional flying shrapnel; Chinese mortars were still coming in. A minute or two later I got up and stumbled after one of the last groups of stragglers, following them to outpost Ava and returning to the MLR through the Ava-MLR trench. The sky was just beginning to show some light. We watched the angels load the last of the casualties into the back of a jeep ambulance. The bombardment gradually diminished, the echo rumbled among the hills and died out. I lay down on a muddy blanket and listened to the jeep drive away, then tried to go to sleep.

There was one more patrol, an ambush. When we got out to the ambush point—among some tall weeds on a little finger northwest of Ava—I went to sleep (Get right out of that womb!), which is something I never did before. The lieutenant in charge crept around the perimeter and checked each man's position, an ordinary procedure. I awoke with a noticeable start when he approached and nearly fired at him. I did, I almost squeezed the trigger. The lieutenant didn't see me because I decided that it would be too obvious if I sat up suddenly. So I lay still with the weapon in a position to fire. He must have heard me jump awake, at any rate, he tripped over me, literally. When this happened I rolled over and looked at him, a display of phony alertness. He whispered, "Are you asleep?" "What? Of course not, sir." "Well, then . . . keep your eyes open." He moved on to the next man. The platoon sergeant, who accompanied him, knelt down and said, "You *better* sit up, boy." Later on someone accidentally set off a trip flare and scared the b'jesus out of everyone. Nothing else happened.

It's occurred to me many times that it would have been so simple and so right for the men on patrols not to put themselves out. Recon patrols I'm talking about. The Chinese leave us alone and we leave them alone, and sit it out until it's time to go home. One man did this, a corporal in charge of a four-man recon at the time that we were on Hill 229. He took the men out of a ravine, not far from the MLR, and there they sat, calling in at intervals establishing check points as though they had actually reached their objective, etc. One of the men informed on him, and he was sent to the rear to be punished severely. But the corporal had a fine idea.

The morning after that uneventful ambush, our new lieutenant, George Dormeyer, came up—he had been living in the CP bunker, learning the ropes. I was sitting on top of the ammo bunker when he arrived. I pointed out the 7th Marine lieutenant to him and he introduced himself. "I'm George Dormeyer," he said, and he began to question the older man in a fine manner. It was obvious that he wanted no combat stories, only facts. He asked one question after another, and the other officer, a large ultra-bucolic Irishman of about thirty, was snowed by it all. As they talked, a 60mm. projectile landed without warning. It landed on top of the platoon CP bunker, of all places. When the dust cleared, Lt. Dormeyer rose and continued questioning. He casually suggested that the other officer turn over all automatic weapons to our platoon, that they would, of course, be returned when we were relieved. A rather startling proposal, and Red put him off. Dormeyer then asked how his boys—Van Horn and myself—were getting on. Red said, "I think one of them went to sleep on ambush last night." "Which one?" asked Dormeyer.

"This one here," said Red, pointing at me. "Is that correct?" said Dormeyer. I happened to be sitting in a kind of arrogant position, and I said, "Of course not." Red got flustered. "Well, he certainly wasn't what you'd call *alert*." So I blew out the back, first because it was absolutely true, second because (through the remarks of some of the other men in our platoon) Dormeyer had been led to believe that I was a good marine and a good squad leader and it was important that he not learn otherwise. So I stood up, put out my cigarette and went into another acting exercise. "The way you cats in the 7th Marines conduct your so-called ambushes," I muttered, "it's not surprising that you thought I was asleep." "What's that, sergeant?" said Red. I went on. "On our ambushes, we *all* lie down." Then, addressing Lt. Dormeyer: "Those jokers last night were sitting up, all twenty of them, like sitting ducks. I could see every one of them, but nobody could see me—which is why the lieutenant here tripped over me." "Go to your bunker, Russ," said Lt. Dormeyer. Later, while he was questioning me, I convinced him that this was the way it had been.

By this time I had acquired some extra gear for the squad: one BAR and a carbine which I had hidden. If the truce had not been signed, I would have stolen a certain machine gun.

During these last days I resembled a ten-toed sloth. So much so that I drew attention whenever I walked far behind the lines to get the hot chow. One day I entered the mess tent wearing nothing above the belt but a flak jacket—heavily bearded and very smelly. An older man who wore no insignia but who was obviously an officer saw the grand entrance and said, "You—get over here." Another acting problem. "Huh?" I snarled, pretending not to know that he was an officer. I was with the forward party and there was no reason that I should have known who was who. There was no one I knew in the mess tent. "What outfit do you belong to?" the officer said, with a pained expression on his face. "Able company, Fifth Marines," I announced, with obvious, but contrived pride. The officer stood up. "Is that how you were taught to address an officer?" Now the transition, a sniveling, quivering hulk, "I . . . didn't know . . . you . . . were an officer . . . sir." "You're a fucking wise guy, aren't you, buddy?" I had overdone the transition a little bit. He proceeded to dress me down like a true Old Salt, like a drill instructor at Parris Island, but I had a ball. If he had asked my name I would have told him I was Aldo Yold.

In a quiet ceremony today, in front of the battalion headquarters, Martin F. Russ, 1216432, was promoted to the rank of Sergeant. Mr. Russ was wearing clean dungarees and polished boots. Capt. Nathan Krupp made the presentation. The new sergeant's friends threw a party later in his honor. The reception took place in the tent of the ———— Squad. Beer, heroin and beans were served. Sgt. Russ is currently employed as a squad leader in the Marine Corps.

GROUP TEN

‖‖‖

The Truce

July 1st, 1953

We are occupying a hill not far behind the lines. The ———— squad, accompanied by a machine-gun crew, are responsible for it, although we have no grenades and little ammunition. But it makes little difference. The Korean war is over. No one will bother us up here.

Last night we sat around a couple of Coleman stoves and drank coffee. In the distance far to the north we could see numerous small fires like ours, in the Chinese sector. No Man's Land is deserted. New Bunker, Old Bunker, Hedy, East Berlin, Little Rock, the Pentagon, the Fan—all deserted and quiet except for the rats.

The truce was signed at ten in the morning, on June 27th, 1953. The news was relayed at once to all unit commanders. After 10 P.M. no one was to fire his weapon. Even an accidental discharge, we were told, would mean a court-martial. Throughout the hot sunny afternoon the Chinese sent over barrage after barrage of propaganda pamphlets. The projectiles exploded hundreds of feet in the air; the cannisters would open and the papers would flutter down to earth like snow. The papers would sometimes fail to separate and an entire packet would streak downward, landing hard. Judging from the height of the trajectory and the angle of the smoke trails, the projectiles were probably artil-

317

lery. The smaller ones—mortars—made a peculiar noise before they detonated, like a loon. Sometimes they went WHOOP-WHOOP in a kind of falsetto. These harmless barrages were mingled with accurate artillery and mortar bombardments. No one was interested in chasing around the paddies looking for pamphlets. It seemed as though the Chinese were merely trying to expend all of their heavy ammunition and pamphlets before the cease-fire went into effect.

The tank road, a segment of which was under direct enemy observation, was bombarded continually throughout the day. Troops were forced to use this road, however, in order to carry equipment back to the supply point for withdrawal. (One of the agreements of the truce was that all troops and equipment of both sides must be withdrawn from the MLR within seventy-two hours after the signing of the truce.) Fortunately there were many old bunkers along the tank road to provide cover during the sudden barrages. Van Horn and I, working together, were nearly annihilated by incoming shells that seemed to walk back and forth along the road. Some of them were 76mm. recoilless rifle projectiles. By nightfall the exposed segment of the tank road was pockmarked with small craters.

When Van Horn, myself and the new lieutenant—Lt. Dormeyer—came up a week before, we noticed that part of the supply route behind the MLR is also exposed to enemy view. A hill mass, or rather the summit of one, barely juts above the MLR hills. This, we learned, was a Chinese hill called Unggok. It is easily distinguishable by the color of its uniformly red soil, seared and bare. Our MLR is still partly covered with vegetation. It was easy to imagine that a Chinese forward observer was watching us from the summit, where it peeks above our MLR skyline. But the supply route was unmarked. It is covered with a huge trellis of chicken wire interwoven with strips of camouflage garland. The road climbs a long gully and ends where the feeder trenches begin. These are not fortified trenches. The company command post is located in this area, but the main trenches are some distance away. The MLR is located along the next series of low ridges, across a rice paddy.

318

UN spotter planes droned above No Man's Land and the Chinese hills during the day, checking enemy activity. Enemy antiaircraft crews sent up intensive but inaccurate fire. The gunners might have knocked down several of our planes had they put a little more range on their fields of fire. In most cases, the little white puffs of smoke following each flash red explosion—barely discernible—seemed to follow the Piper Cub in a neat, harmless line. Twice a shell exploded near a plane; one under the belly, the other beside the tail section.

One large patrol was scheduled to go out after dark, returning before 10 P.M. Van Horn and I volunteered for it, but they had room for only one extra man; we threw fingers and Van Horn won. So I asked the lieutenant (7th Marines) if I could go out on listening post, and was turned down. By 8:30 it was fully dark and the patrol members were lined up behind Green gate, ready to move out. Van Horn and I talked for a while; I was bitching because I couldn't go along. Several rounds of 60mm. exploded nearby and everyone scurried for cover. The light barrage continued and gradually increased in intensity; 82mm. projectiles and occasional rounds of 120 mm. Our reverse slopes were then under continual bombardment until 10 o'clock. The patrol leader, the 7th Marine lieutenant, had seen that everyone was inside a bunker. Van Horn and I had found a deserted ammo bunker and we sat in it. This would have been a hell of a time to get hit, an hour before the long-awaited cease-fire. Five men, including the 7th Marine lieutenant were caught by shrapnel in the —————— Platoon sector. Two men on outpost Ava—in front of Green gate—were wounded. As far as we know, none died.

Van Horn and I are what is referred to as "sukoshi-timers," or short-timers. We are both due to go home before long, a month or two. It is the custom to exclude sukoshi-timers from patrols or other combat duties. Some short-timers have been known to literally hide in caves until it comes time for them to be taken to the rear. But Van Horn and I wanted to get in on the act somehow, this last night. We both wanted to be in the MLR trench at 10 o'clock to see what there was to see. The barrage subsided momentarily and we went outside. A projectile—we believe that it was a 120mm.—thundered into a gully nearby and blasted it. We went back inside. At quarter to ten we went outside again and raced around looking for a feeder trench, found one, and rushed up to the MLR. We huddled in the bottom of the trench and waited.

We could not be certain, but it seemed as though the marine artillery and the company mortars had stopped firing.

At 10 P.M. the hills were illuminated by the light of many flares; white star clusters, red flares, yellow flares and other pyrotechnics signifying the end of a thirty-seven-month battle that nobody won and which both sides lost. The brilliant descending lights were probably visible all along the 150-mile front, from the Yellow Sea to the Sea of Japan. The last group of shells exploded in the distance, an 82mm. landed nearby, the echoes rumbled back and forth along the Changdan Valley and died out.

A beautiful full moon hung low in the sky like a Chinese lantern. Men appeared along the trench, some of them had shed their helmets and flak jackets. The first sound that we heard was a shrill group of voices, calling from the Chinese positions behind the cemetery on Chogum-ni. The Chinese were singing. A hundred yards or so down the trench, someone began shouting the Marine Corps hymn at the top of his lungs. Others joined in, bellowing the words. Everyone was singing in a different key, and phrases apart. Across the wide paddy, in goonyland, matches were lit. We all smoked for the first time in the MLR trench. The men from outpost Ava began to straggle back, carrying heavy loads. Later in the night a group of Chinese strolled over to the base of Ava and left candy and handkerchiefs as gifts. The men that were still on Ava stared, nothing more. So ends the Korean conflict, after some 140,000 American casualties—25,000 dead, 13,000 missing or captured.

Camp Guyol. (Undated)
Danny boy came back from liberty in Seoul a few minutes ago. I haven't forgotten the girl in the photoshop. I wrote out a

simple note yesterday for Dan to give to her and drew a diagram showing him how to get to the place. When you leave the UN parking lot, instead of turning left and heading for the PX, you go straight ahead down that street. It's on the left side, a hundred yards or so from the beginning of the street. (I want to remember where it is; I'd like to see if it's still there five or ten years from now when I come back.) Dan took the note to Kim, one of the Korean interpreters, and had it translated. It was beautifully written out, in ink. It said: "Greetings, young lady! This is my friend, Dan. Please allow him to photograph you. I took a photograph of you several months ago, but I had forgotten to load the camera. Dan will give you some chow, which is a small present from us." Dan returned with the wonderful news that my picture was among those on the wall of the shop.

Camp Guyol. (*Undated*)

Four days after I was promoted to sergeant there was a massive battalion inspection, held for the benefit of Colonel C. L. Torgeson, the regimental commander. This happened some time ago—before Van Horn and I went up with the forward party; that is, before the truce. Lt. Dormeyer had not yet been assigned to our outfit. Van Horn was acting as temporary platoon commander and I was his platoon sergeant. The only other NCO in the platoon was Cpl. Cal Tibbels. Lauroesch had been transferred. Three NCOs altogether. There are ordinarily fourteen. The table of organization calls for one lieutenant, one staff sergeant, four buck sergeants and nine corporals. We were slightly under strength, one might say. To my horror, Van Horn informed me that he would not be around for the inspection; he had managed to include himself in a court-martial hearing at division headquarters that day. I would have to represent the ——— Platoon.

The squad leaders were called together: Pfcs. Hogg, Lo Castro and Williams. The problem was made clear to everybody and everybody co-operated. The men were racing around the platoon area like a bunch of crazy people; borrowing soap, exchanging cleaning rods, bore cleaner, rifle rods, brushes, bore patches, buckets, etc., unpacking seabags to find clean dungarees, and other minute tasks. The place was a mess all of a sudden, and I was very nervous. Then the word was passed around the battalion that the fucking colonel also wanted "junk on the bunk," *i.e.*, all 782 gear—everything we had ever been issued—must be laid out on the cot. A number of complex diagrams were handed out by panting runners, showing the necessary arrangement of all the junk. Many changes were eventually made. Lt. Casimetti fluttered back and forth among the tents, checking the layout. All wrong. Tear it apart, lay it down again. At 11:00 A.M. the captain made a dummy inspection of the tents. All wrong. Tear it apart, lay it down again. For the next ninety minutes I ran from rack to rack, moving all forks to the *left*-hand side of the meatcan covers and pointing outboard, jerking all knapsacks from beneath the triangularly folded ponchos which were showing the brown side out and which must later be refolded to show the green side out, and placing the knapsack significantly upon the entrenching tool cover from under which the entrenching tool protrudes precisely halfway, with the collapsible portion facing downward, not forgetting that the bayonet and scabbard must be laid across the uppermost division of the entire display, arranging the tent pegs symbolically so that each of them lays within a single groove of the air mattress, and making certain that all rifles and BARs are facing the same direction. A whistle blew outside and we marched profoundly to noon chow.

When the men returned from chow, I called them outside, into ranks, and we practiced a variety of troop movements; standing at Quantico attention, the puppet movements of inspection —arms, making certain that each man slapped the front hand guard of his weapon in a noble and sincere manner. I have found that the bolt of the M-1 rifle can be jammed to the rear with more speed and precision if the piece is already cocked. I passed the idea on. The word was that Colonel Torgeson was not happy unless an enlisted man looked him directly in the eye during inspection, something we were never allowed to do at Parris Island. Passed it on. Also, all insignia—emblems, chevrons on cap and lapel, etc.—were to be removed. I told them to speak in as condensed a manner as possible if the colonel asked them a question. If possible: "Yes, sir," "No, sir," or "Thank you, sir." And above all not to smile at him, even if he said something hysterical. Canteens were filled in case of faint feelings. The men had memorized the division chain-of-command, something often asked for by inspecting officers.

The company fell out at 12:45, formed and marched to the parade field, which had recently been made flat by a bulldozer. The battalion, on line, was ready for the inspecting party within a half an hour.

Captain O'Ghoul had given me careful instructions on how to behave when the colonel came around to our platoon. There was much to-do lining up the three squads, exact body movements, correct posture, etc., everybody having fun&games.

The executive officer of the battalion called us to attention. He needed a megaphone. Then we were given parade-rest. The inspecting party strode into view. We stood for more than an hour, watching the colonel and his group move slowly up and down the ranks ahead of us. The metallic sound of each bolt being snapped was almost hypnotic. While noticing how nervous each lieutenant was as he received the colonel, I also learned the exact movements, something the captain had neglected to tell me. At approximately 3:30 the inspecting party neared the end of the platoon ahead of us. I gulped a few times, gave the men a quick check, and went into a trance. I was now on stage at the Moscow Art Theatre, and guess who was directing. No, not Stan. Me. I called the platoon to inspection, a welcome relief from the rigid parade-rest we had maintained. 1041 men (more or less) were waiting, and so was Mr. Chekhov, so I thundered out with the prepared speech. The colonel, a leathery caricature of a marine senior officer glared back. "Good afternoon, sir. Sergeant Russ; —— platoon, Able company. Thirty-six men present. Two men, mess duty. One man, sick bay. One man, division headquarters. Platoon prepared for inspection, sir." He acknowledged my prolonged salute and I snapped the old claw down like a whip. "Take your post, Sergeant," said the colonel. My position was between Himself and three other officers, plus Captain Krupp and also the battalion sergeant-major. The colonel spent at least a full minute before each man.

Col.: What's your job?

Pfc.: Assistant BAR-man, sir.

Col. (taking the man's weapon): I see. . . . Good bore. . . . Have you fired this weapon?

Pfc.: Yes sir.

Col.: What is the battle-sight setting?

Pfc. (making it up out of his head): Thirteen clicks elevation, two clicks left windage, sir.

Col.: Very good. . . . Do you have your dog tags on?

Pfc.: No, sir.

Col.: And why not?

Pfc.: No excuse, sir.

Col.: That's no excuse. . . . Well, where are they then?

Pfc.: In my tent, sir.

Col. (turning to me): Take this man's name down, Sergeant.

Sergeant (scribbling furiously on the pad): Aye, aye, sir.

Frank Rollins, the tough kid with the girl's face, weighs 135 lbs., and is well over six feet tall, and he looked like a chicken being choked when the colonel stepped in front of him. Pugnacci stuttered violently when asked the name of the assistant divisional commander. Andy Kostis was unusually squared-away for the inspection, and his cap was fixed to hide his thick pompadour. He looked so impressive that the colonel, after he had asked the usual questions, tarried awhile and tried to make one of those just-one-of-the-fellas jokes. I can't remember what it was. Andy maintained the agate-eye, complete disinterest, and the colonel moved sullenly on, as the other officers filled in the horrendous dead space with patronizing chuckles. When he had inspected the entire platoon, the colonel stood squarely in front of me and said something like this: "Sergeant, you have a lot of work to do, getting dog tags on your men. I want them worn at all times. . . . You have a good platoon here. . . . Young squad leaders, I

324

notice . . . but there's no reason why you can't pass on to these men the knowledge and experience you have gained yourself. . . . Very good, Sergeant." And he went away. I gave the platoon at-ease and looked at the squad leaders, who were smirking. Dudley Hogg—twenty-eight years old. Vincent Lo Castro—twenty-five years old. Louis Williams—twenty-eight years old. (Sergeant Russ, four days previously a corporal—twenty-two years old.) Har! The fact that I sported a semi-handlebar mustache at the time may have colored the colonel's impression somewhat. We were dismissed. Later, the captain said that the colonel had used the word "outstanding" in regard to the junk-on-the-bunk display of the ———— Platoon.

On Monday, General Pate, the new division commander, came to the battalion area to dedicate the camp. The division band played "Semper Fidelis," "The Star-Spangled Banner," the marine hymn, and "Onward, Christian Soldiers." Lt. Sandler and Sgt. Van Horn stepped out of ranks and unveiled the wooden sign.

CAMP GUYOL
dedicated to the memory of
Edward W. Guyol
killed in action on April 15th, 1953

Lt. Guyol has been written up for the Navy Cross, for heroism, particularly on the night of the Bunker Hill raid. He went out alone during the bombardment and led groups of men to safety.

José Rivera has received the Bronze Star, for retrieving Lt. Guyol that night. It is interesting to note the formality involved in giving a man a medal; also I want to put down the fact that it was I who got things rolling for Rivera and his Star. I went to the captain one day and told him what Rivera had done that night. Apparently everyone had forgotten about it. The captain hadn't heard. I also mentioned that Lt. Guyol, before he lost consciousness, told Rivera that he would write him up for a medal. The lieutenant actually said, "I'll get you the Medal of

Honor for this." This is something I left out of the account, for no particular reason. Whether or not Rivera's act deserved to get him a Medal of Honor is beside the point. For what he did, he should get something. Each man that was a member of that patrol was questioned—by several officers. We were asked to write down a detailed account of the circumstances connected with Rivera's act. A few weeks later, in a company review, he was awarded the medal.

Camp Guyol (Undated)
We of the ——— squad have devoted a good deal of time and energy in attacking not the Chinese but each other; not, however, dalliance in any sense of the word.

Lester Higgins, the burly, mad Negro from Chicago—who looks forward to a career as a gigolo—sustained an awesome reputation for harmless violence. The following business was one of his more overt methods of self-expression.

The men in the bunker are all occupied: some sleeping, some reading, or writing letters. Others are busy cleaning their weapons. Higgins, seated in a dark corner, becomes totally rigid —with alarming abruptness. The dim candlelight accentuates the wild countenance he has assumed. His glare descends on Pugnacci, who pretends he doesn't know what's about to happen. Higgins rises, resembling a statue just coming to life. Pugnacci is away like a rabbit, leaving several parts of his rifle clattering on the ground. Catapulting out of his corner, Higgins is in full pursuit; through the bunker entrance, down the slope, across the rice paddy, in and out of an old trench, back across the paddy, up the slope and into the bunker again. At this point the seizure abruptly subsides. Staggering about exhausted, the two men resume their former activities; Higgins returns to his letter, Pugnacci retrieves the scattered parts of his rifle. This particular demonstration occurred as often as three times a week. I am pleased to report that whenever Higgins caught Pugnacci he tickled him.

Another: Cal Tibbels, the scarred one, had a sort of characteristic prelude to the attack, or should we say, to the dance. Before becoming a kind of Quasi Modo, he sometimes delivered the following succinct preamble:

"I'm . . . going . . . to . . . destroy . . . you . . . a little bit"

If the arch-nemesis of the moment was too bored to flee, Tibbels would grapple with him.

Another: Andy Kostis had been profoundly disturbed by the film *War of the Worlds* and as a result occasionally effected a pretty tremendous transmutation, assuming the nature of one of those vast Martian spaceships, equipped with dinosaur neck, that appeared in the movie. Swaying back and forth, he would circle each of us in turn, providing himself with the following vocal accompaniment: "Nyeu-nyeu-nyeu-nyeu," etc., uttered through clenched teeth. Once it commenced, the noise was continuous, even while taking a breath. He produced the sound as though it were a mechanical vibration coming from the hold of the spaceship. His articulation was so rapid that none of us were ever able to imitate him. Upon locating whoever it was he wanted, the vibrations increased rapidly, like a Geiger counter. The volume and pitch usually accelerated to such a degree that we got irritated as hell. Hovering about, uttering "Nyeu" four times a second—ultimately in strained falsetto of ear-shattering intensity—he selected his hostage and fell upon him, to the relief of everyone present except the hostage, who was merely dragged a few feet.

One more example: Kostis's favorite act was a parody on total recall. It was discovered one day by accident that he reacted very violently when anyone hummed a certain tango.

For as long as the music continued he would stride about with giant steps, often dragging an unprepared partner along with him, executing those 180-degree turns of the tango with bruising abruptness. The demoniac procession would continue until the music ceased. This sounds unlike Andy, I know, but he has his little narcotics difficulties. Something about monkey on the back. Needless to say, no one was particularly anxious to hum that tango after he had his first fit—although, in order to maintain the morale of the —————— Squad, I managed to hum that tune every

327

so often. Kostis's ability to maintain an absolute deadpan amid our howls was phenomenal. Lt. Dormeyer walked in on this once, made no comment. What can one say?

By way of proportion, let it be said that our squad was the most valorous and efficient unit within the battalion. In reserve areas, of course, it is a total shambles.

Camp Guyol (Undated)

Now. To begin with, there is a deal called (laughingly referred to as) Rest and Rehabilitation. I went last month. Flew to Japan from K-6 or something like that, big airport outside of Seoul, I guess. Got a cold id by doze. Hain't fed the pigs. Barn roof a-comin' off tew. Before the train pulled out of Munsan-ni a prisoner train arrived and came to a stop next to us. Crowded with Chinese and North Koreans. Most of them had taken off their outer garments and were wearing only shorts and cap. Strangely enough the caps were Chinese-type with a tin star on them. It seemed strange that they were allowed to keep them. They were singing or chanting songs and keeping time by slapping their hands on their knees. I was sitting in the vestibule, only four or five feet away from one of the windows, all of which were covered with chicken wire. A Chinese and I stared at each other. I wanted one of those tin stars. It would have been impossible to have shoved a pack of cigarettes through the chicken wire, but I pulled them out of the pack and made it plain that I wished to trade. I was spit upon, but it didn't bother me. I guess I wasn't playing the game right to begin with. I laughed—it was a real laugh—and said, "Gung ho," and we stared at each other again. I made a series of terrible idiot faces for him. He was obviously fascinated. It was a tremendous moment. I did an involved pantomime, firing a machine gun at him, throwing grenades, dying, coming back to life, saluting, bowing, leering, weeping. As a representative of the Marine Corps—perhaps he had never seen a marine—I felt obliged to give him an idea of how things were with us capitalist war mongers. Inscrutable wasn't the word for this cat; he was evidently a witless Mongolian idiot. He managed to look bored, but I knew better. He watched.

Marines on R & R go to Camp Miller, outside of Kyoto, Japan, where they are set at liberty after a series of hygienic lectures, getting new uniforms, having military script changed into yen (360 yen equals one dollar). Free for seven days. The transition was so swift it was shocking. Within one minute after walking past the gate, I was catapulting down one of the wide boulevards in a tiny taxi. The cab driver, like Parisian drivers one hears about, refused to acknowledge jaywalkers and nearly hit several. This is the way it was with all of the drivers. We came to the Kyoto Hotel and pulled up under the marquee. A uniformed doorman opened the door. A bellboy took my small bag. I was thinking, of course: Oh, if those salty bastards in the ——— Squad could see their master now. As I remember, the rent came to about $2.50 for one night. A flophouse? Hardly. The lobby was more luxurious than that of the Statler in Buffalo, and not unlike the lobby of any expensive hotel in an American city, except that the clerk made it clear, without any provocation, that any woman I brought in would have to sign at the desk. He was very polite about it. Elevator—serviced—to the seventh floor. I spent considerable time puttering about the room like an aborigine. In the first place I hadn't been alone for a long time, and it was an unusual state; also there were so many oddities to examine—ash trays, running water, mirror, shower, bath tub, electric fan, desk, shutters, wall paper, pictures on the wall, a pot. I sat on the pot for some time. It was night, and fine to look out the window. The city could have been Buffalo.

I went out and found a restaurant, sat down with two marines. Quite a bit like sitting down with one's sister at a dance. There were a group of young dolls seated at the next table. One was particularly attractive. We smiled and I beckoned, it was as simple as that. She spoke English surprisingly well. Her name, she said, was Judy. Would I like to go dancing? Oh, my. On our way rejoicing. As we forward move. Goodbye Marine Corps, goodbye womb—or rather—oh, never mind. We walked through

329

streets the like of which there aren't any in America. Narrow twisting alleys, well lit by lanterns and colored neon signs, many weird colors, crowded with people, Western dress, Oriental dress. We found a ballroom, almost as big as Moonlight Garden at Cincinnati's Coney Island. There were two stages. On one of them, a jumping Nipponese combo was blowing a strange kind of jazz. Ricky-tick, honky-tonk, lie-tee-fie-ti. When their set ended, the curtains parted at the other end of the dance floor, spotlights on, and another jumping Nipponese combo, blowing "Sous of ze Border." The absolute Theophrastus END. These bands must be recorded. Mitch Miller must be told. We drank Tom Collins, about thirty cents apiece, at a table and we danced all right too by gar. The waiters wore tuxedos and the bus boys wore natty whites. "Judy" was wearing a cool print dress and was quite attractive. Mutt and Jeff, of course. She was more than willing to drink, and get loaded she did. She explained that each prostitute was required to carry a card, as a member of a guild. Once a week all members must report to a hospital to be examined for disease. Her card is stamped with the date after each visit to the clinic. We were told at Camp Miller to ask to see the card, etc.

From then on, stayed fractured. Judy was very gracious, and stayed with me for four days. Knowing immediately upon arrival that I would come back to Kyoto some day, I wasn't particularly interested in making the grande tour, even though Judy wanted us to go out to a lake nearby for a day or two. That would have been wonderful (I was a fool not to have gone). Frankly, the city of Kyoto was far too much to try to take in in one week. That's one reason why I've never visited the Metropolitan Museum of Art. If I ever go there, it will be an all-day visit for several successive days. To drop in for a couple of hours would be a bit staggering. Kyoto was staggering. What I did more than anything else was talk, hour after hour, to Judy. And sing American tunes; sometimes she would sing Japanese tunes—awful ones like "Japanese Rhumba" (ay-yi-yi) and "Mushi-mushi Anone." "China Nights," however, is fine. We ate in all sorts of crazy restaurants; she would order. On the fourth morning, walking along the busy main street, I asked her if she would mind if I went away. I think I gave her the equivalent of twelve dollars.

I moved to another hotel, near the railroad station, almost as luxurious. I made the mistake of getting a haircut. The only American in the shop, I sat facing a row of Oriental customers, who watched. After the barber had cut my hair he fell on my neck like a judo expert, literally. I was pummeled, with the cutting edge of his hands. My head bounced up and down, sideways and backwards. It was extremely difficult to remain inscrutable, even though the row of customers were watching; my blushing cheeks were flying all over my face. Once I went into a vast department store and walked up and down the aisles of most of the floors, wanting to buy everything in sight. The music department was the greatest. It's time they heard a new *tone* at Birdland or Bop City. I would like to have bought the Japanese equivalent of a double contra bassoon (the kind only mad people play). The store had a terrace roof; a miniature amusement park. One can see the entire city below, but one doesn't look too long at the city of Kyoto unless one intends to play the double contra bassoon.

The bars in Kyoto are fabulous. There was one called The Brown Derby, on Kawaramachi street I believe. I got friendly with the "hostess," who wore always a black silk dress with a high neck. Her name was Emiko Nagata. She was large for a Japanese, and built like the Aphrodite of Melos without the fatass. A beautiful woman. I walked her to the streetcar station two nights. Without being too obnoxious I tried to go home with her, but it would have been impossible. Her father had been wounded during the war, and her brother had been killed at Okinawa, fighting marines. As she pointed out, I would not have been welcome. Why any American is welcome in a Japanese house is a mystery. After it was plain that she wouldn't be propositioned, and when I returned the next day just to see her, she relaxed and would sit down and talk. I was infatuated with her and she liked me. I relaxed, too, and got to that fine point where I didn't have to talk. She asked me to write her, especially after I returned to America. The last night in Kyoto we went for a hand-holding walk after closing time. We walked past a canal, crossed it on planks, walked through a beautiful park (a park which one doesn't look at too long unless one intends to play the double contra bassoon). I had bought her a pair of earrings and an umbrella. Needless to say I was in AGONY. I embraced her once at the station and that was that.

Kyoto is the most beautiful place in the world.

Having spent one week in one city of Japan, I'm hardly qualified to comment at length on the subject of Japanese women. But I think I understand why so many G.I.s return with Japanese wives, and how great the change must be from living in the company of a Japanese woman to living with an American woman.

September 10th, 1953, Ascom City, outside of Bu Puang

I am writing this at Bu Puang—the Ascom City where we were billeted when we first arrived in December. We will board ship tomorrow. I am thinking how lucky I am. I'll never believe that I had it rough over here. But many of the other men at Ascom City today did have it rough. Some of them lived through mass attacks on East Berlin, Boulder City, Reno, Vegas, Carson. I never saw one. This will be the last entry; we won't do much aboard ship except lie around and dream of the things we will do in San Francisco, of seeing our friends and families at home, of our futures. It would be nice to be able to summarize the past few months, to comment profoundly, to show in a few paragraphs that I have matured or gained in some way, but I'm still part of it, among thousands of men who are going home, and frankly I've never thought too much about it. I dare say most of the men here are glad that they went through the past year, and I dare say that most of them would be at a loss if asked why.

We boarded the Kumchon Cannonball at Munsan-ni three days ago. I sat in the open vestibule for most of the ride. When we stopped at Kumchon-ni I looked around for little John, but he was probably in school. When we pulled out I sat on those steps that protrude from the vestibule of every car. Andy came out later on and stood behind, regarding the vastness of the passing terrain with his cold stare. I wanted to ask him how he felt about things, but I knew he would never tell. The train was moving no faster than twenty miles an hour. An old papa-san was walking along the edge of a huge paddy bordering the tracks. We were a hundred yards from him when he saw us. He wore a long white robe and a black bird-cage hat, a patriarch. When he saw us, he bowed vigorously, waved his stick at us, bowed, smiled, and bowed vigorously again and again. We carried no weapons, he probably knew we were going home. When we came alongside, the old man still bowing happily, Andy, blowing smoke out of his nose, said quietly, "Whatta ya say, ace?"

This morning some of the new replacements landed at Inchon and were brought here, several companies of them. From our side of the sprawling camp, a thunderous chorus arose: "You'll be sor-ree."

They are less fortunate than we who made the varsity and played games in that enlarged playing field, No Man's Land. But they will get the feel of this sad country with its fine people and its awesome mountains and they won't forget either. Nor will I.

There.